On the Way
to Other Country

Best wishes!

[signature]

12/1/01

Other Works by C.W. Gusewelle

Books
A Paris Notebook
An Africa Notebook
Quick as Shadows Passing
Far From Any Coast
A Great Current Running: The Lena River Expedition
The Rufus Chronicle: Another Autumn
A Buick in the Kitchen

Documentaries
"A Great Current Running"
"This Place Called Home"
"Water and Fire: A Story of the Ozarks"

On the Way to Other Country

STORIES FROM A SPECIAL TIME,
WHEN THE JOURNEY HAD JUST BEGUN

by

C.W. GUSEWELLE

 KANSAS CITY STAR BOOKS

These essays appeared first in The Kansas City Star

Published by KANSAS CITY STAR BOOKS
1729 Grand Blvd., Kansas City, Missouri 64108

First Edition

Library of Congress Card Number: 2001093880

ISBN 0-9709131-7-6

Project Coordinator: Monroe Dodd
Illustrations: Jeff Dodge
Dust Jacket Photograph: Loeb Granoff
Design: Jean Donaldson Dodd

Printed in the United States of America
by Walsworth Publishing Inc.

*For Katie, Anne and Jennifer
with love,
and in memory of my friend,
Henry C. Haskell*

*A book of ideas and arguments,
memories and seasons.
A book of lives.*

Table of Contents

I

The Upturned Stone

II

Country Markings

III

Cavils, Insurrections

VI

Counting Losses

VII

The Dark of the Year

VIII

Between Seasons

IX

The Stirring

X

Summertide

XI

Equinox

The Upturned Stone

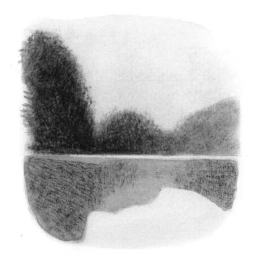

No use trying to explain it now. It was just one of those aberrations of youth — a thing that came over you when the spring sun turned the stones in the vacant lot to warm white loaves and the damp earth sent up a fragrance of all the living and decaying generations it contained.

The equipment needed was a small cloth bag of the size they used to sell five pounds of sugar in. That and a forked stick. It was a simple activity, but endlessly satisfying. On the particular day that your urges commanded, you went out with your sack and stick and turned over stones in the lot, uprooting the heavy loaves one after another and inspecting the shrunken worlds that thrived in the darkness of their undersides.

Sometimes it was a colony of ants, startled by the sun, sometimes a torporous beetle, or that chilling little dragon, the centipede. More often it was only pill bugs, balling up like miniature armadillos when they were touched. But every fifth turn, or tenth, there would be a triumph. The stone would tilt up and there would be a sudden smooth movement — movement with a sense of length to it — and the prize would rear up there on the bare place where the stone had been, eyes glittering, tongue flicking, facing you on his home ground.

They were fine, electric moments, those confrontations between boy and garter snake — full of the ancient symbolism of good and evil, only with the snake the innocent party and the boy the villain of the piece. You moved in with your forked stick and, if you were quick and deft enough, the unlucky creature went into the bag.

It seemed a harmless enough sport, for youth's trusting world did not admit such things as copperheads and rattlers. And always the occupants of the bag were turned loose unharmed, no doubt to the distress of neighbors who wondered at the sudden proliferation of serpents in the garden.

But all that was many years ago. It may be that boys today no longer pry on certain spring days among the stones of vacant lots, testing themselves in that small way for the later, larger terrors. Maybe they have discovered better, sterner tests. In which case — as so often in the dialogue between generations — it would be pointless to try to explain.

A Thousand Dawns

In that still hour, that empty graveyard hour of morning, a boy would wait awake already for the touch of hand on shoulder that announced the choice between warm bed and the dark fog-rising lake where great fish, too, were waking. And never did he choose the bed.

Even in July it was cold in the 4:30 darkness of that far north country. The boy would tremble as he dressed, from the chill and his half-memory of interrupted dreams and other things. And then would creep out, small underfoot, to the rough table where a lantern burned and the big people drank their coffee and, if he came quickly enough, there was hot chocolate for him.

Parents were around that table, and some older than parents, and some whose kinship he hadn't ciphered out. The oldest of all of them, an uncle — very old, perhaps as much as 40 — moved in a cloud of blue pipe smoke and was remarkable for the way he drank his coffee. Impatience was in him to be started before the lower sky began to pale. Yet he wanted that coffee, hot as liquid fire. So he would raise the stoneware cup and take the least amount and set it down, release it completely, then instantly take it up again — forty or fifty repetitions to the minute, like some silent, hasty machine — convincing himself by this that the bitter stuff was cooling as he drank. The boy tried imitating with his cup of chocolate but it burned all the same. The thing took a thousand mornings' practice. He imagined that the inside of the uncle's mouth must be calloused as the pads of a wolf.

In heavy coats they went down then through darkness to the boats, and out across the lake, the men rowing, the uncle's boat leading, a half-mile or more to the chosen fishing place. A breeze rising before dawn would stir a little chop on the water, so that a missed oar stroke would send a cold, thin spray over riders fore and aft. *"A fine morning for northern pike to be running,"* the uncle might call across to the nearest boat. Or, if the lake happened to be still as polished lead, *"A fine morning for the bass to rise."* (Why pike run whereas bass rise is semantic mystery but, subjectively at least, correct.) Always it was a fine morning for something.

Moored among the gray snags of a drowned willow forest, they saw the last stars go out, watched the fog roll up like torn clouds of smoke, revealing the shore from which they'd come, the day advancing in banded blue and apricot behind. Sometimes the lake gave up its fish and sometimes not. Sometimes an immense one struck and vanished, leaving broken line or shattered tackle and a legend to be enlarged. When the new sun rode just atop the water tower of the village at the lake's far end, when, in short, they first began to be comfortable inside their coats, it was finished for that time. That's how they passed those mornings of their lives.

They are gone now, most of them. They forgot to count the dawns, or maybe drank them in too much sleepy haste. And when next anyone thought to look 40 summers had fled.

The boy finds himself the age the uncle used to be, as much gray in his hair as brown, with daughters of his own. The uncle is past 80. Still spends the season fronting on the lake, though. Is commanded by doctors to keep regular hours and husband energy but, because the old passion still gnaws, is frequently noticed joyously to disobey.

The lake has changed. Churned by speedboats and waterskiers, droned over by pontoon planes, its shoreline a jumble of cottages, it is wild no more. There have been changes of role as well.

One morning not long ago, the man who used to be the boy

woke first and padded across the silent cabin, much modernized through the years, to lay hand on a pajama-ed shoulder. Instantly, wordlessly, the uncle threw off the covers and sat up on the bed's edge and began to dress. Soon they were drinking coffee together at the table in that practiced way, bringing cups quickly, mechanically, from table to lip and back again, before going down to the boat.

Perhaps the fish are fewer, for surely they rise (or run) less freely to the lure. It doesn't matter. The two early wakers in the boat are fishing mainly for recollections now, and in that chase their luck is always good.

From there the man and his family struck farther north, almost to Canada, to what is left of pine-birch wilderness. The rough and solitary nature of that place rolled back the years. They arrived at dusk, August coming on and the temperature in the lower 40s, at a small house of hand-notched logs on the edge of a piece of water not even begun to be tamed. A smoking wood stove warmed them and later coarse woolen blankets wrapped them. Out a hundred yards in the darkness, great fishes feeding broke the water with a sound like small explosions. Duck families splashed and chuckled in the reed grasses. And loons spoke of loneliness from moonrise until sleeping.

The daughters are 9 and 8 and both accomplished fisherfolk, but one in particular, the 9-year-old, has the passion in her — in the blood, as it's sometimes said. We teach, and learn, without altogether meaning to. Thus through all the beginnings and changings and endings of many lives there run strands of likeness that are both fearsome and a comfort.

So it happened that in the shank of night, the hour still small, the man sat already dressed, his scalding cup at hand, in the room where the girls slept. One lay turned to the wall. The other's face, in the light reflecting around the corner from the kitchen bulb, was a genetic replication of his own at that same age.

A very long time he looked at them in their dreams, and in his, before he put a hand softly on the arm of the one.

"All right," she whispered. Just that.

And sat up directly, feeling for her clothes — deep, dark-eyed child of morning, the heir to all those memories and now the maker of her own.

Who We Were

Immense, heavy-bodied, they came out of the wrapping dark and flung themselves against the screen of the porch, drawn by the light. Giant moths, apparitions of the night — the eye-winged Cecropia, the rarer Luna, ghostly pale — as big nearly as birds.

Thirty-five years ago, that's been. Nearer 40. Where have those great moths gone? (And where gone the slatted wooden porch swings we lay on to watch them in the last hour's dreaming before bed?) So long it has been since seeing one that I can almost believe they were inventions of the sleepy eye of youth. I've checked, though, and the encyclopedia confirms there really are — or were — such creatures. So where have they gone? Gone to insecticides and lawn sprays, no doubt; gone to the exhaust fumes of the city's passing cars.

Progress is inevitable. The past can't be retrieved, and maybe shouldn't be. But still I catch myself wondering which marvel would be finer to show a child: perfect lawns and passing legions of Pintos and Vegas and whatnot — or a thing that comes riding on silent wings, Persian-tapestried wings, out of the cool spring evening to seek the light.

The seasons were more distinct then, in the dim prehistory before air conditioning — or at any rate before word of its invention had gotten to our street. And summer was most distinct of all. There were electric fans, true. A wet towel stretched over the window at bedside, with the fan drawing air through the cloth, gave some relief. Probably there were arrangements more ingenious than that. But as July drew on toward the breathless hell of August, the miserable panted on the rack.

And, in the final resort, they took themselves to the park. What gentle and polite community there was among the sweaty multitude during those dusks of deepest summer on the grassy public mall. Blankets were spread and vacuum jugs uncorked. There was a discreet mutter of battery-powered radios; sometimes quiet singing. Several thousand people could be found there any stifling night, a solid carpet of tortured flesh running from the flagpole at the top of the mall all the way to the pine grove at the lower end.

Midnight would come. One o'clock. Two. And presently the little breeze would rise — coming not off of baked cement but down across the grassy openness. New life would stir. Strangers, fellow sufferers reborn, would exchange last words and, gathering up their paraphernalia and their sleeping young, go off chigger-bitten to their beds for what was left of night.

What splendid astonishment that was, as a child, to awaken at daylight in one's own room — but with so fresh a memory of deep sky and stars. Now there is air conditioning instead, which I suppose we must be grateful for. And city parks, though they have very many uses, are not for sleeping in.

Leaf smoke announced the fall. The scratch of broom rakes at the curb, men standing together upwind from the blue fog of their burning, the thin voice of the sportscaster lamenting Army's lacerations at the hands of the mighty Irish. Then came eminently sensible folks with their anti-burning ordinances and forbade this ritual practice. No doubt they were right to do so.

But something was lost — some sense of the organic cycle of things. The curbside pile of white leaf ash glowing orange at the heart told more of the year's dying, somehow, than a row of antiseptic plastic bags set out for the weekly pickup ever will. Thus some of us still do defy the law. And always will, if only in a modest way. Once each October, we will furtively set one small heap of leaves afire. It is like some ceremony of the ancients whose enduring practice has outlived the memory of its purpose. For mere disposal, sanitary landfills unquestionably are superior. But disposal no longer is the point. We burn those leaves to save ourselves.

Middle age is not afraid of change. Certainly it doesn't fear its children or their world — a world, after all, that is of its own making. The terror in the middle years is of forgetting, of being left with no special territory to claim as one's own between youth's discovery and the final, patient wisdom of great age.

Such a lot, you see, is gone. The sledding on barricaded winter streets. The great mysterious moths of the night. Most of the fine old elms that shaded us. The relentless heat of summer. The sense of being many strangers unafraid together.

And fled, with those, is a part of the sureness of what we were.

Creditors

It is that time of month when creditors speak. Not yet through their paid agents or summonses of law — it hasn't come quite to that. But for the next week or so, each day's mail will be freighted with their correspondence.

The routine claims of mortgage, automobile, utilities and the like may be suffered with a measure of numb indifference. Much worse are the accounts from the charge-card companies, the entries far displaced in geography and time: a ski-lift ticket, weeks after the mountain winter has passed into flatlands spring; a restaurant meal whose taste is unremembered; some gewgaw long since broken or left in a hotel room.

The entries have gone cold, the tracks of a stranger rumored sometime to have passed on the way to pleasure. It is like that recurrent dream — common, I'm told — of being punished for an accidental crime, or someone else's.

So there arrive all these monthly reminders, regular and oppressive, of the degree to which we've allowed ourselves to become hostages to our appetites, prisoners of our wants. We are washed over by a chill sense of helplessness, and the helplessness is real. For exactly to the extent that we require money and are obliged to think about it we have forfeited freedom and a measure of power over our own lives.

There are alternatives, of course. Many years ago I explored one of them.

I was a young man, waiting with a friend in a street cafe near the Gare Saint-Lazare for the morning train that would carry us out of Paris and eventually toward home. I had traveled half a year; had resigned my place at the newspaper by letter in some vague notion that I would "write." But funds ran short. And even if they had not, there comes in any journey a proper time for going home.

On the next table in that Paris cafe was an English-language magazine, an old *Esquire* left by some other traveler. In it was a long interview with John Steinbeck in which the late author (still living then) reminisced fondly about the Great Depression. It didn't matter not to have money because nobody had any, he said, or words to that effect. And you weren't expected to succeed — it wasn't possible anyway. So, while we were poor then, we were also very free.

The notion seemed wonderfully appealing; it lodged in my imagination. And though I had intended to make my way back to the same city — maybe even to my former job — I went instead, with the $76 that was my total remaining stake in the world, to a woods cabin in a poor and then still fairly remote section of the Ozark borderlands in the southern part of the state.

That was early November of a golden autumn. At first there was a bicycle which soon broke and was forgotten (the country general store was only a four-mile walk away through splendid hills). My cabin had one rough room, a wood stove, wall shelves, a sort of a bed and an open porch facing out a lane toward the unpaved road and the timbered country beyond.

Four hours a day I cut wood with ax and hand saw to feed the stove; four hours walked the woods, carrying a gun to get meat for the table, and four hours wrote, or played at it. That pattern was the habit, although not a law to live by.

Because money was short and the winter long, I kept an approximate journal of expenses. The needs were not elaborate — flour, salt, sugar, baking powder, shortening and dried milk from the store, and occasionally onions or hard red apples at a few cents a pound; eggs from a neighbor lady along the road at 12 cents a dozen. Bulk tobacco, and a small machine to roll my cigarettes.

Sometimes I walked to the home of an acquaintance, an old

farmer whose strength had failed, to spend a morning splitting his stove wood. Payment was in Mason jars of last July's blackberries to fill my pies. On the top cabin shelf was a bottle of sherry of which I took one small glass a day. Over one of those I listened to the radio account of the first man — a Russian — to fly in space.

Much of that winter and spring game was scarce. And yet, while I investigated the preparation of macaroni in all its imaginable forms (and some unimaginable), I really lacked for nothing.

Once, I remember, some city people — a friend from the newspaper and his wife — came to visit. They arrived early on a Saturday evening and we began to talk, forgetting everything else. Such a feast of talk as none of us had ever known. Straight through that night and into the light of morning — a wild, crazy extravagance of conversation. Until we fell down in sheer exhaustion to sleep an hour or two, then woke and ate and took to the woods, talking again as we went.

When they left in the evening, there was a terrible stillness to be filled. Always after visitors it was the same, but that time especially. Several days, a week, might pass without another word spoken aloud.

But then the pattern of the days would reassert itself. The feeling would recede. And, lying down in the dark with the stove creaking and winking through its bolt holes and the big owl booming from his branch at the back of my clearing, I would be able again to consider with satisfaction how free I had managed to become.

Some six months later, in the early part of May, just as the tree frogs had begun to fill the woods with their electronic din and the wildflowers were starting to open, I came back to the world. Because my cash outlay for the winter had averaged only a little over four dollars a month — $4.10 to be exact about it — quite a sum still remained of that original stake. But convention and my new city needs required that I take a job, and so I did. In a fireworks warehouse. No smoking, very seasonal.

For a time the country feelings stayed. I was uneasy in a room with three or four people at once; five or six made a thundering mob. I still rolled my own smokes, spilled tobacco crumbs on friends' carpets and was ashamed. I will never forget receiving from the firecracker king my first week's check, for $60, and thinking that it would buy a whole year in the place from which I had so recently come.

There was still that sense of power, of control over one's life. But then I bought a $200 car and began accumulating books, and from those small corruptions all the rest has flowed — newer and grander automobiles, a mortgage, credit charges, bondage to the oil sheiks of Arabia.

So here I am back at the newspaper, in the same room, almost at the very spot in that room, where I began. And where, if the creditors' earnest communiques this time of month are to be believed, I am destined — good, gray gelding — docilely to remain. Never again, I suppose, will I lie on the edge of sleep, hearing an owl boom and feeling free in that particular way.

Instead, I sometimes wake now, unaccountably, and touch the lady beside me in the bed, then steal into the next room to listen to two small daughters breathing softly, evenly in their dreams. Around me the house and all its appliances tick and purr unceasingly, and I imagine that I can hear the tread of the bill collector on the stair.

Briefly, quite abstractly, those distant winter months may be recalled for their spare uncomplication. But then I remember, too, how that freedom had to be paid for — in the currency of unutterable loneliness.

And, in the end, the long silence and the empty room are the most relentless creditors of them all.

In the Protein Chain

We human beings have an almost limitless and sometimes touching habit of idealizing the circumstances of our existence.

Thus we conceive of hardship to be ennobling and pain to be beatifying, all the more so if they are somebody else's. We honor the willingness to work a lifetime at the same desk in an unrewarding job as a kind of heroism. We have invented the notion of romantic love to explain the commoner impulses of loneliness and procreation that bring us from time to time together.

In this same vein, it pleases us to imagine that a house aswarm with life — grown-ups, children, pets, the more different sorts of life the better, ruling out only mice and cockroaches — must necessarily be a happy and a loving place.

But the reality is seldom that simple.

My own household, for example, presently consists of two adults, two children, a dog, six goldfish and one more cat than the local ordinance allows.

The cats, shut indoors to stop them from eating the neighbor's birds, sit solemn and attentive with their eyes close to the aquarium glass. The dog lies on a rug not far away, pretending to sleep, waiting for the cats to get careless. The balance of our coexistence is fairly delicate. Seeing them that way — all watching and being watched — I suspect sometimes we are not the loving family our friends think us to be. But that we are instead only a dangerously closed ecosystem. Just links in the protein chain.

The latest addition has been a lizard and, with him, a box of 50 meal worms which on alternate days must be delivered up by threes into his lair.

Actually, this one is the second lizard. The first one came home from the country the other day in a bottle. He (she?) was a fence swift, a three-inch creature counting tail and all, with a brown hide like tree bark and the head of a miniature dinosaur. He went into a fish bowl left over from the days before the tank. Earth, moss, rocks and a jar lid of water were provided for his comfort and amusement. A screen was put over the top to hold him in. Once that first night, when we sprayed the interior of his bowl with a plant fogger, he gave a little shudder that we took for pleasure. That was the nearest we came to any communication.

What to feed him was an issue, but not for very long. Because the next morning, shortly after the children left for school, the cats solved the small problem of the obstructing screen and the question of fence swifts' diets became academic.

If you have children, you will understand how such a crisis — with its prospect of blind tears and brooding hurt — can galvanize a parent to a frenzy of self-interested activity. Inconvenience doesn't matter. Cost is no object. Has a lizard been sighted in some distant state? Quick, fly the damned thing in by hired plane and be done with it. Anything to avoid the scene that will otherwise surely follow.

By day's end, the successor lizard was in place. Not a fence swift but a green chameleon. In a pet-store terrarium made for the purpose, with a light on top and a lid that latches.

Thanks to these exertions and expenditures, life was able to go forward. The furnishings of the death bowl were transferred to the terrarium. Much love already has been invested in its occupant. He has become for a time the center of our lives. He has a name. His habits are meticulously observed and reported in detail. Neighbor children arrive in numbers to admire him and help offer up his ration of worms.

Superficially, again, our household seems a loving and untroubled habitat. But even though the immediate crisis has passed, a great sense of danger lingers darkly over me. For, as I've said, I know how delicate the balance really is. We hang by a thread.

The chameleon eats his meal worms and is unafraid. But I find myself overtaken at odd moments by this cold vision, like a waking dream, of things to come.

It is that the cats, having one day finally polished off the goldfish, will solve the terrarium latches, too. And will eat the chameleon.

And the dog, seeing them grow smug and inattentive, will seize that opportunity to eat the cats.

And the children, in grief and fury, will eat the dog.

And the next move will be mine.

A postscript: Returning home from the office immediately after writing the above I found that, while its latches had not been undone, the terrarium itself had been knocked off the table onto its side in an obvious attempt to break the glass.

So it is beginning.

An Unlikely Tyranny

She was a handsome lady with a canary yellow sedan that had cost $25,000 at a minimum and she had not paid that kind of money for an automobile with the intention of being made ridiculous.

But there she was, parked outside the society drugstore in the chic little shopping center, with people going by in tennis dresses and high-fashion warmup suits. And the lights of her big canary yellow car — all its lights, front and back, inside and out, of which there were very many — were blinking on and off uncontrollably. And every time the lights went on the horn also sounded. It was a loud horn, with the proper voice of authority for herding lesser machines out of the way.

So now this imposing conveyance, smaller by only a little than a light cruiser, sat winking and hooting mindlessly and the people in tennis dresses were beginning to stare and smirk.

The lady could be seen moving around a lot inside, frantically pushing buttons and turning switches. *"I have paid $25,000 at a minimum for this canary yellow sedan,"* you could tell she was thinking, *"and this should not be happening to me."*

Her mistake, of course, was in imagining that price made any difference at all.

My own car is of a humbler sort. Its horn is thin and reedy, meant for squeaking servile salutes to the heavyweights as they cruise past. In the first month from the factory the lower half of the plastic dashboard fell down into my lap as I was driving. In the third month I raised the rear hatch which, being misaligned, destroyed a part of the roof and then came away in my hand. The battery, of a size meant for operating portable radios, died with the first frost. In traveling cross-country, I must keep alert for the glint of my $28 wheel covers spinning away into farmers' fields.

At some school event not long ago, the father of one of my daughter's classmates asked how I liked my car. I recited this list of my misadventures and he seemed surprised. He reminded me that he worked at the very plant where that car had been manufactured — a fact I had known, but momentarily had forgotten.

I do not hold him accountable. All cars are instant junk, not just the ones his company makes. And he, least of anyone, should find this surprising.

The only automobile worth the name that I have owned was a 1947 Chevrolet bought when it already was 14 years old, driven another 110,000 miles and sold after that for $100, half what I paid for it. When I say they do not make cars like that anymore, it is not just a figure of speech.

It has become a favorite theme of the futurists that society is on the way to being taken over by machines. We hear this repeated so often and so insistently that we accept it to be a fact, or at least a serious danger. In an earlier day the risk might have been real. But I do not believe now that it can ever happen. Machines, even very expensive ones, have gotten progressively more shoddy and unreliable — to such an extent that they have become incapable of performing even the limited tasks assigned to them, much less of ruling civilization.

When I bought a house with an electronic garage door opener I thought I had moved up in the world. Then the wiring of the gadget went haywire. It responded neither to clicker nor button. For several days, until a repairman came to break in through a window and disconnect the opener, I could not get at my car at all. And I will never own another one of those.

I have stopped taking photographs for much the same reason. Once I bought a camera — paid what seemed to me quite a price for it. I took this camera on a family vacation and devoted myself to making a pictorial record of all our joys, to the exclusion of having any actual fun myself. When we came home I found that the film, the whole time, had been disengaged from the spool inside the camera. Thus, I had no pictures — and no memories either. I refuse ever to spend another vacation looking through a viewfinder with nothing but a tangle of blank celluloid to show for it.

Some friends visiting from out of town last week told of their experience in a movie theater shortly before we saw them.

Projection booths, it seems, are now fully automated. The reel is unattended. On this particular afternoon the patrons were treated to the sight — shown magnified on the theater screen —

of the film burning up inside the projector. The images of the actors faded, replaced by writhing abstractions in orange and red. It was fascinating, my friend said. The audience sat absorbed and uncomplaining, watching the patterns and the vivid colors shift and change. Until finally someone thought to go looking for the theater manager and secure the intervention of a human hand.

Machines are dumb and imperfect things. So are we — but they are even dumber and more imperfect.

It may be that, in time, we will find ourselves and our civilization ruled by something. By greed, perhaps, or fear, or shrunken resources or a changing climate. Or possibly by some demonic ideology of our own concoction.

But with all due respect to the futurists, I cannot think that it will ever be by machines.

The Search for Serenity

Surely, we tell ourselves, there must be some remedy for all that ails us. Our lives grow relentlessly more complex. Work consumes our days, and worry our nights. Jobs must be clung to at any cost, not for the satisfaction they give but because of the uncertainty, in these times, of ever finding another. The mail brings messages from creditors, with word of compounding interest.

The news of the world is depressing. The politics of our country is depressing. Candidates hurl their pronouncements like spears — and the spears turn to noodles in mid-flight. There is worse than ambition in those faces. There is an awful vacuousness. They do not even command trust, much less inspire.

Our schools are in distress. Our churches are caught up in bickering and confusion. Our automobiles are shoddy and the appliances we buy are more apt than not to irradiate us or set our houses afire. Our music has become a tuneless scream. Modern literature has turned to an examination — a celebration — of our deviancies. Cults flower. Cities smolder again in racial anger.

Each hard rain sends a few yards more of Southern California oozing toward the Pacific. The San Andreas fault murmurs and ticks like a bomb. A mountain explodes, sending its plume of ash across the land. A tinpot island dictator empties his prisons into the refugee camps upon our coast, and thence into our towns.

The stock market has become a joke. Money itself has become a joke. Thrift is foolishness. Even sensible people have turned to seeking their fortunes in chain letters and financial pyramid schemes. Giant corporations cling white-knuckled to the precipice of insolvency. Recovery is promised, but the architects of salvation are the same glib, expensively appointed fools who presided over the initial ruin.

What wonder, amid all this, that our children are growing up, growing away from us, hardly noticed? Almost as strangers. Or that friends neglect one another and drift apart? Or that all the other relationships which used to give anchor and continuity to our lives have become tentative and conditional?

It is not that we have become a worse or shallower people. It is only that there is, in such times as these, a feeling of being riders aboard a runaway coach whose driver has lost the reins. And that if only we can manage to hold our places — careen on a bit longer, a bit faster — we will somehow regain control and find the road again.

More and more I am persuaded it is an idiot race. One that is run on the course of our weaknesses, not our strengths. But it needn't always and forever be so.

A fortnight or so ago, I passed some hours with friends in a small town removed three hours from the city. It was a Sunday morning, and at the breakfast table there were fresh strawberries in the bowl. Inside the old house there was stillness — not just empty silence, but the kind of yeasty quiet of things considered, of dreams dreamed, of ideas resonating among the thousand or more books on the shelves of the room.

Outside was the stillness of an old brick street. And beyond that of the town itself, of shops serenely closed, of the empty courthouse square. And farther yet, the stillness of the surrounding land, into which the bells of the churches that morning sent their measured chiming.

For those few hours, the sense of fear and fury was suspended. The people of that place were determined to live their lives with some deliberation. They refused, by an act of choice, to be passengers on the coach which carries so many of us along in terror and dismay.

So choice is possible.

Just in recent days, I was in the company of some other people much like myself, inhabitors of frenzy, beside a still pond in the woods, surrounded by birdsong and the click of insects. And as the day progressed, although what we were doing there passed for work, the change in us all — the look of our faces, the cadence of our movements — was striking to see.

Which must mean that the choice is easier and more available than we often dare let ourselves imagine. And it is this possibility which, to my mind, suggests that we will yet manage to recover our balance and not go the way of crumbled civilizations after all.

I have been struck, over the years, in visiting the places where significant men have lived — Mount Vernon, Monticello, Edison's summer home in Florida — by the quality they seem to have in common, which lies over them even to this day. It is the quality of serenity.

Without some base of stillness at the center, there is no possibility of arousal, no hope of sensible judgment, no basis for self-discipline and no margin for creative risk. In better times, serenity — quiet sureness of purpose — has been the strength of this country. Just as the lack of it has been the fatal weakness of so many other societies on earth.

Most of us will never live in houses as stately and serene as those I've mentioned. But we can seek to construct some such place in our mind — and beginning from that point of stillness attempt to regain control of our lives, our personal affairs and the institutions that rule us.

But it is hard to do, you say. The events and forces that contort our lives already are too many and beyond control. There is no turning back.

Maybe that is true and maybe not. But the search for serenity in our private and public matters, even if the odds are uncertain, still seems to me worth the try. Since the alternative is to remain on board a coach whose driver we now suspect of being mad and whose destination has begun to be clear.

A Plain Virtue

Perfection is widely sought after but seldom found. Surpassing excellence is a quality almost as rare. Increasingly it seems to me that dependability is the only standard — or at least the most consistently useful one — by which the people and things in our lives may be intelligently measured.

I have two tractors at the farm — old machines, both of them, manufactured by the same company and identical in every respect but one. That is, one of the tractors can be counted on for a day's work whenever asked. The other invariably will find some way to break down.

The parts in them are the same, possibly even made in the same year by the same hand. They receive the same maintenance. The single difference between them is that one is dependable and the other is not. On a farm, there hardly is anything to be more despised than an undependable machine when work needs doing.

In the city I have two cars. According to the normal expected life of an automobile they are reasonably new. One was built in this country, the other in a foreign land by people whose cleverness is legend. Neither car is dependable. They were undependable the day they came from the assembly line. Pieces of them unaccountably fall off. Fluids drip from them. A good part of the time they do not operate at all.

Someone connected with the motor car industry suggested, with sympathy, that I must have had the bad luck to get Friday cars — put together in the last hours of the week, when the assemblers were eager to get away to the beer hall and the bowling alley. The thing to do, this source said, is to buy Monday cars, although how one arranges that he didn't know.

I have heard any number of excuses for why my cars do not run, and some of them are splendidly inventive. It is too cold or, alternatively, too hot for them. There is too much humidity. The gasoline is inferior. Or the altitude is wrong. None of these reasons has anything to do with the real problem, which is that the machines are undependable. There is no other word for it — and no cure.

There are people like that.

If you operate a business, you have learned that there are employees who can be counted on somehow to accomplish almost any task set for them. And others who, whatever native talent or other endearing qualities they may own, will contrive some way to fail.

In a newspaper life, I have known writers who could do magic with the language — stories much more wonderful than any of us, their less brilliant colleagues, could make — when the spirit moved them to do it. The problem was that they were only rarely so moved. At other times they could scarcely be troubled to put one sensible word after another. And in a craft that requires dependability above all else, that fault was insurmountable. They were the hares. But in the end they were left behind by a world of tortoises.

It is that way in human relationships, too.

More marriages made in heaven have been wrecked by undependability I suspect, than ever failed because of falling hair, multiplying chins or a want of bedroom athleticism.

Children, it is said, thrive on dependability and are disordered by the lack of it. This does not mean that their emotional landscape must be perfectly level. My children are accustomed to the suddenness of my noisy rages. But they also know that these eruptions invariably are followed within moments by forgiveness and displays of contrition. I am not tranquil, but I am at least dependable.

And it is the same even with friendships.

Almost certainly you have had, at one time or other, an inconstant friend. By that I mean a friend who gave affection when he or she chose to — when it was convenient and suited his or her purposes. But who was quite as capable, the next hour or day, of passing without recognition, as if you were a stranger.

There is hurt in that, and cruel mystery. And there is no better explanation for it than the one used for machines. Some people, like some cars and tractors, simply are undependable. Once that is known, it devalues beyond repair their worth as friends.

Thus the thing that we are hoping our daughters will come to understand, almost ahead of anything else, is the transcendent importance of this quality of constancy, of dependability, in all the small and large affairs of a life. It is, in itself, no shield against unkindness or disappointment. And there is no celebrity in it; the dependable are far more likely to receive quiet gratitude than wild applause.

But it does have the virtue of letting you be known — with all the baggage of your shortcomings and slender gifts — for what you are, not what you seem to be. Which is, all in all, a safer and more explainable way to travel.

Coming of Age in Boulder

Having mastered the elements of rudimentary speech, their first request was for the piercing of their ears. Memory telescopes time, of course — but that is my recollection of it.

In one form or other, evidently, it is an impulse as old as the memory of the species. For the *Encyclopaedia Britannica,* under its entry titled "Mutilations and Deformations," catalogues a really dazzling variety of practices — some of them so deliciously, so arcanely depraved as to forbid decent description. "Perforation of the earlobe for insertion of an ornament," the encyclopedia reports, "is exceedingly widespread."

Widespread in some circles, perhaps. But not among those dear, kind ladies of probity and virtue — mother, aunts, older cousins, remoter family and friends of family — who filled and supervised my boyhood and shaped my values in ways not later easily unbent. Pierced ears, while not actually evil, were a little less than respectable. Pierced ears were for the saloon, the dance hall and worse. Surely I must have agreed for, while it was not a matter of conscious deliberation, never to my certain knowledge did I date a girl with holey lobes. (Well, maybe one — on the sly.)

So I found this demand of my daughters — sweet heaven, of my babies — more troublesome than might a father of different or more cosmopolitan background. Several years I managed to resist, years of tears and ultimatums. Any number of their little friends were having ears violated. I heard the names recited and was unmoved. But the day their mother had her own ears done I knew I was on a slippery deck.

It happened finally in Boulder, Colorado.

On a birthday while traveling; as the alternative to an enormous stuffed dog of serious price and nasty look; done by a stranger, in a department store, with a two-for-one coupon torn from the *Boulder Camera*.

Their mother the procuress took them and I didn't go to watch — was spared that much. So what I know of the procedure comes second hand. I had imagined great physical pain. They reported there was little. (I know the ear lobe is supposed to contain few nerves. But the same is said of the scalp and I believed that, too, until once, bending at the wrong time, I caught a thrown horseshoe just above my lateral occipital gyrus.)

The surgery, it seems, no longer is performed with a stone and a whetted splinter of bone. There is a machine for the purpose now, something like a staple gun. The operator aligns the cold metal against ear, presses a lever and in a single blinding instant of lost innocence the thing is done — the hole made and the first small silver ornament driven and locked in place.

Less painful than the least bee's sting, they said it was. Hardly a pin prick. They seemed somehow subtly changed, more worldly. We drove away from there fast, leaving stuffed dog and department store and hateful city behind. In Latin societies, too, they pierce the ears of their female children at the earliest age. And consider the birth rate in Latin America.

Still, it is important to be open-minded and progressive, able to change with the times. To that end the other day I called my daughters around me and got down some books, illustrated volumes from past years of travel. Surely, now that they had begun, they didn't intend to call it quits at such trifling perforations. So I opened the books — lay before them a veritable smorgasbord of fashionable self-mutilations — and commanded each to choose one.

Here, for instance, was a fetching style from Kenya, the ear lobes stretched and elongated with weights into leathery loops that were tied together behind the neck for convenience.

"He's kidding," one of them said to the other. But

uncertainly, not smiling.

Or notice these giraffe ladies from Burma, necks extended inside wrapped brass coils until vertebrae from the back are drawn well above the shoulders.

"Groady!" the other shrieked.

Or this Tubbu charmer from Chad, a ring passed so cunningly through her nose.

"He *is* kidding." With visible relief.

Or this one with the notched ears and the wooden plates for lips.

"Look, if you want to do that to *your* lips (laughing now) that's A-okay. Us? No way!"

But wait, wait — they were leaving — *you haven't seen the four-inch golden lily feet of the Chinese!*

They were gone, though — all smug and self-contained. A father tries to be liberal-minded and instructive and gets, for his pains, laughter and dismissal. Do they suppose I could not detect, in the manner of their going, just a suggestion of the slinky, swaying coquetry that has always distinguished the ladies with pierced ears. And is it possible that any boy attracted to such a girl could be good enough for a daughter of mine?

Charmed Circles

We pass through this world being reminded constantly of the need to mind one's place. But what, exactly, is that place, and how is one supposed to recognize it?

Assumptions are risky. One may presume too much, and be thought pushy. Or too little, and be regarded as obsequious and a lickspittle. Surely the best policy is to start by considering oneself the equal in worth and ability of most anyone else, and then, through a process of experiment, to let the evidence speak for itself.

As it happens I play tennis — just well enough not to embarrass myself, poorly enough seldom to win. If I find myself staying at some place where a tennis court is among the entertainments, I consult the bulletin board postings for another player who might be looking for a game. And if I notice there someone who rates his level of skill as advanced, I refuse to be intimidated. Instead, I am apt to telephone at once to try to arrange a match.

Usually the result is about as you would expect. I go to the meeting equipped with my few ragged strokes learned as a boy on the public courts. He arrives with his graphite racquet, matching wrist and head bands, a smile like a wolverine's — all fangs and hungry purpose — and a swagger born of a lifetime of lessons.

Last week it was a fellow in his middle twenties, slope-shouldered and dangerous looking. He was from New York, where he had played all winter twice a week after midnight, when, as he put it, the court fee was only $30 dollars an hour. As you might guess, people like that mean business.

During the unpleasantness that followed, the only sounds were the awful explosions of the ball from his racquet and his infrequent little yelps of astonishment when a shot of mine happened to carom back across the net in play. At the end of it, we both knew our places. But they were not taken for granted. They were established fairly. To my mind, anyone who publicly declares himself advanced — at anything — ought at least to be called upon to prove it.

On the day some years ago when I returned to the working life after a considerable time spent aimless and frequently poor but fiercely independent, I resolved never again to address a fellow employee or editor, regardless of rank, by anything except his given name. I do not think I ever made a healthier or more constructive promise to myself.

Between strangers, the word Mister is a convenient device of courtesy. But as it is used among people who know one another and work together, it becomes a caste word — a badge of place. It has no use in the meritocracy which any enterprise ought to be. What's more it is meaningless.

Hierarchies become established by all sorts of accidents which defy explanation. The people who find their way into authority — in a newspaper or any other business — may be wonderfully gifted or they may be incurable dolts. These qualities often seem unrelated to the matter of advancement. We have all known both kinds.

The really fine and talented ones generally have little time or use for deferential protocols. Indeed, my guess is that they find them tiresome. Bosses are only men and women, after all. They have names, like we do. And names are to be used.

There are differences between people, of course. But the differences that count are the ones of character and ability, not of station.

I had a call the other day from an acquaintance who wanted to discuss trash collection. It seems that the truck which makes the rounds of his neighborhood is manned mostly by stout youngsters, with one white-haired old-timer among them. The young men hurl the contents of the rubbish cans carelessly into the truck, then make a practice of sailing the container lids into flower beds or wherever they happen to fall.

The old man, on the other hand, although sometimes struggling with the weight of the cans, invariably takes pains to return them to their place on the drive and to replace their lids — a fastidiousness for which one supposes he has never heard a word of thanks. My acquaintance spoke of this with a fervor that had to do with more than just the survival of his flowers. He rightly saw it as an example of pride of workmanship, resulting from an attitude and habit of mind which may be disappearing.

The job of trash collecting, essential as it is, does not command much public prestige. Yet somewhere that old man learned — learned beyond ever forgetting — that the nature of work counts for less than the manner of its doing. So he goes about his task with care, not remembering there is any other way. His rank is not a consideration. He does it for himself.

To spend too much thought on where one fits into the larger picture — on what, precisely, one's place is or ought to be — is pointless and can be bitterly corrosive. There are, in this world, certain circles of talent or luck or privilege from which we remain forever excluded. For everyone, regardless of gifts or means, there is some such circle.

Always there will be someone abler. Or richer. Or more beautiful. Or more influential. Or better pedigreed. And they will appear to live in charmed circles. But for them, too, there will be other circles, different ones, to which entry is forbidden.

How, then, does one find one's true place?

It does not need finding. One's place is wherever one happens naturally to be. And only gnawing resentment can make it dishonorable.

Other Music, Other Rooms

I t is disheartening to consider the effort we must expend and the pain we are obliged to suffer in order to satisfy the expectations of others. I think of this most often on Thursday, which for the young of our household is music lesson day.

As you may have noticed, flesh born of woman does not spring into this life with immediate genius for playing the clarinet or French horn. And most attempts to learn may be classified, aesthetically if not in law, as unnatural acts — more unnatural for some than for others.

Certain children have flaccid lips and sausage fingers and tin ears. And some are worse than just ungifted. But never mind that. One of our most cherished assumptions is that anyone in this world can accomplish anything he sets himself to. And its corollary is that any child, regardless of his own will or aptitude, can be made to fit the mold of his parents' hopes.

So it is that small boys with spindly shins and eyes wild with terror must strap on pads and run trembling up and down the football fields of the land in pursuit of their fathers' approval. Or that girls still soft with baby fat must be committed to the fearful discipline of East German lady shotputters or Romanian gymnasts.

And so it is, too, that each Thursday, in the hour immediately before supper, my daughters are delivered up to the place of their musical advancement. But with the important difference that the idea of lessons was theirs entirely, not ours.

The music school is a warren of small studio rooms in the basement of an instrument company. In the long hallways outside the rooms are metal folding chairs for students waiting to begin their lessons or parents praying for them to end. Once some years ago I was in a slaughterhouse and I have never forgotten the sound of that. All through the subterranean labyrinth of the music school there reverberates a terrible and many-voiced lament: the strangled grunts of the tuba, the braying of trombone and whinny of cornet, the porcine squeal of cracked reeds and protesting strings. They remind me of the noises of the abattoir and in a real sense they are. For something is being murdered there, too.

Our daughters chose piano which, I have discovered, is the discreetest of instruments. Mostly their mother takes them to their lesson on Thursday, but I am an occasional substitute. I sit on a chair in the hall and now and then look in through the small window to observe them puzzling out a bar of music or bent in studious consultation with their teacher. The sweet murmur of their playing barely can be heard through the acoustically padded walls of the room

Not so, however, with the aspirant in the next studio to the left. That one is a student of horn. Which horn I can't say; it is unidentifiable in his hands. The noises he causes to come out of it — the heaving groans and windy gurgles — have nothing at all to do with music. Last week I think he was playing God Bless America, and what he did to that song would in some societies be punishable by public strokes.

I try to sit very small in my chair, very flat against the side of the hallway. I look fixedly at the studio in which my daughters are quietly mastering the piano. And in spite of that, other parents seated along the hall peer wonderingly at the closed door of the horn cubicle, then inspect me with a kind of furtive pity. After each explosion of flatulence from behind the door, I want urgently to leap to my feet and cry out, *Not mine! I don't know who or what's inside there, but it isn't mine! Mine are in the next studio. Mine are the two pianists.*

From time to time during the hour, that studio opens and

the teacher, a tall, pale man with a crazy look in his eye, stumbles out and shuts the door quickly on the incredible racket behind him.

He stands there in the outer hall, swaying a little on his feet like a fireman who has just fought his way through heavy smoke. He doesn't say anything or look at any of us. He just stares a few moments fixedly at the blank wall. Then looks at his watch. Then draws up his shoulders and hurls himself back into the room.

That man must wonder sometimes at the direction his life has taken, and whether there can ever be any way back.

Just once, in leaving, did I glimpse the monster of studio 5. He turned out to be only a small, roundish boy of 10 or 12 years, trapped in his horn's brass coils, perspiring and hopeless of eye, as much a victim as any of us. Then he sucked in a giant's breath, his cheeks ballooned — and we fled directly up the stairs and out to the car.

As I say, music was our daughters' own idea. They began piano because it pleased them to. They are quite as free to stop. We refuse to make them hostage to our expectations. Their futures must be their own to shape.

Not long ago the younger one came home from seeing the motion picture called "The Children of Theater Street," about the famous Russian dancing school in St. Petersburg. "I've decided what to be when I grow up," she announced. "I'm going to be a famous ballerina."

We were delighted for her, naturally, and offered our immediate congratulations.

But how well did she understand the demands of the dancer's calling? Did she know that, no less than the piano, it would mean a life of unyielding discipline? No more frivolous vacations, no cheeseburgers, no idling in the sun by the pool. Only iron devotion to one's art — days, months, years spent flexing at the barre.

A punishing prospect, no doubt about it. But that is the price of greatness.

"Well . . ."

She turned the matter again in her mind.

"Maybe then," she said finally, "I'll just be famous on our block."

Life Under Glass

The children have received a microscope as a gift. No, that's not exactly true. What has happened is that their father has given them a microscope for himself to play with, which he does fairly often and which, as it happens, he is doing now, as he makes these notes.

His knowledge of science — of any science — is embarrassingly slight. But he has become fascinated by the small worlds that can be entered through the instrument's eyepiece.

The scope, an inexpensive one, is set now on its lowest power, a magnification of fifty times.

A desk lamp laid on its side sends light glancing from a mirror up through the bottom of the slide. Coffee and tobacco, the comforts of travel, are at hand. Today's expedition is into a droplet of water drawn from the murk of a long-abandoned goldfish tank and deposited in the polished depression on the slide. (Experience has shown water from the tap, although more populous than one might wish, to be less interesting than the aquarium's juices.)

Under the lens, that one drop becomes a considerable sea. Things are suspended in it — terrible, spiny clusters that resemble islands of steel wool. But they are inanimate, evidently.

Then, at the upper right edge of the optical field, life announces itself. Shift the field a fraction, and a tiny globule of gelatin is seen to thrust out a curious "head" and then to dart away quickly, as if on some remembered errand, in the direction the head was pointed. It goes with purpose, and its speed, on the scale of its environment, is nothing less than fabulous.

If memory serves, one of the spiny islands is drifting somewhere to the left, approximately on the creature's course. Shift the field again. Yes, there the thing is. The swimmer seems not to see or sense it there and, as if deliberately, plunges straight ahead into the awful tangle, writhes there a while, and then is still.

The whole sea is still as well. For in that droplet not another living thing can be found — only the drifting stalks and fragments of some that might once have lived. Sometimes it is like that. Life does not uniformly teem. But the next sample, taken from a different sector of the fish tank, is broth of a richer sort.

Instead of a single protozoon, there are now whole colonies and cruising schools of them. Animals of a different species, these — lightly speckled, able at will to clench and then elongate themselves in tubular shape, with a fine beard of cilia whirling about what one takes to be a mouth.

The glass depression in which the droplet lies is, to the naked eye and to the touch, ground out and polished to a perfect smoothness. Under the lens, however, it looks quite different. Magnified, its rim becomes a jagged and forbidding coast, distinguished by countless unnamed coves and prominences, broken headlands and shadowed fiords. One of these coastal features might well be named Point Desolation. For there, it seems, the weak and hurt among the swimmers appear most often to be borne up by the tide, to cluster in considerable numbers and finally to die.

An afternoon easily can slip by thus, with the eye held rapt to the scope.

One forgets to smoke. Coffee grows cold in the cup, as it has now, and must be replenished. While doing that, the maker of these notes will have to consider whether to tell here — to invite ridicule by telling — something that he has just seen under the glass.

The kettle boils. And, yes, he will tell about it — but in the most factual way. Just the event itself as it occurred, or seemed to, without any discussion of the implications. Without concluding anything.

Moving the field of the glass ever so slowly, he had set out from Point Desolation, bearing southeastward down into that quarter of the sea where, on another map, Australia might have been. There he came upon two protozoa of the race described above. Or it may have been one animal in the process of becoming two. First they seemed a mass together, but soon divided either into two individuals or autonomous halves of the one. It makes no difference which.

Swimming only a short distance, then, these two blundered into the threadlike tendrils of some filamentous object and commenced immediately to thrash and struggle in an attempt to free themselves. These exertions, which only caused them to become worse entangled, grew progressively more feeble. The outcome seemed obvious. But with a last violent contortion, one of the creatures managed actually to break loose. Immediately it darted some little way off and stopped there, its middle parts rising and falling rapidly.

The note-taker duly recorded this behavior, observing — at least to himself — that, were it some other, larger species, the animal might be described as panting with exhaustion and relief. Then he put his eye back to the glass and noticed an unaccountable thing.

The free creature, the escapee, had turned again toward the danger zone — had drawn close to the entangled one, actually touching it finally with its forepart but eliciting only a faint movement.

"Look out!" the note-taker cried aloud.

But it was no use. With a slight wrong movement, the creature had come up against a filament again. Another instant and it was entirely enmeshed. The thrashings were repeated, although more briefly. Then a final quiet settled over that zone of the sea.

It was not something one is glad to have seen. And it is not something the note-taker is entirely comfortable to be reporting here. He does not know what it means. He does not want to know.

That much decided, he will now take a square of paper tissue and dry that specimen slide until it squeaks.

Country Markings

The intention had been to spare them hurt. To that end I had years before invented a gentle fiction. Then, on a recent sun-washed day, I found how clumsily I'd made the hurting worse. It began with the smallest question.

We had seized the weekend, my two small daughters and I, to make a beginning on a long-planned project in the woods. The exact nature of the task is unimportant. But it involved hard working with our hands, the three of us together. And now, at midday, in a perfect state of comfort with the sun warm overhead and the breeze cool against our faces, we sat on mossy stones, listening to bird songs and sharing our lunch from a sack.

"Where did you bury them?" the younger one suddenly asked. Not morbidly at all. Just wanting the information. And she spoke their names — the names of the first dogs in her memory, and among the greatest ones in mine. The two little rabbit hounds, dead those five years.

"Over there," I said, and pointed. We looked together across the glitter of the pond. "Up on the hillside there. It was a favorite place of theirs."

"And where are they now?" The question had been asked before. And again I spoke the fiction which, through usage, had come to be expected.

"Running somewhere, I suppose."

"Oh," she said. Reassured by the telling of it, she and her sister turned their attention back to lunch.

The day moved on. The afternoon light softened and the

breeze fell. Woodpeckers sent their urgent rappings across the stillness. Small fish rising made circles on the dark water. We had finished our work — or that part of it we had set for ourselves. But we were together in a flawless hour, and to leave quite yet was unimaginable. So we contrived a make-work task, carrying and placing flat stones for a path across the shallow outlet of the pond.

We were some yards apart when I heard a sharp, happy cry. It was the younger one again. "I saw a dog," she announced to us. "There, through the trees." Her small face was turned toward the hillside.

"Just one?" her sister asked.

"It might have been two." She meant to be truthful, but hope was remaking the truth in her mind. "I'm pretty sure it was two!"

"Do you think it could be them?" her sister asked. Older — but a child still.

My daughters were looking at me. "Could be," I said. And wanted those words back immediately. Knew the cruelty of my mistake. The small one started away up the hill, then. Excitement chimed in her voice. Excitement and unreasoning faith. She was calling them by name.

"They can't hear you," I said. But she went on a little way in spite of that, unwilling to believe. The older one and I walked back together along the pond dam to the dock, where she lay down on her stomach, staring into the black water. For a long time she didn't make a sound. Just lay there, face down toward the pond, her tears sending out silent rings where they struck.

"Why didn't you call them?" she asked finally. She put it as a *question. In those few minutes, though, she had come far toward puzzling out the answer for herself.*

It was a while before I could reply.

"Because," I told her then — the truth at last. "There'd only be heartache in it."

Homestead

The old house straddled the hill between the black line of cedars and a thicket of wild plum, looking out across fields gone mostly to weeds and berry tangles from disuse.

There were holes in the roof — you could stand in the living room and, looking directly overhead, watch spring clouds passing across a considerable reach of sky. Squirrels lived in the attic and raccoons under the floor. A persistent trumpet vine, sometime in past years, had sent an exploring tendril into the bedroom between the window and the sill. The tendril had grown into a woody cable as thick as your thumb, forcing the window open. Other shoots followed, maturing, flowering and dropping their parchment leaves in the silent seasons of that room.

I came on the place while trespassing, following my two beagle hounds across the fallen fences of that country 20 years ago.

There was some broken furniture in the house. But clearly it had long been untenanted. The first dwellers, most likely, were under the fieldstone markers in a grove in the field to the west. The last had gone somewhere else to live. Trespassers before me, hunters in the winter, had sheltered there and built a fire on the kitchen floor.

Miraculously, the place had not burned. Wildfires used to sweep that country every fall and spring, set deliberately to kill the ticks or to clear the undergrowth from woodland pasture. One of these had claimed the barn — consumed it to its native stone foundation. But the house itself had been spared and waited now, wrapped in a drowsy-threatening hum of resident wasps, for a different sort of end. Wind and rot work more slowly than fire, but in the end they are quite as thorough. The place hadn't many more years of life. In the back yard, a rusting tractor of ancient vintage had, from the look of it, already coughed its last.

We rested and dreamed there a part of an afternoon those twenty years ago. Then a spring squall blew up and we hurried off, the beagles and I, to the surer shelter of our cabin three hills away.

Seven years more went by. And in the curious turnings that things sometimes take, I found myself a landed fellow — the possessor in fee simple not just of any land but of that very place. Owner of the neglected fields, the cemetery, the foundation of the burned barn, the broken tractor and the ruined house itself with its appurtenant raccoons and squirrels and wasps and interior trumpet vine jungle.

Shortly after that a family came. Tenants is the usual term, but friends is the more factual one. Warm, good people with more courage than most of us, and with their own dreams as a pattern to work from. It was early October, with hard winter only a few uncertain weeks away, and, standing in the living room, you still could see sky and clouds. They were racing the season.

First the roof. Then the well, collapsed into itself in a wreck of sodden boards. Then the broken window of the bedroom where the vine had lived. The projects were taken in order of their urgency. And, mercifully, the Indian summer held into middle December.

Now that, in turn, is going on a dozen years ago. What changes those years have brought! The house that was so manifestly doomed is once more tight and dry. Its reincarnation still is in progress — may always be. Its thirsty old boards, for instance, will be needing their third coat of paint before this season's out. But it's a light and happy place. A refreshing breeze stirs through it on the hottest day. And there are even children growing up there again.

There is hay in the barn — oh, yes, the burned barn has a successor — and two thousand or so new bales lie in patterned rows in the green, rehabilitated fields. Beyond the hay, cattle rest in the shade at the edge of woods. Sound fences define the margins. An orchard has been set out. There is a dooryard vegetable garden, full of promise — though just now needing rain. Even the ancient tractor has been gotten running again.

It is the discouraging pattern of this world that things wear out and lose their usefulness and are discarded. We inure ourselves to inevitable decay. Roadside junk yards and appliances with a three-day guarantee have lost the power to chill with their implications.

Yet, say what you will about human beings' capacity to wreck, there is also, in the best of them, an abiding instinct to preserve and to restore. Thus a farmstead that was dead, beyond use, has embarked upon a second productive life. And all because of the caring presence, the courage and the special talents of a very remarkable family.

I like to think that I own the place still, but that's of course an empty conceit. It's no more mine, now — and maybe less — than when I came on it as a trespasser. My name is on the deed, that's true. But in all the ways that are more important, it belongs to the people who live there and have shaped it to their hopes.

The Meadow Harvest

A friend of mine is a country man, by which I mean only that he lives in the country and partakes of country pleasures. He is in every way as capable and as cultivated as any of us who call the city home. The only things about him you might think of as being countrified are the gentleness of his speech and the grave courtesy of his manner which, in these strident and angry times, I have always taken to be the most civilized of virtues.

I greatly enjoy his company and flatter myself to think that he likes mine. That's just a guess. If he didn't, he would never let me know.

Anyhow, I met this friend on a rural lane the other day while I was out berry picking. There is nothing I know of that rewards a little industry more generously than wild blackberries, fresh-picked and eaten for breakfast in a bowl of milk with a sprinkle of sugar on the top.

In an ordinary year, the crop is so profuse, the thorny canes so heavy with fruit, that success — as with the writing of prose — is limited only by the time you have available to spend and the pain you are prepared to suffer. This spring, though, after a profuse bloom, a late frost had come to strip the brambles nearly bare. So, in spite of a half-hour's hunting, the bucket still was empty and my friend noticed that.

"Let me show you a patch I know about," he said, and gestured over the next hill. "There'll be berries there if there are any anywhere." (He had just come from finishing the season's haying, a hot and tiresome job. And his dinner was waiting for him at the house — though he didn't mention that, and wouldn't have. I learned about it later.)

With him leading, we crawled through a fence and set off

along a timber track down toward a moist and grassy meadow. "My dad and I used to always come here," he said as we walked. "In fact, the last time we picked berries together it was here."

The father, also a soft-spoken and gentle man, had been gone two years. He had lived a long and vigorous life and had given much happiness to his family and to others. He died on a stifling mid-summer day and was found beside a tree where he had stopped to rest, his pail of blackberries beside him.

I remembered that, of course, and remarked that it seemed as easy a way as any for things to end.

"I guess so," my friend said. "If someone has to go. But it's been hard. We all miss him so much." That's another thing about the country. People, if they know and trust you, are not ashamed to speak their feelings.

We came out into the bottom of the meadow, with the sovereign berry patch just ahead. Lush and heavily foliaged it was — and barren like all the others. The ruinous frost, it seemed, had settled there, too. Except for the sweetness of the prize, we might have turned back. Instead we followed the meadow up the side of the next hill and there, near the woodline at the top, found a thicket whose fruit had ripened safely above the killing cold. And further along the ridge to the right, an even larger and more prolific growth.

Thorns clawed our arms and chiggers colonized us. Shortly, though, the pail was half full and heavy.

Would my friend share the harvest? No, not one berry. His time and his secret meadow he'd willingly share, but only if he could give them freely. He went off then toward his own house and his lovely wife and his dinner gotten cold from waiting.

I felt a bite of envy as I watched him go. It is a fine thing, and anymore a rare one, to be able to pass your life in a single stretch of country and know it well, to devote your years to that, to receive its careless gifts and bury your sadnesses in it.

My country friend is a lucky man. Best of all, I believe he knows that.

The berries were eaten the next morning, with other friends, beside an open window in the rain. And they were wonderful — as fine as anything you ever tasted. Where you find them, and whom you pick them with, has a lot to do with the flavor of wild blackberries.

Bad Fences: A Country Correspondence

God did not will that the way of cultivation should be easy.
— Virgil

(There follow here certain letters, shortened a bit but otherwise unedited, which were exchanged not long ago on a rural matter.)

Robins Hill Farm
Appleton City, MO
June 13

Dear Charles:

Yesterday afternoon a bunch of cattle (approx. 30 head) come up from the east on that old road & got in the soybean patch & we're sick about it. We back tracked them down the creek to a pasture belonging to a man name of Argus Mooner (some of the cows had brands A M) & there was a fence with limms on it looked like it had been down sometime.

So we called the man's they were & he wasn't home but his wife & 2 boys come over & helped chase awhile. She acted kind of mad about it, as she'd been to the beauty parlor & was afraid she'd mess up her hair. It was so hot Ralph wore out & got down at the far end of the patch & I had to come get the car & go bring him back

About 3 a.m. this morning the dogs barked, I got up & the cattle was back. I didn't wake Ralph & by morning they had eat it off clean & left.

Ruint!!

Thought we had better let you know.

Yours truly,

Ula

Kansas City
June 15

Mr. Argus Mooner
Rural Route
Appleton City, Mo.

Dear Mr. Mooner:

Here for your record is a copy of the letter concerning the estraying of your cattle into my soybean field. If it is agreeable with you, we will wait until harvest to calculate the dollar loss.

Sincerely,

Charles Gusewelle

Robins Hill Farm
June 18

Dear Charles:

Argus Mooner come over this morning & looked at the patch & said he was sorry about the trouble it caused & all. Seemed real nice about it.

Canning berries,
Ula

Appleton City
June 18

Dear Mr. Gusewelle:

I feel there should be corrections made. The cattle ate the tops of the bean plants, but in no way can it be construed that the stand was destroyed. It is entirely possible that the plants will send up another stem and produce beans. In fact, in some instances the "clipped" beans have out-yielded unclipped or unmolested beans.

Sincerely,
Argus D. Mooner

cc: Mr. Ralph Roberts

Robins Hill Farm
June 20

Dear Charles:

We read the copy of his letter & was hopping mad. Last night we got to thinking about it some more & got tickled, but now I'm mad again. I've got half a mind to get a lawyer — say that Ralph wore his self out over it, & I'm a-worryin, & that it's messed up our sex

life, & sue him for unrecollectable differences on that
if nothing else.

Still mad,
Ula

Kansas City
June 25

Dear Mr. Mooner:

One passage in your letter of last week particularly
engaged my interest. That is, your mention of
instances in which "clipped" beans have out-yielded
unclipped. You have opened up here a most
stimulating area of inquiry. Due to the recent nature
of the incident my reading on the subject still is
limited. But have you by any chance seen the reports
of the excellent work done in recent months by Dr. C.
J. Humus at Beltsville? His monograph, "Incidence of
Double-Podding in Soja max, Clipped and
Unclipped," was, to my mind, most challenging and I
can commend it to you without reservation. I think we
will agree that Chet Humus was, and is, pre-eminent
in his field.

In the name of fair play, I would propose the
following arrangement: If the "clipped" beans should
in the end outyield the rest of my beans, as you
suggest they may, I will pay you a royalty of $1 per
bushel for each bushel of beans that the clipped field
produces in excess of the average of my unclipped
field, plus a modest fee (as we shall agree between us)
for your cows' services in manuring my field, less my
charge (at $3 per head per month, pro rata) for one
day's pasturage for 33 head of cattle.

Moreover, I would hope — if it seems advisable from my continuing reading on the subject — that perhaps later in the summer I might arrange (again, for a fair fee) to engage the services of your herd in "clipping" my remaining 25 acres of soybeans.

Please let me know if the above suggestions strike you as equitable. Meantime, I shall continue to pass on for your consideration any further technical materials that may seem of interest.

For example, I have in hand a most intriguing summary of a piece in an obscure journal, *Everyman's Horticulture,* by Jerzy Dubik. If I do not misread Professor Dubik's thesis, it is that the interaction between the cellular structure of *Soja max* and cow's rumen can, under certain circumstances of temperature and soil acidity, result in the production not of soybeans but of *cucumbers.*

Or was it blueberries?

Never mind, I shall locate the journal and read the monograph in its original.

Awaiting your next, I remain

Neighborly yours,
Charles

Division of Extension
Agronomy
Kansas State University
Manhattan
June 29

Dear Mr. Gusewelle:

Your letter regarding clipped soybeans has been referred to me. We don't have research information on this matter in Kansas. Therefore, I hesitate to speculate on advantages or disadvantages of this practice. But if it were sound, I am certain that soybean producers would be using it regularly.

In summary, do not mow your soybeans. I doubt that it would pay.

Sincerely,
Verlin H. Peterson
Extension Specialist,
   Crop Production

Embassy of the
   Czechoslovak
   Socialist Republic
3900 Linnean Ave., N.W.
Washington, D.C.
July 2

Dear Sir:

Referring to your letter dated 22 June concerning some information about professor Dubik in Czechoslovakia I recommend you to write to:

Ministerstvo zemedelstvi
Tesnov, Praha 1.
Czechoslovakia

Very truly yours,
Josef Velek
Commercial Attache

Kansas City
July 5

Dear Mr. Mooner:

I'm afraid I will not be needing your cows' services on that back soybean field after all, since the advice seems to be against grazing them. This is a disappointment, as I had hoped we might really be onto something there.

Also, I would like to apologize for having passed on some wrong information in my letter of June 25.

I have discovered, on further investigation, that Jerzy Dubik was not a plant scientist at all. He was a minor Slovak poet, and the document to which I referred turns out to have been a manuscript page from his memoirs, rejected for publication shortly before his passing in 1926 of, I believe, a social disease.

It came into the possession of a distant cousin in this country, in a trunk of old papers, and some time later was inserted as a page marker in the copy of *Everyman's Horticulture* at a section dealing with the control of aphids in floribunda rose.

As for the passage in question, it seems that Soja was the given name of the poet's former wife, who, during pregnancy, had been fond to excess of cucumbers and blueberries. We are left, then, with a reminiscence, nothing more. The fault was in my translation. And in the author's penmanship, which, due perhaps to failing health, was in places barely legible.

So please forgive the error. In the course of all this I have had the privilege of examining a slender book of Dubik's verse, printed (undated) at the author's

own expense in Prague. To my mind, it is doggerel.
The man's obscurity was richly deserved.

I understand the drought in the neighborhood
has lately been broken by two or three nice rains. So it
looks like we will have a good year for soybeans in
spite of everything.

Cordially yours,
Charles

(This correspondence was terminated abruptly when Mr.
Mooner passed word through the town barber that, if he
received another letter from me, I would be shot on sight.

(His fences still are bad. We see one another across them
from time to time, at a considerable distance.)

Morris

I have heard neighbors down in St. Clair County, out on
the blacktop east and south of Appleton City, swear that if
Morris Underwood ever moved away or quit fixing things
they would just have to give up farming. For some of them
that may be exaggeration. For me it is absolute truth.

Morris has had a run of awful luck. Several years ago — two,
or maybe three — his old house on the hill burned in the night.
The Underwoods set up a trailer where the house had stood.
Three times lightning struck the telephone. The phone people
told Morris that what he needed was a wall model. So with the
fourth strike the lightning burned up the phone and the trailer,
too.

Morris and his wife have retreated temporarily to his

workshop, living there until the trailer is replaced. But they are not going to move. There have been Underwoods on that hill for longer than anyone can remember — so many generations of them that, on the maps, the hill is identified by the family name. And Morris will be there for the rest of his days, which is a mercy for all of us who depend on him.

This has been the haying season, and in haying time there is a wonderful variety of machines to be broken. The minor breakdowns are doctored where they stand, with a piece of wire, a spare bolt, a hammer, wrench and a whispered prayer. Next in order of seriousness are the *shade tree* jobs. The disabled implement is pulled to the edge of the field, under the leafy canopy of a friendly oak, for several hours of strenuous tinkering.

Beyond that, there is only one thing left to do: Take it to Morris. What Morris gets, then, are mainly the critical cases and sometimes the terminal ones. And in this haying season we have been breaking machines almost faster than he can get them running again.

First it was the second tractor — the one that pulls the hay rake. Then the mower. Then the rake itself. Then the mower again, its inner parts. And finally, most ruinously of all, the hay baler. The thing roared and grumbled mightily. Some of the gears turned; some didn't. Deep in its iron heart we had somehow wounded it terribly. Another neighbor acquainted with that machine came to help with the diagnosis. He looked. He listened to its metallic howl. Then he pronounced the fateful verdict: "I believe I'd haul it over to Morris."

Our places face one another diagonally across the blacktop. Morris has a long time to see us coming — out our quarter-mile of gravel lane to the road, another quarter-mile along the blacktop and then up his own lane to the top of the hill.

But whether he actually *does* see us coming I can't say. Maybe our despair goes ahead of us and announces us in some psychic way. Or maybe Morris just figures that there is a better-than-even chance that if he walks outside — any time of night or day — he will see us coming with something broken. In any case, by the time we turn up his lane he is usually waiting there on the top of the hill. And always he is smiling, not because he is glad for our misfortune but because he knows we are bringing him a new challenge.

He is a large, powerful man with great blunt hands that can move as delicately as a surgeon's. There are many kinds of genius in this world and Morris Underwood has true genius in his hands. There is no other word for it.

Even before you can stop with the machine in tow he is walking toward it. And magically, it seems, he already has in hand or in his pocket the exact tool that he will need for the first exploratory step of his doctoring.

I have never seen him refer to any diagram or manual. He has no need of them. The way that machines are put together and the way they function are mostly governed by a sort of lovely, uniform logic. Cylinders must fire in a certain order and in an engine, any engine, certain things must happen to allow them to do that. If a shaft is stuck fast in place there must somewhere be a key, a pin. Not sometimes but *always*. There are laws in mechanics as invariable as the laws of nature. Morris's mind and hands are in harmony with this fine logic.

You either have the genius or you do not. Most of us, in matching the tool to the job, assume that the larger the problem, the larger the force that must be brought to bear. But what we would address with sledge hammer and crowbar, I have seen Morris Underwood approach with a screwdriver as small as a watchmaker's and needle-nosed pliers that looked like something from a dentist's tray.

Our tractor he repaired with a penknife — and it has run perfectly since. In the mower, a dry bearing had wrecked the shaft; he had it working again by morning. One arm of the rake had worn in two. He burrowed under his scrap heap for a length of pipe and set to work with hacksaw and welding torch. Two hours later he pronounced the rake better than it had come from the factory, and I haven't any doubt that is true.

The baler, our last casualty, was in graver distress. Something was twisted and torn in its innards. It would neither take hay in the front end nor discharge finished bales from the back end. When commanded to do either, it shook and chattered and made pitiable groans.

Morris walked around it and came back to the side where he had already decided the focus of the problem lay. His anticipation was plain to see.

"I've never worked on one of these," he said — speculatively, but without the least fear. "When I get done I'll know something won't I?" Then he took out those tiny pliers of his and began probing under the grease for the pin that he knew, beyond any doubt, must be there somewhere.

When I get done I'll know something. It struck me, hearing him say that, that he had just expressed about as well as can be done the creed of a useful life. To have a gift; to apply it joyfully; to welcome problems for what they can teach; to go boldly onto new ground so that, tomorrow, you will know something that you don't know today.

It hardly needs saying that the hay baler is back in operation, humming like a Rolls Royce and leaving rows of perfect bales behind.

If it had been a jet airplane engine that we'd taken him, though he had never seen one, the result would have been the same. He would have looked at it, and probed at it with some small instrument until he had discovered its inner logic — the logic of all machines. And in due time he would have put it right.

Our unpaid account with Morris has gotten embarrassingly

long. The trouble is that when you go with your broken implements directly from the field you rarely have a billfold or checkbook in your pocket. And when the settling-up does come, as eventually it will, undoubtedly he will ask too little. Genius seldom commands its fair reward.

Morris has recently taken a job as night deputy marshal, keeping the law between the hours of 10 p.m. and morning in the town of Rockville seven miles away. Sometime, I suppose, he sleeps. And yet he still manages somehow to deal with all the problems his neighbors bring him. So that again this season as before, the business of farming in that corner of St. Clair County manages to go forward.

The Solitary

Vast the field, with woodland bordering. Small the distant creature in its center.

Draw closer and you will find it to be a horse — a red horse alone in a pasture of a farm from which the people have gone. The field, clipped close and brown with summer grazing, is empty except for the single animal. The woods also are empty, the cattle having been taken from there to some other place.

It is all the horse's kingdom now — all the clipped meadows, the rocky prominences and brushy ravines. A mile in any direction to a fence. His solitary province.

The horse has not actually been left and forgotten. He is only unused. A new farmer will come there soon to live. After some months the cattle will return as well, and then there will be use for him aplenty. But none of this, of course, does the horse know. He understands only that a great quietness has come to rule.

One day there was a stir of life in the barn lot. The house doors forever opened and closed. Voices could be heard, and some recognized. The next day the other animals, excepting only him, were collected and rode away inside trucks.

And the day after that the voices stopped, the silence came.

In the horse's experience such a thing never has happened before. He is mystified by it, perhaps a bit alarmed. He stands alone now in the center of the farm's largest field. But the path worn by his hooves just inside the fence's perimeter tells how many times previously he has measured, then measured again, the dimension of his solitude.

He will, as I say, be provided for. That much is assured. He does not yet know this, though, and so may be considering, with what passes for foresight in a horse: *Will there be hay? If the house is not lived in, who will bring it? And if no one does, what of me? What will become of me, forgotten here?*

In the yellow evening, though it is only the last of summer, he smells the air for snow.

Two walkers may be noticed now to advance into the edge of his field. The red horse lifts his head to watch them approach, then takes a questioning step or two in their direction. But plainly he was not the reason for their coming. They just walk on by.

Always before when people have come toward him afoot across a pasture it has been for the purpose of catching him up. And, after catching, to work him. Not easily to be caught was a fine sport, at which he was an expert. Oh, he would suffer himself finally to be touched and bridled, but only after making clear that the discretion in the matter was his.

But to be passed by with scarcely a notice; just to be left standing with no attempt at catching . . . that is an event of a different and mysterious and disappointing sort. He watches the two people pass out of that pasture, down a wooded path bearing toward another meadow. He makes a sound in his nose and looks about the empty field.

And then he does something — this large, solitary, famously hard-to-catch red horse — that he has never done before. He follows after them, falls in step behind. First at a discreet distance. Then closer, until finally he overtakes them, treading almost on their heels. The walkers stop and turn. He hesitates, but for an instant only. Then comes shouldering directly up, not just permitting himself to be stroked and patted, *demanding* to be.

The people speak to him by name. The sound of it is familiar. Why, it is his own name! So he is known, after all. He is remembered.

That is slender evidence to base a winter's hopes on, but for him, for now, it is sufficient. The people walk on. He just stands, feeling no further need to follow. Then turns away, satisfied, to go about some errand in the deeper woods.

Is there a single word to describe what was in his mind for those few moments?

Looking into the eyepiece of a microscope I have seen one-celled animals, primitive and gelatinous things, swimming in a daub of water on the specimen slide. Watch long enough and, if there happen to be two of them, sooner or later they will make their way to one another across the empty regions of their droplet sea.

In our house, the dog follows us from room to room, refusing to be alone. The cats, defying the proper nature of things, sleep pressed against the dog.

Do these creatures understand the meaning of loneliness? Does the red horse despise and fear his unbroken march of empty days?

Is there anything or anyone of us alive that doesn't?

In the Place Given

The soil on his hill is sandy and underlain shallowly by rock, inhospitable to growing things. But my friend has stirred that earth and worked it fine, and there he has made his garden. The many rows of it lie long and straight.

He does not garden for amusement, although the doing of it gives him pleasure. He is a country man, for whom that is serious country work. To make fruitful his considerable patch of tilled ground will assure the fatness of his family's table all through the summer and beyond, on into the season of snow.

To fail would be a genuine inconvenience. So he takes no chance of failing.

He plants the best seed, ordered in the dark of winter from a catalogue he studies with care. Cheaper seed can be gotten. But since the germ of his whole harvest is in those packets, he considers correctly that seed is not the place to save.

Some gardeners cannot be patient. They begin too soon, and their seed rots or sprouts weakly in soil from which the cold has not quite gone. Or a frost blackens their young plants. But he proceeds by the wiser schedule of men who better understand the cadences of growth. Intuition directs him — intuition and old rules. Certain plantings must be made in the dark of the moon and others in some different lunar phase. Country people, who garden with a purpose, accept this with the faith of generations. We call it superstition — and then observe our own ill-timed plantings mysteriously grow spindly and barren.

Aesthetically, his garden is a work of pleasant geometry. The plants in it are arranged with an eye to their eventual size and fullness. So that looking at it later, in its maturity, one sees in the whole an expression of orderly thought, of elegant logic.

It is not, however, merely work of the intellect. There is much hard labor in it — wagon loads of rotted straw and manure to be hauled from the calf lot in the spring and worked into the ground to both nourish growth and hold moisture. And, after that, repeated cultivations to keep the rows clean of weeds.

But enough details of gardening. You have, I think, a picture of the man: provident, foresighted, and with the discipline to carry out his plans.

Returning now to the first point, which was the arid nature of the soil atop the hill where my friend lives. I have seen other men try desultorily to make garden in that exact place — men who occupied the house before him. Nearly all of them failed. Too droughty, they said it was. Or too stony. It drained wrong. Or was too exposed to the withering winds of the summer. Always there was some good explanation.

But this man I speak of seemed oblivious to all these reasons why what he had to do could not be done. That spot on the hill was the one that happened to be available to him. *"I'll make my garden there,"* he said without an instant's hesitation.

And so he has done, for three years now.

This summer, with his plantings safely in and flourishing, he began another project. Nearby the garden he is constructing a root cellar. Having first dug a room-sized pit, he has poured a cement floor, inclined so that it drains through a tile at one rear corner. Now he is laying up the sides of concrete blocks. And when the roof is finished he will mound it over for insulation with the earth dug out to make the pit. Entered by a short stair and doorway on the garden side, it will afford safe winter storage for the produce put up in jars by the women of his house.

It is a large task, the building of a root cellar. Of course, if one hasn't the gift for wringing abundance from unpromising ground, or finds enough reasons not to try, one is spared the problem.

My friend goes gladly to his work.

Her Wisdom

A little cloud came slipping up the sky. The day had just begun.

Farming the land, my wife's mother used to say, is a bitter business. I always dismissed that as an old lady's maundering. She was, after all, well on toward 80. And as it happened, she was also right.

One small cloud on a clear day, that's all it was. Hardly worth the notice. Next spring's wheat was on the ground, broadcast with the fertilizer. Nothing remained except to turn it gently under. And then, if winter didn't kill it and the spring rains didn't blight it and the weeds didn't take it or the hail shatter it out before the harvest, and if the price for it didn't take another dive — if none of these calamities ensued — all a farmer had to do was sit back and wait for it to grow. And afterward count his profits.

But that little cloud slipped higher up the sky, and then drew closer. A wind came out of it, blowing hard from south and east.

How slowly the tractor moved! You cannot know the true meaning of slowness until your eye has measured the progress of an antique tractor pulling an ancient disc over a 40-acre field, with a deluge forecast and more seed and fertilizer than you can handily afford lying exposed atop the ground. The machine's advance is undetectable. A glacier's movement would be, by comparison, breakneck.

The little cloud spread out to cover half the sky. And then the whole sky. And turning sooty dark it spat a rain. A small rain, at the first. But after that a larger one. The rain came marching like a sloven dragging her wet skirts across the field. The disc blades caught up the earth in gummy clods. The tractor tires began to slip and spin on the turns.

Spells of that thenceforward through the day. Wind and shower. The day cooling. Lunch a sandwich eaten in the shelter of a truck. The eater of it chilled and sodden to the skin.

And yet, amazingly, the dimension of the task diminished. Slowly the tractor might move across the field. But move it did. That is, it moved until it stopped — just decided, with a stricken groan from the region of its gear box, that it had labored long years enough. Old machines do not cost much. But old machines break often, and, by their breaking, indirectly cost a lot.

No matter, though. Because the rain came then anyway, the separate drops of it coalescing into sheets, beating like a trillion buckets emptied on the part of the field turned under and the part of it not.

The truck could be seen, then, departing from these catastrophes, withdrawing up a lane that ran a river. Stopping at the house, inside which the man warmed himself beside the stove. And where, looking out in disappointment, he watched the storm contract again into a single cloud, a little cloud scarcely worth the notice, that slid down the sky ahead of a watery sun.

A bitter business, was what she used to say of farming.

Old women have wisdoms worth knowing, if only the men who married their daughters ever had the sense to listen.

Lighted Windows

The quiet life is the lonely life. Go long enough without the regular commerce of other human beings and there comes to be no joy sweeter than a silence broken.

Along a certain country lane I know are two houses in whose windows after nightfall lamps always can be seen to burn. Those are the saddest lights I know. The welcome they offer is altogether an abstraction. They burn for no one. No one is expected. And no one ever comes.

The keepers of the two lamps are friends of mine — friends of many years. One of them is alone because of loss. Her house is full of memories and full of articles that remind her of people she has loved, nearly all of them gone now to death or distance.

The other friend lives by himself by a kind of choice. His wife has work in the city two hours away. Years ago the arrangement was logical. He actively farmed the land, and so — in the solitary march from one weekend to the next — had no alternative but to pass a bachelor life. He aged, though. And gave up farming — rents his land. But by then the habit of silence was fixed and deep. So he remains in the country alone, for reasons now less easily explained.

When first I put down roots in the neighborhood we built fence together, that man and I. Several miles of fence. It was in early March, no season for the task. But circumstances made our labor urgent. Ice froze to our jackets while we worked. We built fires of gathered wood to warm by. When we came in across the fields at dark, me bouncing behind in the tractor box, his house would be empty and still. He would go first into the front room to light the window lamp. Then we would sit together in his kitchen and drink a whiskey or two while we warmed.

His enjoyment of talk was obvious. He told wonderful stories of great fish and fine bird dogs. Then I would go back to my own cabin to sleep away the tiredness and the cold. And the next morning, at first frozen daylight, we would drink coffee and repeat the day. Until one afternoon we looked back along the fence and saw that it was finished. And with no more reason for evening visits, we drew apart into the silences of our respective lives.

His lamp still burns, though, lit at almost the same hour of every night for most of 20 years. If he is unaware of loneliness, it must be because he cannot now remember the absence of it.

Not so my first friend, whose house is nearer along the lane. The keenness of her missing people is undisguised. She is very unguarded, very loving. She speaks of me as her adopted son, and from her endless kindnesses and considerations you could easily believe it true. She comes to sit in the evenings — brings flowers from her garden for my wife, and feathers from her peacock's tail for my daughters, and edibles for me.

Ours is a sorry sort of gratitude. For the talk inevitably ends and she goes away to her house, and the next day or the one after we go back to the city. And her window light burns for people who pass and do not notice, who cannot guess at the sorrow and goodness that house contains.

I understand perfectly the punishment of such extended silences. I lived half a year on that lane, before even those people came to live there. I, too, was unvisited. I learned to depend for companionship on a wood stove's creaking, a tea kettle's piping, the voice of hounds baying trail a long way across the night.

Then my life changed. And I came to live where people talk endlessly — too loudly and too much. Where the confusion and the clamor of the days might be insupportable — except for knowing the alternative.

I was lucky. I came back again from silence. But along that lane where the lonely lamps send out a cry unheard, most people likely never will. The distance is too great, the time too short. And even the habit of pain is hard to break.

The Other Side of Winter

In recent days we have begun taking in worms. Yes, it has come to that. First stray dogs and cats, then lizards and fish, then turtles and neighborhood children. Now worms.

The initial specimens were bright green and horny at one end. The man in the tobacco barn where we picked them up called them tobacco worms. If we'd found them on tomato plants, he said, the same creatures would properly have been called tomato worms.

Like the dung beetle, we are what we eat.

But call them, for convenience's sake, tobacco worms. We found a container for them and, disregarding the surgeon general's warning, provided them their ration of the weed. They gave no sign of noticing their new surroundings. The food was what they were used to. They seemed entirely content to get on with the business of becoming.

What they will become, if the tobacco farmer knows his worms, is a moth of the family *Sphingidae* — hawkmoths, or sphinx moths, as they sometimes are called. In this season of their lives they gnaw bitter leaves and are loathsome to the touch, their beauty, again according to the tobacco farmer, perceived only by hungry channel catfish.

But the best is ahead. In another season they will be nectar drinkers. Ungainliness forgotten, they will come riding on agile wings, swift as birds, silent as shadows. And they will own the dawns and summer dusks of the garden, taking nourishment from the throats of only the sweetest flowers.

Not many days later, on a country road, I came across a different worm. A bigger variety, the size of your largest finger, pale chocolate in color, with rows of bright crescent markings down the sides.

This new one's future is a mystery. He was crossing the pavement, so his leaf of preference is unknown. He lives in a bottle beside the others. And leaves of several kinds have been supplied, in the hope that he may find one or another of them palatable and so be enabled to continue his slow march toward the destiny that lies on the far side of a long sleep. Even as a worm, that one is quite beautiful. What he might become in his final transfiguration can only be imagined. But surely it will be something very splendid.

We watch, now, for other worms. When driving, we find it hard to raise our eyes from the rushing surface of the road.

The nights have cooled. Before the freeze, any creeping thing that means to live to achieve a finer state of being had better be about survival's business. The last leaves must be quickly eaten, the twig found, the cocoon spun. At every hand, in these far, clear days and brittle evenings, one can sense — if one does not actually hear — the cumulative stir of all these hasty becomings. And if one is a realist, it is necessary to wonder: *What has any of this to do with me?*

Search as I might, I can detect in myself no amazing possibilities waiting on the other side of winter. To wish for wings, if one hasn't them already, is both pointless and painful. If I creep now, and am what I eat, I will not learn to fly.

That is what the worm must think, too, if it thinks at all.

The difference is that the worm is wrong.

Artifacts

L ike shadows passing briefly on the land, they left no mark. All that remains of them lies buried in the fields and thickets of a piece of ground which long ago became a farm. For a century, the plow has stirred the earth. And in the things the blade turns up, those vanished ones — those fled shadows — find momentary voice again.

At the eye's corner, the farmer notices something out of place. A chert flake glinting after rain. Or a smooth stone where, in a life's acquaintance with that field, he remembers no stone before. Bending, he takes it up and brushes away the clinging dirt and turns it in his hand.

Two springs ago an ax head, or possibly a maul — an expert would know which — was found there in the furrow. The speckled granite had been shaped to perfect symmetry, then grooved at the sides for hafting. The thing seemed almost to speak aloud: *Try to duplicate this. And, in your failure, know that we were a capable people.*

Farmers, being respecters of tools, save these lithic implements; have been saving them so long, in fact, that several generations of the finders have gone to join those shadows. It beggars imagining how much stone was worked, by how many hands, over how many twilit millennia. Nor is there any guessing, because the excavators have never come, what other older and perhaps more astonishing things might still lie undisturbed below the plow zone.

Having the great good luck to know the present farmer as a friend, we were able on a recent evening to put our tent at the head of that field and light our small fire and watch the darkness come.

The features that much earlier made the place an attractive

resting spot for some hunting band can have changed but little. From its crest, the field — once probably meadow — runs down in gentle decline past a copse of woods to the thickly timbered margin of a flowing stream. Darkness gathered earliest and deepest there in the wooded bottom, out of which there came at intervals the boom and chortle of a great owl speaking. While up on the hillside the wideness of sky, the early starlight and the corona of the still-unrisen moon on the horizon gave a sense almost of day prolonged.

There was a feeling also — and how to say this without its sounding a contrivance — a feeling somehow that, although alone there, we were in a companionable place. Once, stepping several yards away into the night and seeing my wife and daughters moving darkly around the fire, it struck me that I would be not much surprised to see other fires, many of them, making points of light all down that hillside and other figures bending there.

At the beginning of sleep a pair of coyotes beyond the creek set up a manic yipping. Sometime in the middle there was a brief beat of rain against the canvas of the tent. And at the end of sleep, in that long hour before dawn when the morning is deepest blue, two geese came croaking low across the field and bent away southward toward some remembered water — vanguards of the great migration.

There is not much else to report. We breakfasted, and scratched a bit at the surface between the corn rows, finding nothing of importance: some chips flaked off in the shaping of a blade; one rather larger piece that, with imagination, could have served as a fleshing tool; a fragment of the lower jaw and teeth of some small creature whose antiquity could not be told because of the impossibility of knowing whether the plow had turned it down or brought it up.

Only these sketchy leavings to tell of so long an occupation before us. Disappointingly slight, they seemed at first. But were they so little after all?

All around lay the careful order imposed by the farmer's hand, and conspicuous there on the hill an orange tent, the proof of us. But strike the tent, as shortly we would, and all that remained would be the charred circle of the fire, to be erased by the creeping grasses of a single season.

Suppose the farmer's stewardship were to end. A few seasons more — not many, you may be sure — and the field would go back to whatever it first had been, with all his old harness buckles and later tractor parts sleeping speechless in the sod among the brambles. House and fences, too, would be consumed in the slow burn of time.

The owl and the coyote would cry to no listening ear.

If, much afterward, some very different kind of people were to come to make encampment on the hillside, it is probable they would consider the ones who had passed that way before but who, like brief shadows on the land, had left no mark.

And they would be speaking, among many others, of us.

On the Way
to Other Country

They came to me foundlings out of the frozen woods of a lonely winter and we spent the next 14 years together, those little hounds and I. All of their lives and nearly a third of mine.

As with any friends, it hurts very much still to think of them gone. I suppose in all that time I spoke more words to them than to anyone alive except my blood family.

We passed that first season together in the woods and they fed me — brought rabbits to the gun. Then we came to the city, which was perhaps the ruin of us all. They took distemper. I took malaise. We became citified, the prisoners respectively of wire fences and office walls, and it was all downhill from there.

One of the hounds, the one called Shorty, was outwardly very phlegmatic and content, always sat very close. In his heart, though, he was insecure. He groaned when you scratched his stomach.

The other, his brother, was the larger and more able and yet, somehow, never quite healthy. The distemper left him uncertain on trail, where once he'd been unfailing. But the hound's passion still was in him. And in later years, asleep on the rug at the foot of the bed, he would run and yelp in his dreams. I liked to imagine sometimes what country he was seeing, and whether he would ever see it again.

One autumn morning of his last year — he was alone by then — he slipped through a carelessly opened door and was gone for two days. Walking had become a labor, and yet somehow he traversed some 50 blocks of city streets and city traffic — ended up in the stairwell of a business in the industrial district, at a place where there were friendly hands and a can of dog food kept against just such an emergency.

How he'd gotten there — more exactly, *why he'd gone* — remained a mystery. Maybe he was trying to make his way to open country again. Maybe, by some instinct we know nothing about, he understood that Shorty had gotten there before him.

That one's name was Slats.

I buried them on a piece of wooded ground that as pups we used to run together, on a hillside sloping to a pond. The scene of many triumphs. And one day not long ago, out walking, I came across the place again. Not quite by accident — nothing ever is entirely by accident.

Moss of the woodland floor had crept up to cover the two piles of stones. The day was one of those on the dividing line between winter and spring . . . sun and scudding clouds, still a little edge of March in the air.

The trees were budded, the birdfoot violets just coming. I couldn't tell you how many exact such days those two and I had spent in that woods together. And for all the love that life has granted me, I felt lonelier then than in any time I readily remember.

One wall of the room in which I sometimes write — where I am writing this — is covered entirely with photographs.

Of a man I used to work for, and in whose home I spent many hours of boyhood. Gone now.

A scene from some battlefield of a generation ago, with Russian women bending over their dead in the rain and mud. All gone — gone even before I ever saw that photograph.

Of an old poet in Topeka, Kan., reading from his manuscript beside a window 20 years ago on one of the last summer afternoons of his life.

Of a friend in a duck blind, also gone. The blind and the man both.

Of other friends met in foreign countries, and still others

moved away to distant states, unlikely ever to be seen again.

Of children grown beyond that moment, and almost unrecognizable in the pictures.

The two little hounds are there in one of the photographs, side by side in a brushy covert. Their heads are raised, their eyes fixed off alertly at some distant point from which a sound has come. They are very young and very eager. They know that life is sweet and they believe that there is nothing beyond that moment.

That is how I look, too, in the pictures on that wall. It is how all of us look — all of us arrested in time by the camera some years ago.

For a hound, today is an eternity. Maybe, like them, we would do better never to consider the shortness of the race.

III

Cavils, Insurrections

(Note: This piece was written in 1980. Though some of the numbers have changed, the inequities it speaks of have worsened.)

What is a person's labor worth? From the beginning of human commerce, that has been an essential question. Much history has been shaped by it. Wars and ideologies have proceeded from its asking. Medieval peasants considered it as they tilled the princely lands and trembled in expectation of some further levy by their lord. Centuries later, it was the question that set Karl Marx brooding in his garret.

And what is the answer?

The minimum wage in the United States now is $3.35 an hour — a sum which southern textile manufacturers, California lettuce growers and the operators of restaurants nearly everywhere hold to be excessive. One hears the argument that in certain categories of work — dishwashing, for example — the imposition of a minimum wage only results in fewer jobs and worse hardship for the least skilled. This is stated as if with the inevitability of a natural law. But to the degree that it is true at all it is the result of deliberate choice, based on the premise that holding down the menu price of lasagna and lobster Newburg takes precedence, as a social goal, over the need of dishwashers to live by what they earn.

On the bulletin board in the office where I work there appeared a page from a magazine showing the incomes of some of the country's leading corporate executives. Their compensations ranged upward from a mere $3 million a year for the chief officers of several oil companies — well known servants of the public weal — to $5,213,700 for the head of a corporation engaged in the production of motion pictures and other mass entertainments.

Bear in mind that the minimum wage earner may expect, in a year's ordinary work, to receive $6,968 for the labor he performs.

By the process of simple division, one discovers that the value put on the contribution of the movie magnate is exactly 748 1/4 times that accorded to the minimum-wage worker. Or it may be expressed another way. Arriving at his studio office at 8 o'clock on the morning of January 2, the film chieftain will by 10:47 of that same morning have earned an amount equal to the salary of the dishwasher or common farm hand for the whole of the year ahead.

It may be argued that the farm hand, say, lacks the valuable talent of the movie magnate in dealing with temperamental stars, impatient stockholders and other high-level corporate matters. But there also is undoubted art in dealing with temperamental hay balers, balky mowers and aged tractors which can be kept running only by improvisations akin to magic.

Obviously these are very different sets of skills. But can one reasonably be said to be seventy-five thousand percent more socially useful than the other?

Further, if the restaurant dishes go unwashed or if the hay does not get baled and put in the barn the minimum wage earner can expect to be turned out into the street. In fact, he may *absolutely count on it. This happens less often with captains of industry. If the head of an auto manufacturing company elects to build cars that no one will buy, do not look for him in the bread lines. He is more apt to be seen on television, explaining to government committees why the public — including farm hands and dishwashers — ought to indemnify him against the results of his own stupidity and miscalculation.*

I did not set out intending this to be an insurrectionist tract. The only purpose was to examine the interesting question of what an individual's labor is worth. But it turns out to have been the wrong question. The issue — in this society or any other which man has devised — is what power is worth. And to ignore that is in most cases fatal to our expectations.

(An afternote: In the ensuing two decades, the minimum wage has increased by $1.80 an hour, to $5.15. Over the same period, however, the average annual C.E.O. compensation has increased to between $6 million and $10 million, with the top earner receiving a ludicrous $45 million a year.)

The Piper

Ihave lived my life in one place and, traveling out from there, have seen the world. That kind of continuity is a luxury available mainly to those of us who are without a driving ambition.

Do not misunderstand. I have known fiercely ambitious people, and have been very close to some of them. I hold no brief against ambition. It is just that, never having been very much possessed by it, I am forever amazed by the control some people permit it to exert over the shape of their lives.

An acquaintance not long ago spoke of her sadness at having to move to a different and distant city. For the first time in her memory, she said, she had been entirely contented in her home. She had changed it to her own taste — had made it hers. She was devoted to the city. Her children were happy in school and had established warm relationships which it was a sorrow to see ended.

Her husband, she said, entirely shared these devotions, these regrets. And yet . . . and yet the move was a requisite of advancement. The opportunity simply was too good to pass up. She said that in the wistful way that people speak truths in which they have not quite persuaded themselves to believe.

"Anyway," she added, almost defiantly, *"we'll always really think of this as home."*

She was wrong, of course. It will not remain their home, in any truer sense than the place they came from last or the one they are about to go to. So long as advancement remains a value worth pursuing, they will have no choice but to obey opportunity's commands. As with any refugees, their only true home will be inside themselves.

Again, I am not suggesting this is reprehensible. Only that, according to my own bias, it is a sad and dangerous way to order one's life.

Among writers there is frequent talk about the importance of the *sense of place*. Like the jargon of any craft, that has an arcane and expensive sound. But it is more than a writer's phrase. A sense of place is important to us all. In plain English, it is that sum of your memories and experiences, that feel for detail and texture, that unspoken but abiding surety of *at-homeness* which enables a human being to understand one particular fraction of this world more exactly than any other part. And, if he or she just happens to be a writer, to describe it with such vigor and detail that even a stranger there will have to say, *Yes, that's exactly how it must be!*

The sense of place is a tool, then. But it also is nourishment.

Having been so long in one town, there is hardly a street in it upon which, or near which, I cannot now place some moment of my life. Or of a friend's life. Or some remembered fragment of my family's story. I know the people who live on those streets, if not by name at least by nature and temperament. I know their instincts and their habits, because they are my own. The themes of our lives, though different in detail, have been broadly alike. When we meet and speak to one another, there are things which it is unnecessary to say because we begin from a base upon which much already is understood.

Many forces have been at work to make ours a transient society. The ease of travel is one. The growth of giant corporations, shuttling their workers and administrators about like pieces on a chessboard, is another.

Mobility is the inevitable way of life, we are told. We have been told it so long and so incessantly we have almost forgotten that in many respects our lives still can be controlled by volition and conscious choice. In short, the statement is true only if we allow it to be — for ambition's sake, and in the name of corporate convenience.

Ambition can be a persuasive piper. I'll confess that there have been moments in the past when his playing came faintly to my ear, as from a great distance. But I was never entirely sure that what I heard was music, or what the piper's fee might be. And so I stayed.

As a younger man, if I was asked how long I'd lived in this place and had to answer, "All my life," I spoke those words with a bit of the provincial's shame. The answer still is the same. But I have seen enough frantic goings and comings, become content enough with my choice, to say it like a boast of incredible good fortune.

So it has been a long time now since I heard the pipes at all. And, with continued luck, I never will again.

A Malicious Myth

Salaried labor is neither the natural nor even necessarily the desired human condition. That is, very few of us — given our free preference in the matter — would choose a lifetime of steady work.

The creative idleness of youth is altogether sweet and satisfactory. Have you ever heard of a child jerking awake at night in a cold sweat, wondering how tomorrow's time possibly can be filled?

Then we grow up and take jobs — mainly because of the practical need to support ourselves, but also because it is what we are expected to do. And at that point a relentless process of acculturation begins whose purpose is to transform our attitude so that, instead of viewing work as an unavoidable nuisance, we will come to see it as something nearer a state of beatification.

Unless most of our waking hours are spent at the office or factory, we are led to believe, our talents and our self-esteem will deteriorate and our lives soon will come to be empty of any meaning. Nothing in the experience of our early years bears this out. Moreover, some of the shining achievements of humankind have been wrought by people who avoided steady employment as a matter of principle. Still, the warning is repeated until it acquires the weight of fact.

Surely it is unnecessary to ask whose interest is served by having this myth believed.

If being employed were truly a holy condition, then one might expect its holiness to be respected under any and all circumstances. But that is not the case, as the several million people put out of work during occasional recessions will gladly testify.

Suppose one quits one's job for one's own convenience — simply walks out the door for some reason sufficient to oneself. That is regarded as a faithless sort of behavior which may cause the miscreant to be labeled as undependable and a floater. If, on the other hand, the company discharges employees for its convenience — because of reorganization, or a changing economic climate, or even to redeem the mistakes of incompetent management — then that is simply sound business practice. At such times, very little is heard about the sanctity of steady work.

When, in the evolution of law and humane convention, it became no longer allowable for people to be sold into obligatory service or for children to be made to take the place of burros in the traces of mine carts, some subtler means had to be found for assuring a reliable source of labor.

The result has been an outrageous distortion of the work ethic, from the original mild claim that labor can be good and satisfying to the bizarre notion that one's job is the most important thing in life — more important than one's family or friends, more important than any other interests, more important than health or sanity and even, when the occasion demands, more important than honor itself.

Needless to say, anyone who can be made to believe that can be counted on to answer the bell.

Have you ever looked directly in the face of someone who, without forewarning, has just been fired from his place of work? A confusion of terrible emotions can be seen there: disbelief, rage, fear, shame and self-contempt. Hardly less awful is the face of someone who has been living for months or years in the dread of that happening.

We have been taught our lessons well. So well that even retirement — when stopping work is not only permissible but actually encouraged and in some cases required — has become a diminishment and, as medical studies have shown, a physical peril.

It is impossible to tell someone for 20, 40 or more years that the job is everything — that one's identity and true worth are determined by what one does — and then expect that person to march away gracefully and find fulfillment in the golden sunset. Either one has been duped from the start and made a fool, or else one's real value has become suddenly, vastly less through receipt of that letter of appreciation and gold watch. There are no other possibilities.

You do occasionally come across people whose interests have flowered and whose lives really have taken on a new and larger dimension after dispensing with the encumbrance of regular employment. These examples are elating, but they are regrettably few.

Human beings can endure under almost any circumstances. But civilization, which has to do with more than just endurance, depends on the mistakes and resulting wisdoms of one generation being of profit to the next. The prices of groceries, shoes, automobiles and condominiums being what they are, probably we will not be able to spare our children the unpleasantness of reasonably steady work. But perhaps they will understand more clearly than we have that an occupation is only one aspect of a rich and constructive life — an essential aspect, but certainly not the paramount one.

And I would suggest to them, as a first principle, that no one ought ever to work at a job he cannot imagine leaving.

Men in Long, Black Cars

Probably it is no accident that the argument that the poor are without ambition is advanced most vigorously by persons who are not themselves poor.

This isn't to say they have never been poor. Indeed, individuals who have risen from hard circumstances often are the most rigid in their view of poverty as a moral condition. This is a form of self-congratulation. For it suggests that, in their cases, being poor obviously was not the result of a spiritual defect but rather only of temporary bad luck. And it reflects all the more credit on their achievement of having clawed their way into the middle class.

The notion of the poor as innately flawed and feckless is equally useful to people of very great means, providing a kind of social logic for wealth and inheritance and also relieving them of any possible discomfort of guilt.

The slightest honest observation, however, makes nonsense of the thesis.

There are stupid and lazy poor people, of course, just as there are stupid and lazy rich people. The size of one's house or bank account, or one's position in the commodities market, says nothing at all about one's industry or intelligence.

Each morning at a particular hour — and not an early hour, either — I observe a long black car passing along a certain street. In the front is a uniformed driver. In the back is a man speaking on the telephone behind tinted glass. I can't imagine whom he is talking to, nor do I know anything else about him, except that he is either too lazy or too inept to operate his own automobile.

In Nigeria, years ago, I knew a man who swept the floor of the Lagos airport and slept on a straw mat which he unrolled at night in a corner of that place. Poor, the fellow was, even by the standards of his own country. But he was not without ambition. He meant, someday, to own a bed and to be able to afford a room so that he would not have to bear the indignity of passing his nights on a public floor.

Some men want to own factories and sports franchises. That man wanted to own a bed and a room. Is one ambition necessarily superior to the other?

Again, a long time back, I met a citizen of the Spanish city of Seville who, though poor, had set himself a clear goal. By day he directed tourists to the attractions of the city. By evening he did a little casual procuring. From midnight until 4 o'clock in the morning he worked as a baker's helper.

He was a man of the lowest class. He bought his children's rope-soled shoes on credit, and paid the interest for years. But with the savings of his father's life, and the savings of his own, he intended one day to buy a bicycle for his son, thus affording him a degree of mobility no one in that family had ever known before.

A modest ambition, his — but it struck me as a visionary one.

As a rule of history, it has been possible to know the quality of governments and societies by their view of the poor. It seems as fair a way as any to judge a society still.

The poor *are* different from the rest of us. But they are different not in their persons or in their wants and dreams. Only in the details of their lives. Charles Dickens and Victor Hugo and Feodor Dostoevski — all writing a century and more ago — understood this oddity of the human condition, and the power of luck and mercy in shaping us all.

One waits now for some sign that the sleek men who govern America today have read those books.

Poverty's Family

The five of them appeared suddenly in the art gallery's tea room — just came directly in with a kind of outlandish swoop as bandits might arrive, or a tattered group of Gypsies.

Two slight and sallow men, one maybe 40 and the other a boy perhaps half that, in old trousers and shirts rolled up at the cuffs. Both with shaggy hair, not for style but for need of cutting. A large woman in an expanse of red slacks. A smaller, older one in print dress and wool sweater. And a girl the boy's age, somehow disabled in her walk, wearing a striped smock six inches too short, handed down from somewhere.

All these, evidently, a family.

In the tea room, aquiline ladies and a lesser number of suited gentlemen were taking their cups of chicken creole and cakes and other refreshments from china service. Framed prints graced the walls. Sunlight reflecting from a sculptor's mirrors positioned on the outer grounds streamed golden through the windows.

On the floor above and the one below were assembled the arts and elegances of the ages.

And in the precise center of all this the family took up station, pressed together as a single unit of five bodies, looking at once intimidated and angry and embarrassed. Waiting for something or other. A hush descended. The aquiline, refined faces turned.

"What are they doing here?" one of the ladies hissed. "How in the world did they get in?" A piece of a brownie suspended on the tines of her fork. Immediately she regretted speaking.

The boy detached himself from the others. She watched with horror as he bore straight down upon her and thrust a scrap of paper in her hand.

"What is it?" she cried. "What's this?" She pushed the paper back toward him. He stood there not speaking. Possibly unable to speak. And gave her the paper again. She peered at it, trembling with fright and indignation.

"I don't know what it *means!*" she cried again, almost a whimper. "What do you want? What is it?"

The boy took his slip of paper and retreated crestfallen back to the group.

"It was something about dishwashing," the woman said. "At least" — with great relief — "he didn't ask for money." But she had been deeply shaken and commenced a sudden, irrational tirade against racial minorities. Although, as it happened, the people huddled there in the center of the room were in fact white.

Her companion, another woman, ventured to intrude a timid word or two of moderation.

"Don't give me that bull," the first lady screeched. "I won't listen to that bull!"

The family waited, shoulders touching, facing outward as if

against likely attack. Someone had to be gotten from the kitchen. That person returned then with an application for employment, two sheets, closely printed. They sat down at a table in the "No Smoking" part of the room and all lit cigarettes and looked at the application, then at one another, then back at the document, trying to puzzle it out.

Someone had sent them there on the promise of work. But it was evident that they would not be employed. Evident to the man from the kitchen. Evident to the patrons. And beginning to be clear, by now, even to the applicants themselves.

A sense of relaxation passed over the room. Faces turned away. Interrupted conversations were resumed, and forks clinked discreetly against china plates. But the episode had not yet quite ended.

The girl of the family went to the serving counter — actually had the audacity to go through the line. And came back with her chin up and a crazy, defiant look in her eye, carrying a cup of coffee and some sort of roll. The roll was broken in pieces and distributed among the five. More cigarettes were lit. Then the boy also went for a cup of coffee. It was getting out of hand.

Time passed. Much time. Finally someone had to tell them that there were no dishes to be washed. And they got up, still moving all pressed together as Gypsies might. And went out of there, but not in haste — looking squarely in anyone's eye who dared, butting their cigarettes in various ashtrays along the way.

Out past the sculptor's reflecting mirrors to the gallery drive, where a rusted blue pickup truck was parked, with three folding wooden theater seats affixed, facing rearward, in its open bed. And some got in the truck and some got in the folding seats behind. With a lurch, a squeak of tires, they vanished as abruptly and as strangely as they had come.

And now I must confess an odd, an unexpected thing. The tea room seemed so much emptier after they had gone — flatter, with less vitality.

I am no artist, but it occurred to me then that if a painter had observed these events, looking for subjects for his brush, there can be no doubt at all which ones he would have chosen. He would have considered all those mannerly folk and their handsome clothes and fine profiles and would have found little there of interest. Instead he would have gone directly to that family of awkward poor. And, if he had been gifted enough, he would have made something luminous of them.

Artists have always known which faces belong in galleries.

The Gatekeepers

For a century or so, the term "cub" served adequately to describe the raw beginner in the craft of newspapering. But now everyone demands dignity and respect as his due, so the cub's job has been redesignated. It has become an "entry level reporting position."

Perhaps today's newspaper managers imagine that this impressive-sounding nomenclature will be helpful in deflecting bright young men and women from otherwise wasted careers in medicine and the law. And maybe they are right, though I doubt it. Several years ago, when the pillars supporting the newsroom ceiling were repainted various luminous shades of yellow, orange, green, blue, red and purple, I heard it soberly explained how this would enable us to attract a better quality of journalism school graduates. The effect, I must say, has not been noticeable.

The words "entry level," however, sound rich with promise. They imply a doorway — well-guarded but accessible to a chosen few — with unlimited opportunity beyond. If only one can secure "entry," the way will naturally lie open to fame, Pulitzer prizes and speaking engagements at Rotary luncheons.

The reality of course is quite different. One might as accurately speak of the lad at the gas pump as an entry level oil tycoon, or of the author of a passable college English theme as an entry level novelist. Entry level journalists are, all in all, no better or worse than cubs have always been. They arrive with skills unpolished and with very little practical sense. Some of them eventually learn the business well and some are incurable fools. The best often remain reporters all their lives, by their own choice. The worst usually gravitate to some other line of work where fortunes are more routinely made, perhaps proving they were not such fools after all.

In any case, the notion of lush pastures waiting just inside the "entry" is purest fantasy. But the phrase seems to be the fad of the moment. The bulletin board is cluttered with announcements relating to entry level news positions — some newly open, others just filled. And it is saddening on two accounts.

First, in any office — not only this one — the bulletin board is a battleground where egos relentlessly and bloodily contend. It is of some importance how many pieces of paper one can manage to have posted there over one's own signature. That is a measure of the ebb and flow of individual fortunes in the corporate hierarchy.

It is especially useful to be seen as an offerer or bestower of entry level positions. For one can scarcely be a gatekeeper unless one has, himself, already entered. These memoranda thus advertise that their authors are safely across the threshold and, it may be assumed, on the way to something big.

More saddening than that is to hear vigorous language made deliberately stilted and bland.

What business do serious journalists — whose tools are words and whose main virtue is straightforwardness — have talking about "entry level positions"? That sort of mealy euphemism may suffice in the personnel office or in the card file of an employment agency. But it has no place in the vocabulary of people who earn their living by being plainly understood. Like surgeons, newspaper folk are supposed to deal in precision. If ever I heard a surgeon describe my condition and his intentions that obliquely, I would leap from the examining table and flee his office for my life.

Fashions come and go. Among some in our craft, it is the fashion now to affect the language of the market researcher, the management manual and the factory floor — to speak of the newspaper's content as "the package" and of the newspaper itself as "the product."

One wonders how they suppose their readers speak.

"When you go out to close the car windows, dear, would you mind bringing in the product?" "We've trained Rover to fetch the package." "Hand me yesterday's product, please, to wrap the garbage in."

As I have gotten grayer, I have found myself approached more often by young people attracted to this business and eager for advice. I have very little of use to tell them. Except to find a newspaper that still calls itself a newspaper, operated by men who call themselves editors, not news managers or somesuch. To accept employment as a cub reporter — nothing else, however fancily described.

And if interest lasts, talent grows and success follows, to give the Rotary Club its money's worth.

Broken Angels

In telling the news, accuracy is indispensable. It is the basis of all credibility — a commodity beyond price.

But accuracy also is like a delicate crystal figurine which, once shattered, may be all but impossible to reassemble. Try to put the pieces back together and what originally was an angel looks more like an octopus. Try them another way and you get a chimpanzee. What you are *least* likely to get, no matter how many times you try, is the original angel.

Newspapers used to ignore their blunders, unless their mistakes were of a scale apt to generate proceedings in a court of law. The attitude was that it was better to be wrong than to *seem* to be wrong. That has changed. The pendulum has swung to self-flagellation. Newspapers wear hair shirts and, when caught in an error, lash themselves publicly with willow wands in the hope that these vigorous displays of penitence will persuade readers that they have not spent their 25 cents foolishly.

The correction column of almost any newspaper is the place to look if you enjoy the spectacle of grown men and women scrambling around on hands and knees, hunting for shards of the figurine and trying to make the damnable object whole again.

The seeds of rage and controversy may lie concealed in an item of seeming innocuousness.

Man chokes on legs

Attempts failed last night to revive a visiting conventioneer from Biloxi, Miss., who strangled during a meal in his fourth-floor room at the King's Palace Hotel here.

According to authorities, death came to the 42-year-old software salesman while eating a plate of frog legs from the hotel grill.

"He just kind of hiccupped and turned purple and that was it," reported the man's wife, who was with him when he suffered the seizure. A member of the fire department rescue squad said that the wife, when asked if she had tried Heimlich's maneuver, told him to "watch your mouth."

The victim's name was withheld pending notification of other surviving relatives.

And that would seem to about cover it. But, alas, accuracy's watchdogs do not sleep. The correction column tells the rest.

Because of a writer's carelessness, it was wrongly reported yesterday that a man choked to death on the fourth floor of the King's Palace Hotel. The hotel has only three floors. The victim, from Itta Bena, not from Biloxi as the story alleged, was identified today as Buster Leroux.

Surely, now, Mr. Leroux will lie in peace. But, no, the thing won't die. The correction must be corrected.

According to Mrs. Vernabelle Leroux, who contacted the newspaper by telephone from Itta Bena, she was not in a hotel room here when her husband, Buster, strangled on a plate of frog legs. Police confirmed that Mr. Leroux's companion at the time of the misfortune was not Mrs. Leroux, as initially reported, but instead was Miss Bunny Dee-lite, an exotic dancer employed in the hotel lounge. Hasty reporting and shabby editing were, we regret to say, to blame for the confusion.

And still another day.

It has been brought to the editors' attention that, in listing the survivors of a Mississippi conventioneer who died in a hotel room here, the names of the children of Ms. B.D. Lite, entertainment executive and associate of the victim, were included by mistake.

Ever onward toward absolute truth.

The manager of the King's Palace Hotel contended today that frog legs were "not even in season" the night a guest died in one of the hotel's rooms. The error resulted from an inexperienced reporter's failure to read the menu. Authorities said they would reopen the inquiry into the cause of death of Buster Dee-lite of Leroux, Miss.

By now Buster is notorious, his family has been shamed and Bunny is a talk show headliner. And the subscribers don't know whether it's a newspaper they're reading or a Mad Comic Book.

The labors have been stupendous. The backs of the offenders have been satisfactorily flayed. But the shattered angel has not been reassembled in identifiable form. Sometimes it is best just to sweep up the glass and swallow the next frog.

Beyond Progress

"Pain's a delusion."
"Oh, is it?" said the Savage and, picking up a thick hazel switch, strode forward.

— Aldous Huxley
Brave New World

A man with whom I have worked for several years, and whose abilities I admire, has talked of leaving the craft of newspapering — of quitting it entirely, not in anger but in sadness and perplexity, and taking up some other occupation.

He is still, relatively speaking, a young man. He has not worn out in long service, as some of us are apt to do. The trouble is that the march of technology has made the trade of journalism almost unrecognizable as the one he entered. Quite simply, he has come to the limit of his tolerance for adaptation. I realize that this same stress has overtaken workers in many other occupations as well, but since newspapering is the one I know that's what I'll speak about.

One brings to one's line of work, and then attempts gradually to perfect, a set of skills which — however great or modest — one counts on to serve for the whole of a career. Once these have been mastered, the *process* of one's work becomes second nature. After that it is unnecessary any longer to give much thought to the rote details of how the job is done.

Then the new machine arrives. Or, as in the case of today's newsrooms, a succession of new machines.

They bear no resemblance to the previous tools of the craft. Emitting small whistles and beeps, they wink bluely from cathode tubes and are able to communicate at fabulous speed with other, larger and even more complex machines. These devices come accompanied by squads of people possessed of the arcane knowledge required to govern them and keep them operating — more or less.

Daily, however, one is reminded that one's own skills have become obsolete. (If proof is required, I submit the case of another co-worker who, after some 20 years in the company's employ, was greeted by his new machine with the salutation, "Good morning, temporary person.")

These other, different skills can be learned — that's not the issue. The operation of a computer terminal, though the language of the art is made deliberately frightening and complex, is a task well within the abilities of any reasonably adept first-grader.

The problem is that computer technology has a half-life measurable at most in a few years, more often in months and sometimes only weeks. After that machine, there will come another. And then another, each sufficiently modified from the one before that its functions have to be mastered anew. So that a career becomes a sequence of swift and grudging retreats from one unfamiliar machine to the next.

But if one can learn to use them, what is the harm?

The harm is that nothing is second nature any longer. The mechanical process of doing one's job comes to occupy the mind, leaving less chance for consideration of the longer, larger questions of why to do it or how possibly to do it better. That this happens at all — in whatever degree — is a deplorable loss.

I suspect also, though it cannot be proved, that people may be psychologically injured by making them dependent for their livelihood on devices whose inner workings they cannot hope to understand. The pen and pencil we understood. Even, in an approximate way, the Underwood manual typewriter. But not today's machines. They belong to an alien discipline. They are built and tended by people who, while highly skilled in that narrow specialty, have no comprehension of the business of words and no real inclination to learn.

And no end to this is in sight. It is that realization which has brought this colleague of mine to the point of despair. If one could master the skills presently needed, then count on those to serve for the remainder of a career, then it might seem possible to carry on. But that is a foolish hope. Always there will be a new machine. The recurrent obsolescence of our skills is inevitable.

My colleague has discussed these things with the keepers of the computers.

"The machines have made your lives easier," they say — as if easier, even if true, were the highest good. They do not hear, or want to understand, what it is he is saying. His pain, they assure him, is a delusion.

He knows better. He knows his life has not been improved and that his pain is real. But he will not set upon them with a hazel switch to prove the point.

Like those in any occupation who have been battered by more of such stress than it is possible to stomach — and their number these days must be very great — he will save himself by going out the door.

The Correspondent

"Mist curls around the hills like spun sugar," she wrote to us from the Burma Valley in Rhodesia. *"Lush fields of winter wheat and maize lie ready for reaping. The countryside is breathtakingly lovely — and riddled like a cancer with terrorists."*

That was her first dispatch, in June of a past year.

The name of Sarah Webb Barrell will mean nothing to you. Nor did it have meaning for anyone here at the newspaper, except for those two or three editors who processed her work. This business devours talent with an awful carelessness.

She was a freelance journalist, one of that considerable tribe of loosely attached writers — mostly based abroad — whose contributions can provide the grace notes and small but useful insights amid the daily run of foreign news. They are selling courage and resourcefulness and the ability, when they find a story, to tell it sensibly and with style. And most of them are selling cheap. Once in a very great while a freelancer manages to become successful and sought-after, but there are few of those and Sarah Barrell was not one of them.

She introduced herself by letter from Africa. She was contributing to a paper in San Francisco and also a French news magazine, and hoped to add us to her slender list of clients. Would we look at her stories?

It costs nothing to look. There is no commitment in that. Freelancers do not ask or expect promises, and they know that it is a buyer's market.

Then that first stunning dispatch came in the mail. Her report went to the heart of the political and, more important, the human issues. It squared with the facts as we knew them. She wrote like a dream. We replied with a hasty word or two of praise and a small check in due course. More pieces from her followed and they confirmed that she was a careful reporter, incapable of a clumsy word.

In one of them she wrote of ". . . *the brown-gold winter veld of northeastern Rhodesia, where the land still speaks of the emptiness and the promise of Africa.*" Then she went on to describe how that sense of promise was giving way, under the pressures of the terrorist war, to feelings of hopelessness and despair.

At some point — I can't say just when — I decided that Sarah Barrell must surely be a beautiful person. I had no notion at all of what she looked like, but anyone who wrote that well, that sensitively, simply had to be in some way beautiful. (I afterward learned that in fact she was a fashion model in New York before deciding to make her way with words.)

Her stories continued to arrive, several a month. They never disappointed. But not all of them were published. Events compete fiercely for a newspaper's space. When a city is buried under snow and the domestic economy totters, Africa can seem very far away. Then came a newsprint shortage, imposing further brevity on us all. Sometimes Sarah's offerings lost out — for a reason, or just by accident. And for those, of course, nothing ever was paid.

Once she apologized by letter for having let some weeks pass without a story. (I doubt, really, that any of us had bothered to notice.) "I've been in one of my periodic manic-depressive slumps," she wrote. "But I seem to be over that hurdle now." I attached no importance to it and turned, instead, to her piece that accompanied the letter — an angry, tender account of the refugees from the war.

Another time I inquired in a general way if she had any plans to return to this country, thinking that our newspaper — any newspaper — would be foolish not to try to attract a writer of such gifts. She read between the letter's lines and wrote back, pleased, but saying that she meant to stay in Africa a while longer because "it is still unexplored for me."

Sometimes checks or tearsheets went astray in the mail and she wrote or Telexed to ask about them. And when I knew that she was planning to be afield with the military or traveling in a dangerous part of the country, I would write asking that she please take care of herself. What else can anyone do?

That was about the extent of our correspondence.

One month, then, her dispatches stopped coming entirely. The next word any of us had was a letter from a Rhodesian law firm, making some dry inquiry or other about "the estate of the late Sarah Webb Barrell."

In the days that followed I managed to learn more — but only a little more — about her. Her parents lived in a town in West Virginia. She was 33 years old and had written from the conflicts in Lebanon and Southeast Asia. She had been one of the last American journalists evacuated from Cambodia.

Not long before, a friend of hers in the Rhodesian security forces had been shot to death accidentally by his own men during an encounter with terrorists. She was much affected by that, and told other friends afterward that Rhodesia would be her last war. She made preparations to come home the next week.

But sometime during that week — whether disheartened by the friend's death, or frustrated by her career or just beaten down, finally, by all the craziness of too many violent places — in her rented apartment in Salisbury, Sarah Barrell ended her life.

I have looked at the accounts. In the more than a year she wrote for us, our payments to her amounted to the grand total of $740. That for the privilege of being little valued and less remembered.

We did not deserve her. Our readers did not deserve her. That wretched African war assuredly did not deserve her. She wrote like a dream, and she had only just begun.

The Tyranny of Change

The dangerous thing about change is that change has no memory. About matters of the past, change is an imbecile. The principle, I think, is general. But let me speak of it in the context of farming, which is a subject I have come to know.

Suppose that a man has acquired a tract of land — fields, buildings, livestock and all. A farm intact. Reasonably, then, he sets about considering how he can turn this acquisition to his profit. Suppose further that there are, among the creatures whose ownership passed with the farm, a dog, several horses, some cattle and a hired man.

This new owner discovers that the dog is lame. He does not know — cannot be expected to know — that the dog grew lame in long and faithful service. He may have been told that, but he is unconvinced or has forgotten. The relevant fact to him is that the beast is of no more use.

He finds, too, that some of the horses are broken of wind, that the once prize-winning bull is long past his prime, that the cows have grown aged and that the hired man, who has tended that herd and those fields for many years, has limits to his ability or his strength. Once he was a sturdy, young figure of a man. But he has left his best years among the stones and thickets of that piece of ground. Now he is tired or infirm or demoralized, or all of these, and his previous master has gone.

Between that former owner and all his chattels, including the hired man, there had existed a sort of unwritten compact. They had spent themselves on his behalf. And by allowing them to do so, he had incurred a debt of loyalty which he acknowledged.

So it was that the dog dreamed his days away on the porch of the house, and the bull was kept in spite of his inability to service the cows, and the cows were kept despite giving less milk, and the horses were allowed to graze unridden, and the hired man was paid as always, although other, younger men had to be employed to help him with his work.

Then came the new farmer, the representative of change, and with his arrival all the debts were canceled.

And he had, besides the deed to the property, a lively sense of his own interest — which made it clear that the lame dog must be euthanized, the aged cattle ground for hamburger, the wind-broken horses made into dog food and the hired man turned out to make way for an abler replacement. Or, if not abler, at least someone known to the new farmer himself.

They arrived, then — the new dog, new horses, new cattle and new man.

Their vigor and their productivity were marvelous to observe. And, over the years, a sort of unwritten compact grew up between them and their master. It was that they would spend themselves in his service and, in return, would later have claim on his understanding and his loyalty.

The contract was given and accepted in good faith. And that is how matters might have worked out, except that some years later it happened that the farm changed hands again. The new farmer inspected his lands and his holdings and observed that the dog had become crippled, the other animals were less than young and the hired man, too, was showing evidence of wear.

Now, he was a perfectly decent fellow, this next farmer, but he had no knowledge of any contract, nor any memory of the past.

The rest you can guess.

I suspect, although I have spoken of it in connection with farming, that this aspect of change can be more generally applied. I think of my own father in his work. He was employed by a large utility and had many friends among his co-workers. His formal education and thus, I suppose, his specific merchantable skills were limited. But there was no limit to his loyalty or his diligence. Apart from family, his job was his life.

He was 47 years in the service of that company, retiring honorably and dying not many years afterward.

But I remember the torment, the anxiety, that periodically assailed him. For he served the company under several sets of leaders. And it was axiomatic that, each time a change occurred at the top, he and many others like him in the ranks had to begin again as chattels without identity. And in our house, as I expect in a thousand others, there was in those times a prolonged and brooding tension of people fearing for the future.

Change does come. Nothing remains the same — or can. But as change ceases to be an event and becomes, instead, the theme and the dominant feature of modern life, the memory of the past becomes ever shorter until finally it is extinguished altogether. Men do not have histories any more — at least not histories that are known and remembered. There is only the present, in which our strength and our talent must daily be rated and measured anew.

It is a corrosive and inhuman state of affairs, against which it is said to be useless to rail. Since change is inevitable, we are told, there is nothing to be gained by fearing it.

My experience has been that we fear it for good reason.

Extravagant Dreams

In times like these — and, for some among us, in any times — the margin of a life can be drawn very fine.

Two men were drinking coffee in a breakfast place. And because their table was separated from mine only by a low divider, I was party to their conversation, though I'd rather not have been.

The younger of them, in his middle 20s, was in a state of desperation. The facts, as they emerged, were these. He had a job of some low-paying sort, and had received a small paycheck. He also had a wife, pregnant several months. They lived in rented rooms and their possessions were few: dishes, cooking pans, a bed. The rest was furnished.

The check in his pocket would cover rent and food, not more. However there was a complication. He had gotten a traffic ticket some weeks earlier for parking illegally. But having no money to pay it he had ignored the citation. Now, as he understood it, a warrant had been issued.

Meantime, he had gotten another ticket in the neighboring state — that one for driving 11 miles over the speed limit on the street he took to work. That offense was more recent. No warrant was out for him, but he was obliged shortly to appear in court to answer the charge.

All together, considering the whole range of possibilities for human mischief, the young man's transgressions seemed not so grave. But the dilemma he confronted had overwhelmed him with despondency and confusion. (Perhaps he brought to the problem something less than the optimum mental equipment. His manner of speaking suggested that might be so. All the same, the problem before him was very real.)

He could use the check to square his accounts with the law.

However he would then have to default on the rent, and he and his wife would be turned out of their lodgings. In his mind, that was the certain consequence. Alternatively, he could pay the landlord but ignore the delinquent parking ticket and the impending court date. In which event he would surely be sent to jail. And, being jailed, he would lose his job and would be unable to pay any future rents, so ultimately they would be roofless in either case.

These details he set forth for the other man at the table, with whom he seemed only slightly acquainted. That one was older, in his mid-30s, with several missing teeth and a day's growth of beard and a disheveled T-shirt. Not someone whose advice would inspire confidence. Together they silently considered the impossibility of the situation.

Then, as if to wish the truth away, the younger man gave himself up to improbable dreaming.

What he really wanted, he said, was a place to live that had a kitchen, a living room, a bedroom and a bath.

And a refrigerator, the other man said, insinuating himself briefly into the dream.

Right! With a refrigerator and stove.

Maybe even two sleeping rooms? Since your kid is coming.

Sure! (It cost nothing to imagine it.) Two bedrooms. And a TV.

That's right.

And not just a bathtub, either. A tub with a shower in it. As she got more pregnant, a shower would be better for his wife. The doctor said that.

Yeah, well . . . The older one's voice went flat. If it was him, he said, he would pay the law and stay out of jail. The dream, having gotten too extravagant, no longer held his interest. He went to sit alone on a stool at the counter, an obvious authority on shipwrecks but with no ropes left to throw.

And the younger one, having perhaps 40 more years to endure in the world, went forth to choose between the inescapable evils of the first of all those days.

A Better Contract

Rootlessness is more than just a way of life. It is a condition of the mind. And it has consequences.

You have known transient people. They appear from somewhere and happen to stay a while, like tumbleweeds blown up against a corner of the fence. Then an undefined restlessness seizes them. And with the next faint breeze of opportunity, they tumble on.

That pattern of behavior has come to be accepted. The social scientists have explained it. Corporations have accommodated to it. Mobility, which used to be called by a plainer word, drifting, now is seen as a respected strategy for career advancement.

The costs of it are ignored.

Not the least of the casualties is loyalty — that understanding of shared interests and mutual obligation that ought to, and often used to, and very occasionally still does define the relationship between organizations and the people they employ. Loyalty can neither be commanded nor bought. It is the result of longer investments of time and trust. People on the move — just passing through, so to speak — may carry with them fine skills. But whatever their other virtues, loyalty seldom is among them. And the corporation, knowing it cannot expect loyalty, offers none in return.

Neither feels the least responsibility toward the other. And both are the poorer for it. If the organization fails, that is no concern of the transient, who simply blows on to the next fence corner. By the same token, when employees drift on, taking their skills and their experience with them, the organization feels no sense of culpability or loss — only inconvenience.

But losses there are, on both sides.

The transient never knows the security of being fully understood and valued, with all his strengths recognized, all his defects known and accepted. He accumulates no record, no body of accomplishment. Like a football coach, he is measured always by the current game.

For its part, the organization, while its ranks are continually replenished, does not mature — cannot amass that fund of accumulated experience upon which, in any institution or enterprise, constructive growth depends.

Peer into most corporate offices of the land and you will see there an amazing combination of the young, just beginning their careers, and older but rootless folk, lodged briefly at one more of their many stops along the way. I hold no brief against youth. Or against well-traveled veterans, for that matter. Mercenaries make fine soldiers, though seldom fine patriots.

Any military commander who fielded an army so composed, mainly of Hessians and raw recruits, would be thought foolhardy. And any citizenry that depended on such an army for its protection would dare not sleep. Yet the arrangement has come to be accepted as usual and customary in our working lives. And I am convinced no good can come of it.

At some point, people who work for hire must say to themselves: *This is the place to which I am attached, where I will discover my abilities and my shortcomings. Imperfect it may be — as what isn't? — but I commit myself to the long task of its perfection.*

For that to be a sensible way of thought, of course, organizations must embrace a similar ethic: *These are our people, with all their strengths and defects. They are our resource. By their growth, we grow. By their discouragements, we are diminished.*

The elements of loyalty, stated in that way, sound trite and terribly dated.

But subtract them and what is left except communities of strangers, bound together by nothing more than ambition and temporary convenience? And where — in this society or any other — is the evidence that that has sufficed?

IV

In Changing Light

Leaves on a midnight street, running ahead of the wind, agile and brown as the massed runners in some Levantine demonstration, shouting a dry slogan, passing under the street lamp and on away deeper into October.

Squirrel's footfalls on the shingle roof, hurrying to or from a barren branch where the nut no longer hangs.

Wildfowl riding down the long slant of the season, crying to one another and to sleepers a far song that is sometimes heard and sometimes only dreamed.

Owl's hooded eye fixed on something that moves in the moonstruck grass.

Train's whistle hooting faint from beyond cities and across many stubbled fields.

Cattle in a fold of pasture, bedded close together. Lonely people, bedded far apart.

Gardens withered. Seeds saved.

Despairs all suddenly forgotten. Joys remembered and numbered now in the silent dark.

Other things remembered, too. The oddest confusion of them.

Leaf fires smelled a long time ago. And the voice of the stadium crowd on a frosty night. And the feeling of being young — the exact feeling of it. And the feeling of first remembering that feeling as something not quite any longer true. The terrible attraction of maps, maps being feasts in prospect. And the way in which, unnoticed as it happened, the passion for going became a passion for going home. But home to what, exactly? And then that question answered.

And the answers to it sleeping now under the very roof whose shingles the squirrel crosses on his pointless errand. In the house where the cat squints from his chair. Beside a bureau in whose drawer the seeds are saved. In a room whose window looks down on the crowds of leaves shouting dryly as they run with the wind on past the street lamp and out of view.

October is a memory and a summation.

As with anything concluding, it pays to notice the details.

Cat Knows

I remember that my mother always thought the autumn sad.

The light would take on a keen, far-reaching clarity. The shadows would sharpen at their edges. The days would shorten, and she would speak of loss. Just what was being lost, then, I never quite understood. I was only a boy, intending always to remain one. Boys have no sense of anything. They have no premonitions.

In the gallery one recent afternoon I saw a painting. It was of a garden seen in that particular quality of end-of-season light. A woman is standing among the flowers — summer flowers, at the last of their bloom. The air of her garden is very clear and pale, the shadows sharp and deep.

That is a painting of a century ago.

There was another, more than 200 years before that. In the same pale air, reapers are bending with their scythes, cutting and shocking grain. And still another, even 400 years older, by a Chinese artist, of people passing through mountains beside a stream. Ink on a paper scroll, that one, without color. But the quality of light struck me as unmistakable all the same.

Very much older than any of these was an Egyptian piece in stone, of a man holding by its wings a bird that he has caught. And possibly it was only the coolness of this day some 4,000 years afterward, but I believed I could sense the wind coming down raw out of the Libyan desert and soughing among the stone reeds and ruffling the feathers of the bird in his stone hand. As you will know if you have ever been there, the autumn comes to Egypt like a draught of cold wine. Women with clay jars tread the paths from well to village through shadowed afternoons from which the awful heat has gone. The harvest is in the granaries, and that is the season's joy. The regret is the smallness of the granaries.

Through the autumns of all those centuries the light has been the same. Artists cannot resist it.

What troubled my mother, I believe now, was that she must have had — which I have not — a painter's, an artist's eye. She sensed things passing in the light. Summer's garden starting to curl and dry. Summer's children lost to school again — and, so soon after that, lost to other cities, other lives. Summer's birds flocking, yearning south. Summer's dresses hung away once more.

Rationally I can observe all this, and understand the meanings. But I am unaffected by it. That afternoon a man sitting alone on a bench in a park near the gallery, under a maple whose leaves had gone from green to dusty silver, was no sadder than a man alone at any season. A little farther on, children coming freighted with book bags and lunch boxes seemed a cheerful sight, in no way melancholy. Their babble pierced the day's late hour. Now that cicadas have fallen silent, other chirrupings are clearer heard.

A neighbor was in his yard with a sharp-toothed rake, scratching up in tan piles the duff of another year's failure. Nothing will grow there, he declared. That piece of ground is accursed. He said it in good spirit. My mother, in the mood that autumn always brought upon her, would have found no humor in it. Only omens. She could not abide the sense of things declining, going brown.

I am now of the age that I remember her from childhood. Yet autumn's approach does not affect me so. The sound of voices calling from great distance, of dry leaves rustling and blown things bumping at the pane are signs that I can hear without reflection. That may be because I feel surer of spring than she ever did. Or because my eye for the changing light is less acute.

Or because, as when a boy, I am not susceptible to premonitions.

On the window ledge that day the cat was waiting to greet me. Or I thought that was his purpose. But when I spoke he didn't answer, didn't move. Just sat like a white statue — something made in marble by an Egyptian, and very old — frowning out at the pale light on silver leaves.

A long time he sat, as if transfixed by the vision of a world for him sadly changed. I put my face beside his and looked out, too. But could not see what it was that so engaged him.

Abruptly then he bounded down. And fixing me with a look of pure disdain, as if to say that there were things I could not hope to understand, stalked off to take his winter place in a tufted chair.

My mother, now that I think of it, kept cats always as a girl. And may have learned from them.

The Perfect Spiral

The way between office and home, followed invariably as any rabbit follows its run, passes alongside a high school playing field. Through the stifle of summer the field lay silent and unmown. But as I drove by the other afternoon it had come alive again to the shouts of half a hundred or so boys in helmets and football jerseys. Balls arced across the sky. A shrilling of coaches' whistles cut the air.

The game of autumn had begun. And like the broken-down tramp who from the porch of the country poor farm hears across the reach of years and distance the moan of a passing train, my nostrils flared a little and I felt again the old ache of something sweetly remembered. Bittersweetly, I should say. To be honest with you and with myself, those memories are few — and for a reason.

If there is pity in you, pity that person who cannot be what he or she most hungers to be in this world. The writer with a tin ear for the music of words. The painter without an eye for form or line. Pity the boy born too small and a bit too slow afoot to play the game he loved.

Football? I cared more for that than for most things I've known in life. More than my later work. More than anything, I suppose, except my family and a friend or two. I drew out plays and rehearsed them mentally to the roar of the imagined crowd. Great players and their exploits were catalogued in my mind. Like them, I threw the perfect spiral.

That first year, at 100 pounds or so, I was sent home by a coach who did not want my maiming on his conscience. He told a gentle untruth — said he'd run out of shoulder pads. So I returned with pads of my own. He telephoned my mother. It was, she wisely told him, entirely his affair and mine.

To summarize, then, I did grow a little in subsequent years, and got a little quicker, though never fleet. But I was determined and I was loyal. No one, I think, arrived at practice sooner or left later. And I was less fragile than it appeared. By the final season these humble virtues — willingness and durability — had earned a place not on the starting team but at least securely on the bench.

And now my lean stock of great moments, if your patience permits. There are only three.

There was in the city that year a player for another school who had made a considerable reputation. He had the speed of a deer, the elusiveness of a shadow and a neck that started a bit above his ears. He later went on to have some small success in the professional league.

The previous week he had run for six touchdowns in a single game. At some point in our contest against that team, with the score already lopsidedly against us, I was sent as cannon fodder into the defensive backfield. This feared runner was dispatched on a sweep around end. I am not sure I ever saw him. But I knew he was coming because I could hear my teammates screaming his name in panic, the way men in battle might shout warning of a live grenade. And this so numbed me with dread that I lost the use of my legs and fell to my knees in a posture almost of supplication.

What may have passed through his mind as he broke into the clear field and noticed this curious sight before him — one kneeling figure between him and the goal line some 60 yards away — can only be guessed. It must have confused or fascinated him. For instead of simply stepping around he came directly ahead, straight as a wire, and stumbled over me just as I was trying to stand up.

We became entangled. I reeled a few steps with him on my shoulders, then went down under his mass. Later this accidental collision was translated into a crushing tackle. And I remained discreetly mute while others told how I had smeared so-and-so in an open field.

That was one great moment.

In our team's repertoire of plays there was one which, since I am left-handed, was suited especially for me — though I remember only once being sent in for that purpose. It was an option to the left, in which the halfback had the choice to run or pass. Execution was perfect. The way down the sideline was open. Had I chosen to run, I might be running still. But I saw a receiver crossing deep downfield, clear of the defenders. So I threw the pass instead. A flawless spiral.

He was an all-star, that teammate — a large fellow, handsome, a polished dancer, popular with the girls. He had everything. But when my pass floated down to him in perfect stride, my one pass, he dropped it. Just dropped the damned thing. And came back to the huddle afterward with a little scowl of irritation, as if to concede that even gods can err.

Someone mentioned his name the other day and said his life had not turned out so happily. Only then, putting things in perspective, was I finally able to forgive him.

The remaining moment came in the last game.

We had installed a new deceit — a play in which the flow of action went in one direction while the quarterback, after faking, turned back to give the ball to the runner over the middle of the line.

The struggle had raged scorelessly. For one series of downs the reserve quarterback and I were sent in to give the regulars a rest. The new play was called. And in my mind the following picture is clear: a gaping emptiness where enemies should have been; the sprawl of bodies at either side; the unbroken smoothness of grass lying open to the goal, with the end zone bleachers behind. I passed through that yawning hole without a hand being laid on me. But also without the ball. The quarterback had turned the wrong way and, in his mortification, had fallen on it.

A series or two later, while I watched from the bench, that play would be called again. And the team captain would run unmolested for the only score of the game, thus becoming known — and being known still — as the one whose touchdown beat the city champions.

Those few memories are what's left of a career. But they come awake each time I see a crowd of bright jerseys on a playing field as late summer gives way to fall. Not too many years ago I asked for a football for Christmas and my wife, mystified but indulgent, obliged. I went immediately with a friend to try it out. The friend's small daughter came along to watch.

It was a first-class leather ball, a wonder to throw, with the official emblem of the professional football league on its side. Presently the little girl was heard to ask, shyly, if I happened to play for the local professional club. As in the old matter of that crushing open-field tackle, I didn't lie. Just remained discreetly mute.

And, fading back, sent up another perfect spiral.

Mirror and Door

Has there ever been a time, however long ago or fleeting, when you felt reality growing blurred and when it seemed necessary to hold on, by force of will, to the sense of the moment and of your proper place in it?

The literature of children is rich with the possibilities of other worlds, just out of reach but entered sometimes by accident — worlds on the other side of the looking glass, or beyond the last row of clothes in a dark wardrobe, or at the far end of the tornado's funnel.

One night my younger daughter dreamed a long dream of trying to pass through a fluffy wall of something like cotton, but more resisting. At last, shortly before morning, she managed to break through into a fine place where flowers sang and animals could talk and where flying was the easiest thing imaginable for a little girl. Waking, she launched herself from the bed and crashed, of course. We found her weeping softly there, not from injury but from bitter disappointment.

That came to mind the other day when, just for the least part of an instant, I felt myself losing hold and slipping toward the edge.

A business errand had taken me to the small college town a half-day's drive away where I once spent four years — years remembered now across considerable time as having been wonderfully irresponsible and happy. Finishing the errand early, I thought to pass an idle couple of hours roaming the town and the college grounds.

First I went to the room I'd lived in that freshman year, sharing it with three other baffled and homesick youths. Their faces and names had been long forgotten. But immediately on stepping inside the room they rose up clearly again. There were introductions around, and one of the present occupants turned out to be the son of one of the boys I'd shared that room with those many years ago. He looked a good bit like his father.

Then to the basement of the town hotel and the saloon (a jarring word for so innocent a place) where we had loitered, under-age, some fine and lazy evenings. Nothing at all had changed. The place exhaled its same odors of fried food and beer and powerful disinfectant. It still reserved — but never exercised — the right to refuse service to anyone. An underclassman still was grumbling at having to produce his fraudulent proof of age. Some of the faces in the back booth looked familiar, but were they fathers' faces or sons' or whose? I didn't join them there, or even hail them or make any sign at all, for fear of seeming ridiculous.

Then to the campus itself.

I discovered that the memory, mine at least, is strongly geographic. As I walked there, conversations long blown away on the wind of age came back in fresh detail. Faces, too. Then moving on a few steps among the trees, higher on the hill, the words and the speakers would change.

The library at first seemed small and unfamiliar, until I sat in a particular chair in the bay window at the northern end. Immediately I could say just what splendid story I had read there

— could speak long passages of it aloud — in an issue of Atlantic Monthly magazine, by an author now dead. Could remember the color of the magazine, which was blue, and the quality of light through the windows that specific afternoon.

To the gymnasium, then. And again, footfalls sounding off the wooden floor brought the past alive. In this spot — no, here, exactly here — I had slept on a folding cot that first night really gone from home, waiting with a hundred other freshmen for word of our lodging assignments.

And what about this place, 30 feet out and angled from the basketball backboard? It seemed wrong by a step or two, so I moved and the picture came clear. It was the first afternoon of team trials. From that spot on the floor the ball had made its long arc into the basket. Unfailing — five times running, then seven, nine. It was beyond any explanation — a freak thing, never to be repeated. But it did happen and was witnessed by the team coach who, believing himself possessed of a secret weapon, rushed to conclusions that he would have a long season to regret. The team picture still is on the gymnasium wall, proving that this was not merely imagined.

Then out again onto the upper drive that fronted the buildings. At the bottom of the long sweep of hillside the residences waited, as in a picture — one I had seen several thousand times before. It was the noon hour. Students were hurrying down to the meal.

For just that fraction of a moment it would have been a terribly easy and natural thing to follow after them — to sit down without explanation at my regular place at the table and let it all begin again. That is as close as I have ever come to stepping through the looking glass. It wasn't the fear of falling that held me back, any more than it will prevent my daughter from dreaming her dream again.

The truth in the end was that I really didn't choose to go.

And the moment I understood that, the two worlds drew apart again distinctly. Memory was not a door anymore, only a mirror after all.

In the houses on the street below, chairs scraped and the tenants — all strangers — sat down to their meals. And I, safely back inside my own middle-aged skin, went off to dine with their professors.

The Teacher

We are contemporaries now, or so nearly so that the few years between us no longer make a difference. Our heads are equally gray. But whereas my thinning hair must be arranged with care to cover scalp, his still blows in careless indiscipline.

He is slender, almost slight, and fine-featured. If you were to pass him, books and a sheaf of papers under his arm, you would know him immediately for a man of ideas. Possibly you would take him for a poet or writer of some sort, and you would not be far off the mark. But while he has lived with writers' words and thoughts for most of a lifetime, he is in fact a teacher.

The freshman class I sat in, beside an east window looking down the hill through trees, was only his second at the college. I don't know what age we imagined him to be, but certainly quite old. The distance between 18 years and 27, between students and professor, is immense and all but unbridgeable.

Being both a bachelor and a junior faculty member, he lodged in a tiny apartment in one of a row of cottages — drab colored and cramped, as I remember them; perhaps some sort of military surplus — pinched in among student quarters along the street that faced the campus. As we passed beyond our freshman studies and began to diverge in our aptitudes and intentions, the classes became smaller. Often several of us — the ones with a writing interest — would meet in the evening for discussion or readings in his one small sitting room, wedged in there among all his dangerous stacks of books to drink coffee and suffer his honest criticism or, worse, the lack of it.

"*Well . . .*" he would begin, after some extravagantly inept offering. Just that. The silence would suggest what he might eventually say in private, but was too humane to utter publicly.

In a later year — it may have been our last — he married. A dark-haired and rather exotic woman, as we saw her then. And, like him, very old.

Their lives progressed first to a large frame house near the athletic field, on the edge of the small town. And then to an even larger brick one, mellow with age and lived in by faculty before them, along a fine old street in the town's center, where they have been so long settled now among books and memories and collected things that it is impossible to imagine them anywhere else.

They had sons. The boys kept a boa constrictor and probably other creatures I am reluctant even to think about. Cats bore their careless litters on the rug. Those were years of controlled confusion — of household emergencies, of fierce political issues in the town and the world and the college itself. And amid all this there were new books to be read, new courses to prepare, the endless student papers to be critiqued.

Now that confusion is all but behind, replaced by a degree of predictability with which I suspect they are not yet entirely comfortable. The sons are substantially grown. And it is not surprising, since they were reared in a house of ideas and speculations and disputation, that they have grown into young men of adventurous and independent mind. But the house seems empty without them. All its many rooms lie silent and orderly, waiting for the chaos to return. But it does not.

The boa constrictor survives and at least one of the cats also remains. There is a sense, though, of vitality suspended, of some splendid and terrible force absent. The stillness now seems strange, even to a visitor.

As is plain by now, what began so long ago as a student's admiration has grown over these years into a larger and richer friendship. When occasionally I have gone back to the college, usually it has been for the nominal purpose of visiting with students about some topic having to do with newspaper work. But that is only the thin excuse for seeing my friends again.

They are remarkably unchanged. It is impossible to imagine that they have raised a family, for they seem not to have aged at all. They remain as engaged in ideas and as full of optimism as ever. He still affects a certain severity, but I know him too well, now. The humor in his eyes gives him away, to me if not to his students, of whom he speaks with pride and occasionally with something that is nearer disappointment than reproach. He still expects the best of each of them. He still hopes the best *for* them.

I love to visit there, and feel very much at home. Sometimes other faculty friends gather, many of them his contemporaries and so, now, also mine. A fire mutters and hisses on the grate. The talk is vigorous. There still is no question raised that cannot be answered out of one of the books on the many shelves in that house.

But my feelings are more complicated than just friendship. There also is gratitude. For I cannot adequately say how much of later importance those four years as his student communicated to me — about language, about the uses of reason, about other values that I absorbed but cannot precisely put to words. Sometimes, over breakfast before leaving, I have made a faint attempt to convey that. But hearing it said would only embarrass him, and so I find myself trailing off awkwardly onto some other subject.

I see him with his colleagues, the other professors, and I know that he is respected and well-liked by them. No doubt the successive presidents of the college have understood, too, in some detached way, that he is capable and that the faculty is stronger for his contribution.

But he does not fill the academic journals with weighty tracts nor has he been driven by any zeal for hierarchical advancement. So he will never be one of the celebrities or cult figures of his profession. What he has, instead, is a gift so uncommon that it cannot be ranked or measured, much less required of every teacher who stands before a class.

He merely has the power to transform lives.

Transactions

A part of each of five successive afternoons we spent together. Mine was the desk at the front of the room. They occupied the 22 desks facing. The arrangement suggested a lopsided relationship — possibly of wisdom, but certainly of power.

Not many times in a life is one supplied a captive audience and then permitted, in fact encouraged, to discuss one's occupation and experiences, imposing a kind of false order on the largely fumbling process by which one has contrived to make one's way in the world.

The faces you look into, in such a situation, are at first undifferentiated — at best impassive, at worst openly skeptical. The students are sitting there for credit. They are reasonably sure that earning it will be a pain. You and they inspect one another across a gulf of years, but the view is unclear, the distance too great. And in the attempt to generate some energy, your voice turns brittle and shrill with certainties.

Then, so gradually as to be almost unnoticed, a transformation occurs. The faces become distinct. The masks of skepticism drop away, and you are able to see there the confusions and troubles and unguarded expectations that used to be your own. The geography of the room seems to change, without really changing at all. The desk at the front draws somehow closer to those other 22. One stops uttering pronouncements and begins speaking a different, plainer language. And in that moment the energy, instead of being manufactured artificially, starts to flow the other way.

The week's subject was writing. And writing of any sort — even the kind I do, but especially the finer kinds — is an unpredictable enterprise. It may not, in the final reckoning, be teachable. The forms can be learned, and the techniques. But beyond that, nothing is promised. Just as knowing the rules of the game of basketball is no guarantee of being able to throw the ball through the hoop.

With that disclaimer in mind, we worked at it together. Talked a good deal first, then worked at what we'd talked about. And by the week's end we had something to show. They wrote 22 pieces for me, and, by way of fairness, I wrote one for them. An unequal trade but, under the circumstances, the best that was possible.

We explored together the notion that writing, like most of the other matters of a life, is a transaction. You give something of yourself away and get something in return. And the getting and the giving must be roughly in proportion. At the end, when we read our compositions, made up of feelings and bits of our experience, we knew one another far better than we had at the beginning. Which is one of the higher purposes that language can be put to.

No more than a few of my young friends in that class mean seriously to be writers. But all of them are interested in words and ideas and, if only passingly, in the way in which writing gets done. Becoming older, as I can assure them they'll do, they will know me for the fraud I was — that any writer is who pretends to understand in an orderly way what it is he tries and mostly fails to do. But accidental scraps of what we talked about might be useful. At least they will credit me with being well intentioned.

For my part, I will remember each of them for the honesty of their effort and for the feelings and experiences they risked giving away. So, quite aside from anything we accomplished as writers together, the transaction is complete.

They asked if I would sum up in words something about them and about that week. The promise now is kept.

The Cat and the Stranger

The house in which I am lodging now, a guest, has emptied of its racket and confusion of several years ago. The sons have grown and gone: And the rooms from which one or another of them used to be displaced to make way for visitors are untenanted now. Not empty, mind you. Just not regularly lived in anymore. The rooms still are the boys' own. Their books remain on the shelves — some of them, at any rate. Their saved articles from the various stages of youth still are to be seen on the walls and desks and on the fine old carved ledges above the doors.

These leavings are not preserved morbidly, as shrines. It is just that 20 years and more of occupancy make durable marks. If nothing else, nail holes in the wall must be kept covered. And what better way to cover them than to let hung things stay in their place

So if the boys ever were to come back here to live — back from Africa or the far west or the north country or the other side of town, wherever their luck has taken them — they would find the evidence of themselves remaining. In the natural way of growing up and growing away, however, that is unlikely to happen. Or, if it happens at all, not for long.

My friends, their parents, pretend to be untroubled by the stillness. Their own lives race forward, creative, occupied with ideas and values and the untiring defense of sense in a world tending ever toward senselessness. Or maybe they are not pretending. For with all their tenderness they are realists. They grew up and went away themselves. They know it happens.

Even so, I have to think that sometimes, in the quiet of the evening, they must look up from a book or the stack of papers to be graded and listen for a footstep on the stair. Or, in passing the open door of one of those upstairs rooms, that they might, just for an unguarded instant, find it odd to see the bed unslept-in. They don't speak about that, though. Humanity's a game of losses. And grace is learning to take yours with a poker face.

With other creatures it's different. With a cat, for instance.

Today, with this bit of writing to do, I turned on the lamp in one of the unoccupied upper rooms and arranged myself and my working things at the borrowed desk. Above the door at the left were two footballs. On the bookcase behind, a model ship. On the table at the right, some arcane mechanical construction and also an empty bottle of Irish beer. On the desk's top was a wind-up alarm clock with its spring run down. And in the desk drawers were — among many other things — a box of broken crayons, a fuzzless tennis ball, assorted small bicycle parts and a folder marked *"Personal Letters,"* into which I had the decency not to pry.

Having oriented myself by these investigations, I began to work. But before very long I sensed a presence near at hand. It was the cat of the house, sitting in the doorway, sizing up the situation with cool green eyes.

The meaning of what followed could not have been plainer if the cat had suddenly been empowered to speak her thoughts aloud.

By her puzzled expression, it was obvious the look of me sitting there at the desk was somehow slightly wrong. And possibly the smell of me as well. Yet, at the same time, she found it good to see the room again in use — the lamp burning, the chair sat in, papers scattered and one of those man animals busy with his incomprehensible occupations.

So she rose, the cat did, and came a bit uncertainly across the threshold.

I put down my hand and she examined it and slightly shied away. It was not the proper hand. But then she relented and let herself be stroked. The foot and leg, too, were somehow wrong. She turned those green eyes up directly into my own with a speculative look. *Who the hell are you?* she demanded to know. *You're not the one who used to sit there — who ought to be sitting there again.*

But then she appeared to have an afterthought.

Better an old boy than no boy at all, her manner seemed to say. Anyway, a room needs to be lived in. The lamp shone warmly. The clutter of papers and the click of the typewriter were reassuring. So she flung herself against my trouser leg, and rubbed there companionably. And then, quite satisfied, demanded to be let outside to explore the autumn yard.

I will be sorry for her sake — for her sake only — to gather up my things one day shortly and leave the room to silence and her memories again. Cats do not know how to conceal their losses. Cats, contrary to their reputation, can't lock their hurts behind a poker face.

If you imagine otherwise you don't know cats. Or losses.

Marks of Sense

It is not for nothing that travel is said to be educational. Keep your eyes open while on the road and you are apt to learn something. For example, driving a stretch of western interstate highway not long ago I received a powerful lesson in the value of punctuation.

There, where the pavement ran away to a fine point on the horizon between hemispheres of scorched grass and tumbleweed, a sign rose up, shimmering in the heat at middle distance.

We drew closer.

The sign said: "See Live Rattlesnakes Pet Baby Pigs."

We would have liked to see that, all right. But the afternoon was stifling and many miles still lay ahead of us so we drove on, imagining as best we could that nest of vipers charming the piglets with their gentle touch.

Soon, then, there was another sign.

And that one said: "See the World's Largest Prairie Dog Turn Right at This Exit."

We watched for him, but the exit ramp when we came to it was empty. Evidently the singular rodent had made his turn there earlier.

Some miles farther on, a blinking light called our attention to a warning about "Slow Men Working."

We looked them over as we passed. It's true that there seemed to be a good deal of water drinking and leaning on the fenders of pickup trucks. But as far as we could tell, those men were no slower than road crews usually are.

A man I used to work for was a minimalist in the matter of punctuation. He spent much time in special vigilance for something he called the *Breath-Pause Comma.* Over the newsroom in those years could be heard a sibilance of heavy breathing as reporters strove, by trial and error, to purge their compositions of the offending mark.

In a sense, I suppose that man was right. There is no denying that a breath pause in the middle, worse yet a pause memorialized by a comma or even something more definite, would rob the above-mentioned road signs of much of their magic.

Still . . . I cannot help believing that, all in all, the benefits of punctuation outweigh such occasional losses.

(Notice, if you will, how three dots after the word "Still" give that statement the studied reflective air of something arrived at after long consideration. When the fact is I thought it up in about two seconds at 6:15 in the morning before breakfast in a motel room in Goodland, Kansas.)

These signs seen while traveling remind me of the toneless peroration one hears in the last moments before taking off in a commercial airliner.

Gafternoon ladies genmen welcome board Hard Luck Airways golden fleece service in event of sudden drop cabin pressure mask fall press over mouth nose breathe normally flotation device underseat open emergency exits inflate escape slide serving hot lunch cold drinks seat backs upright position behalf Captain Hardy entire crew enjoy your flight anybody wants to go to Cuba say so now.

That monologue, it has always seemed to me, would profit greatly from being punctuated.

I once made a winter crossing of the Atlantic on a Dutch passenger ship of light tonnage upon whose dining room wall was displayed the notice: "If Chair Moves Remain Seated If Table Moves Remain Calm Hold Plate and Glasses."

We strangers looked at one another apprehensively around the table. Clearly we had set forth upon a mad sea, in the hands of a drunken helmsman. And the babble of those instructions, resulting from their lack of semicolons, added to our general sense of insecurity.

Would it be going too far to suggest that proper punctuation may be the foundation of civil order and even possibly of civilization itself?

One sees from Tehran or Baghdad from time to time the pictures of demonstrators with their jaws locked in the open position. And one knows beyond any doubt that the noises they emit are unpunctuated. Demands are heard for some people to be killed and for others to live a long time. But all this runs together in a blur. You lose track of who was supposed to do which.

That is how societies and even revolutions come apart.

The kind of people who make war on commas are the same ones who would advise baby pigs to trust rattlesnakes and ask passengers to sit calmly in their chairs while the ship goes bottoms up.

By their run-on sentences will you know them. Beside roads and on the walls of drowned vessels will their writings be found.

The Hasty Craft

In a year long past, when all of us were boys, some friends of mine went off to the wheat fields for a season to join a harvest crew. That always struck me as a splendid kind of adventure — to ride the ripening wave of grain all the way up the continent, starting at the Mexican border and ending, just as the autumn began to turn, somewhere on the plains of Canada, having seen the whole miracle of that bounty unfold.

Some things you have to do in youth or you will never do them at all. Another sort of work had claim on me that summer, and so I missed my chance.

Oh, I have seen the harvest — bits and scraps of it. The newspaper used to send a reporter out to western Kansas for a couple of days in middle July to file a florid, thinly researched dispatch, full of the rumble of great machines and contrived suspense about the weather. The assignment usually went to one of the less-experienced hands, the senior reporters all having been so many times already that they prayed heaven never to have to interview another combine operator or elevator manager or county extension agent for the rest of their newspaper lives.

But for the novice the assignment was a plum. It got you out of town, away from the obituaries and the club notices. It promised a chance for writing — *real* writing, as opposed to the rote compilations of marriage licenses issued and divorces filed for.

Thus unleashed, we set out to get it all down: the scarlet sunsets; the country beer halls where the harvest crews came in at night, powdered over with pale dust from the grain, sun-peeling skin hanging like torn wallpaper from their crimson backs; the sudden storm that dashed some farmer's dream to chaff. Always the same storm, the same sunsets, the same carousing and dusty men — in all the stories, although the years and the bylines changed. And afterward, reading our reports in print, we wondered why, in spite of all those adjectives, they seemed so insubstantial.

The reasons, apart from our inexperience as near-beginners, were the old ones of the journalistic craft, but especially the fatal combination of haste and loquacity — too much said about too little known. That is the defect, the structural defect of this business, which experience cannot cure.

The journalist passes from one topic to the next, from the wheat harvest to politics to social issues to the problem of nuclear deterrent, with an appearance of facility or even of authority. But the line between facility and mere glibness, between authority and fraud, is very fine. For, when he sits down to attempt to make sense of his notes, the questions are always the same: *What, if anything, do I really know? How do I proceed in the face of all that I do not know? How may I arrange the words, the ideas, in a way that will seem to have substance and, at the same time, will not expose my larger ignorance?*

As they mature and achieve a certain stature in their trade, reporters may take on a manner of brassy self-assurance. But you will not find a one of them with any sense who does not, in his secret heart, live with the dread that the next paragraph he writes will unmask him as a dilettante and fool. Not a malicious fool, mind you. Just someone too sketchily informed.

Passing by car not long ago through a northern state where the wheat was just coming ripe and the harvest would soon begin, I had cause to stop and visit several hours with colleagues at the newspaper in a town of medium size. The vision of those yellow fields rippling away in every direction from the town had wakened an old memory of missed adventure. And I wondered how that paper meant to cover the harvest, which surely was one of its major stories of the year.

Well, the newspaper, as it turned out, was owned by Dow Jones & Co., and therefore controlled by men in a distant metropolis for whom the adventure of grain is represented by numbers on the futures board. Ad revenues were down. The staff was lean. Write more, the survivors were advised by the home office — *more quantity*. Selling themselves by the pound, they had a harried, hunted look.

Yes, he planned to cover the wheat harvest, one of the young reporters said. He'd always thought it might be wonderful to follow the harvest all the way up the continent, but he'd never managed that. And never would.

Instead, he'd have a day to do the story. With luck, two days.

Some things you do young, or you never do them at all. After that it's everywhere the same, a hasty craft.

The Wind-Chill Factor

Twelve cents was what he wanted — a quite specific need. Twelve cents, no more, no less.

The arctic wind blew keen along the street of business buildings and made the bus sign rattle on its pole.

"I'm trying to go home," the man said. He looked at the coins in his hand. "And I'm twelve cents short."

Sometimes, for reasons not afterward explainable, we shame ourselves. In a sidelong sort of way I examined the fellow, with an air of studied disinterest, being careful not to meet his eyes. Thirty years old, he appeared to be, or maybe a bit more. Certainly not aged. The coat he wore was worn but warm. His trousers bagged around his broken-over shoes. One earpiece of his glasses was patched with adhesive tape.

Down on his luck he was, no doubt of that. But not hungry yet. Not looking frightened yet. In short, a man no worse off than tens of thousands to be seen afoot in the land of opportunity in a season of hard times. And better off than some of them. He didn't need a dollar. He didn't need a meal. He didn't want a drink. Twelve cents would suffice, thank you. A dime and two pennies to put him on a bus, so the bus could take him home, wherever that might be.

"Can't help you," I heard a stranger say. Some brittle stranger with a briefcase and a vested suit. Quite astonished, then, I recognized the voice to be my own.

The trifling appeal had been summarily denied. I tried hastily to examine the reason in my mind. But it wasn't my intellect the man had addressed. It was my instinct, my heart, he'd sought to speak to. And in that instant, for whatever reason, my heart had been bad.

And by the time my head commanded me to feel remorse, the man was gone. Without either anger or surprise, evidently being long past both, he just let the wind blow him on along the sidewalk toward the next corner, where people waited for the crossing light to change. And of course I didn't follow after him. Mercy that scuttled along behind, in guilty afterthought, would surely be contemptible. Or so I argued to myself.

Someone was coming to collect me in a car. But colder, suddenly, than I'd been before, I left the curb and retreated up inside the heated office entryway. From there, however, the man's progress could still be seen.

The traffic signal changed. The people at the curb all went across. One last pedestrian came hurrying to make the light, but was intercepted by the man with the mended glasses, broken-over shoes and 12-cent need. This new passer-by bore no briefcase, sported no vested suit. In fact, he was dressed not much different from the petitioner — rough shoes, worn jacket drawn up against the cold

But his response was immediate, and had nothing to do with intellect. He just took some change from his pocket, counted out the coins and pressed them in the other's hand. And then strode on without a word, having done a thing too slight to merit thanks.

The first man turned, then, and came back along the street. I would like to report that he stopped other passers, one after the other, and extracted money from them and pocketed it with a smirk. The fact, though, is that he simply waited for the bus. When it came he boarded it, having exactly the required fare, and rode away toward home, wherever home was. And only then did I feel comfortable to go down to the curb and watch for my own ride.

Daily, in numberless small encounters, we are defined.

Doom in a Parking Lot

Timing is everything. In work, in sport and in our relationships with one another, the handicap of a beginning made too late is apt to mean disappointment at the end.

Maybe that is just the skewed notion of someone who has spent too many years in dread of deadlines, a slave to the clock. Yet what is true in the industry of news strikes me also as being a rule of a general sort applying to most of our affairs.

The moments tick past, all seeming much alike. But one of them is different. It is that moment — not easily singled out except in hindsight — beyond which success in an intended venture is unlikely, if not impossible. Certainly it is a rule in nature, an implacable law you might even say. The breach of it is severely punished.

Passing from office to car the other afternoon, one of the first raw days of the changing season, I noticed a wind-blown bit of color against the pavement of the parking lot and went over to examine. It was a monarch butterfly, a fine example of its kind. I bent to pick the insect up, thinking it dead, although its wings appeared to be undamaged, their orange and black pattern still vivid and unfrayed.

Just then a gust of wind tumbled the butterfly a little distance away across the asphalt. I pursued it several steps and reached again. And again, just as I did so, the wind sent it spinning. But not by accident.

For I discovered then that the creature was alive after all, and was eluding me by a small act of volition. It clung to the pavement until my hand came near. Then its legs released their grip and the chill breeze sent that animate scrap off to where it found a new purchase.

Unbroken the thing was. And perfectly aware of me there. And yet, unaccountably, it could not fly.

The monarch is a rather wonderful bug. It is the most famous of the migrating North American butterflies, long-lived and a capable navigator, making each year a massed journey of nearly two thousand miles from as far north as the Canadian sub-arctic down established flyways to wintering grounds in the southern United States and Mexico. In the spring, some of those same migrants bear north again, faded by now, their life-force ebbing low, to deposit the eggs that will guarantee the future generations of their kind — and then to go to dust among the grasses of some meadow.

The milkweed plant is their only food, upon which their eggs also are laid. Wherever in either direction that plant has been carried by men — to Bermuda, the Canaries, to Hawaii and even Australia and New Zealand — there too the monarch has managed to find its way on the ocean winds and establish thriving populations.

I have read an account of a scientist at the Royal Ontario Museum in Toronto who set out some thirty years ago to research the monarchs' migratory habits. He tagged and released three thousand live specimens, of which only one was later reported found. So in another year he tagged *ten thousand* of them, receiving but 30 replies. What was becoming of all those tagged butterflies?

It is reported that the gentleman then went south himself and personally ate a quantity of monarchs in the field, finding them to have a flavor not unlike dry toast. Presently he discovered that his paper wing tags were subtly disrupting the color pattern that protected monarchs from predators. What was happening was that the scientist's butterflies were being singled out and eaten by birds. Those of them, that is, that he himself was not eating.

The next time around, with the help of volunteers, he doubled the number of marked specimens to twenty thousand, with correspondingly better result. There was no mention of whether the researcher ever gave up his crazed dietary inclination.

The monarch, then, has passed from prehistory to this day, undaunted by vast distances, by storms aloft or the exclusivity of its dependence on milkweed, by darting birds or munching entomologists. It is, for all its apparent fragility, a hardy creature. And yet here, in a city parking lot, was a monarch undamaged but somehow plainly disabled. By what, though?

I had a layman's intuition which, several days later, I was able to confirm in a book. The temperature was at fault. The monarch can endure much cold, but in a state of immobility. Below 45 degrees — and until warmed again by the sun — it loses the power to fly.

For reasons unknown — because of a late courtship or perhaps out of mere lassitude — that butterfly had stayed behind the main body of the migration, had lingered a day too long in some northern glade. Finally it had turned south. But on this afternoon I've mentioned, a front moved through and the temperature took a sudden drop into the lower 40s. And so, on that stretch of urban pavement, bad timing had overtaken the laggard.

Chilled to paralysis and awaiting the sun, it had escaped my grasp by the one slight means available to it: by letting the wind push it beyond the reaching hand. But there would be no more sun. The cool afternoon would be succeeded by colder rain, and then by snow. The chance was lost. That small untimeliness, the error of a single day, was fatal.

Having managed in good part to separate ourselves from nature, human beings are governed by a discipline less stark. Even so, even for us, a clock is turning. It counts out the critical moments of lost beginnings.

Always   October

Autumn is the season I would miss. Rich in the moment, and rich in memory, there is nothing about it that does not stir me to the heart.

Autumn is expectation. A good many years ago the clarity of sharp October air conveyed across the night to the porch of the house where I lived a sound of marching bands — a thump of drums and after that a weighty whisper of many voices rising. Low over the roofs of the facing houses could be seen a white moonglow of lights. And I would go to where those lights were, with a friend or not, and press my face against the frosted wire fence that enclosed a field upon which larger boys played a violent game.

Out there was fame. A mystery then and a mystery still. But the pursuit of it was a wonderful thing to see. In time I grew. Not enough, but sufficiently to play the game. To play it even on that same field, with others watching through the fence. And already I envied them — the watchers — because I knew and could have told them, though I didn't, that the *doing* never would be quite as fine as the *expecting to*.

Autumn also is the season of leave-takings, of adventures begun.

The other afternoon, crossing a little park, I walked through a slow rain of golden leaves. And immediately I was in a different park, a place of 30 years ago. A girl was there, in a swing, and we were making our goodbyes. I could tell you her name, although assuredly I will not.

We meant nothing, or practically nothing, to one another. We were younger than people of my age can be believed ever to have been. And I was going away to somewhere. Our grief was purely ceremonial. She didn't mind a bit that I was going. And I was glad to be. But the situation imposed upon us certain dramatic obligations. We played our parts in promises and sighs. And after that we never met again, or ever particularly cared to. Probably she does not even remember. But if by chance she does, and should happen to read these lines, I must tell her that the picture of that day, that park, of her, is a part of the landscape of this season of my year. And will be always.

That is a less extravagant promise than some we made while the leaves fell around us on a golden afternoon. But at least it is a true one.

Still older, then . . . much older. I will not forget my father, on the last afternoon of his life, raking up a pile of blown leaves for my daughters, his granddaughters, to play in. That memory is not bittersweet at all. I watch him watching them. His hair is white and thin. He is an old man, as I will be. He is preoccupied — his blue eyes clouded by an intimation of where he is bound. The leaves scutter off the pile and across the clipped grass. The children cry out in delight. It is his moment of completion.

Blackbirds flocking. Wildfowl passing in the dark. Asters blooming against a tan bank at roadside. Farm fields stripped bare, awaiting some further plan. The empty sky, the long silence, the sharpness of late-day shadow, the smell of leaf smoke. I am devoted to all of that, and find no melancholy in it. Only a palpable fullness.

People who live their whole lives in anticipation of some future eternal spring mystify me utterly. Each to his own taste, of course. But if I had my way, I would prefer at the last to walk off, solitary and well-jacketed, across a land of always October.

Leaning into Winter

The afternoon had a no-nonsense look about it. Clouds rolled up in the west, sooty as coal smoke and full of fury. The sun went out. Across the city there were sudden sharp reports, as in a small war, of tree limbs snapped off and flung to earth.

To townsfolk it seemed a considerable storm. But a bit to the west and north, out in the nakedness of levee land where the gray river came tumbling past with standing waves above the current and whitecaps atop the waves, it was more than merely storm. It might have been a cataclysm.

The air was full of bits and scraps of things — tatters of time and the changing season. The wind gripped and tossed a bushy tree and stripped it clean before the eyes. Shredded stalk fields stirred and rose up entire and rode away on the blast. Then the clouds opened with a hammering of rain and hail. And, after the torrent, ground water shone with a dangerous glint in the furrows, like molten lead.

And the birds! Never have you seen, or will you likely see, as many blackbirds as came out of the north that afternoon — from the direction of the raging wind. A river of birds against the curdy clouds. A river that made the true river, the one running powerful in its channel, seem little more than a rivulet.

Pulsing and chittering that airy river came, with a wind of wings that could be heard even above the wind of the passing storm. A vanguard of those travelers settled in the tops of the lowland willow jungle. But didn't stop there; hesitated only. From as far away as one could see, the others — in the *thousands of their millions — still were coming.*

The storm will be forgotten. There could be a few days yet of deceiving gentleness. But those birds were hurrying somewhere. Individually their brains are negligible. But in the aggregate that much intelligence commands respect. So our minds, with theirs, are set now on winter. And like seamen ashore still rolling with the deck, we are leaning already to receive the hammering of its imagined gales.

The Long Patience

Their world and ours are not the same. We are proximate in place and time; we occupy the same space. We are, one to the other, presences sensed. And sometimes there are encounters. We coexist — nothing more than that.

In the blueness of a frozen morning, just before dawn, something large is moving across the ordered turf between houses and curb. The blueness pales. The large thing divides, becomes a pair of smaller ones. Two raccoons, glossy and fat, are foraging there. Then a light goes on in a window of one of the houses. The masked faces turn. And quicker than the telling of it, those two late-moving shadows have vanished over the curb and into the storm sewer. A woman shivering in robe and slippers comes out to get the newspaper.

Her lawn is empty, as it ought to be. The shadows were never there.

Not many blocks away, in the trees of the boulevard median, a rookery of crows is waking. The crows do not consider that they are city birds. They have no notion of what a city means. But they know well their chosen tree and the sky paths leading out, far out, from it. And now, as the dawn yellows, they rise up all together on their dark wings with a sound like a blanket shaken. And in the beds of the houses along the boulevard, there comes to the ears of half-sleepers a cry they think they've dreamed.

Later, in the rush hour along a main street, a driver will brake his car abruptly to miss a dog. Behind him in the hurtling traffic, tires will screech and horns impatiently blare. And he will look across his car's hood into the face — not of a dog at all. The face, instead, of a red fox vixen. Her slanted eyes fixed on the danger of him and his machine. Her lip curled up to show the teeth that hold some small, furred thing she is carrying on her way to somewhere.

For just that instant they examine one another. There is no recognition, only mutual surprise. Then both pass on to habit's destinations. Their worlds separate again, and they forget.

Through the many years of living in our present house I have been locked in a contest with an adversary whose identity I still do not know, and maybe never will. First I noticed a hole, a burrow of some sort, just under the edge of the asphalt driveway. Then I saw that it was getting bigger, and that the asphalt was beginning to bend and crumble at its lip. I shoveled dirt into the hole and packed it hard, considering the problem solved. But when next I thought to look the hole was open again.

In later years I have taken stronger measures. For several autumns, now, I have gotten large stones and, with a heavy sledge, driven them into the burrow one atop the other so tightly no mortal force could dream of dislodging them. The winter snows come. From time to time I inspect the place for tracks or signs of digging. But there are none; all is in order. I put the matter out of mind.

Then spring arrives. And, sure enough, there comes that day when I find my work undone. The den is open and all my stones are gone — not tumbled and strewn at the entrance but simply gone, vanished. And every spring the hole gets bigger. A few years more and I will be able to crawl inside, if I dare, which I won't.

I have no idea how deep it is, or what lives there. But the side of the driveway is sagging worse, and I have given up. Something has decided that place must be its home, and in the face of such determination what use is it to struggle?

In the way that cities go, the houses of my neighborhood may one day be swept away and the entire area — streets, flowers, memories and all — paved over for a shopping mall. Then, the next season, the hole will appear again. And it pleases me to imagine that the financiers and paving engineers will be as mystified before it, and as powerless, as I have been.

It makes one think, does it not?

These creatures were here before we came. They saw us arrive, winching our cannons across the hills to contest ownership and points of law. They watched as we drew our plats and laid out streets and made our buildings and poured all those millions of yards of cement. In spite of that, they still are here.

And tomorrow?

Go to any very old place on earth where men have lived. Go, say, to Heliopolis in the high valley of Lebanon in the Middle East. Two thousand years ago and more, it was a center of culture and commerce. Men were rich there, and powerful there, and vain there. Now their voices have been blown away on the wind that keens among the broken columns. And if you look closely between the stones of the ruined temples, you will find the burrows of the survivors, the creatures who witnessed it all.

Like the dweller under my driveway, they do not ask about tomorrow. *They have always known.*

The Astronomer

Plainly it is not possible to have passed unmarked through more than 70 years of earthly time. And yet there he sits, the famous astronomer, very much a young man still, deep in his accustomed chair with a lighted globe of our world at his elbow.

Some bug or other has made him indisposed. He has come down from his bed in pajamas and slippers and an orange robe, and even in his discomfort there is about him this boyishness of voice and manner and movement that is pronounced, though in no way affected or contrived.

He would not, he says, want a visitor to have traveled such a distance for nothing. *Distance,* indeed! His profession mocks the word.

The solar system I roughly comprehend, as no doubt you do. But beyond its frozen outer reaches lie abstractions that most of us are unable to imagine, or maybe to confront. I had read his books beforehand; had been made uneasy by them.

Our galaxy, the Milky Way, contains perhaps one hundred billion stars, of which our sun is only one — a modest one. The nearest of all those stars is Alpha Centauri, whose image, at light's speed of 186,300 miles a second, must travel four years and four months to reach our eye. But that is the beginning of wonders, not the end. For beyond ours lie other galaxies — the nearest of *those* so distant that, as the astronomer has written, if it had exploded a million years ago, the light bearing the visible news of the catastrophe would not reach us for yet another million. And beyond that one, more galaxies, an estimated billion of them in the part of the universe we see. And that part perhaps the least fraction of the whole.

And beyond the whole, what? Conceivably other universes, although our nomenclature would need to be changed to accommodate that concept. And all of it bounded by what? Existing in what setting? Beginning where and ending where? Why, *everywhere,* of course. And if everywhere has limits, they must likely be described in terms of other planes of time or matter.

The layman wants answers, wants conclusive diagrams. But the astronomer is content with mysteries. Or, if not precisely content, is at least not frightened by them.

Five minutes by car from his living room is the Lark Observatory, on a prominence of land thrust eastward into Lake Michigan. It is a vast machine, rearing spectral white above the shore. In the unheated domed chambers at the top are the instruments. There is a kind of awe to be felt in the presence of a great telescope. This has nothing to do with its scale or complexity, though these are impressive, but rather with its purpose. It is able to transport us visually across indescribable reaches of space and time, revealing the birth and death of suns, allowing us to witness events that occurred long before our species or any other walked this planet.

That is very close to magic and closer still, perhaps, to theology.

The weather that night happened to be unfit for viewing. The observatory's engineer explained the workings of the place, and then we went out in a raw wind onto the catwalk encircling the dome. Eighty feet or so below, winter waves beat cold against the point. Across a bend of land and water, Chicago could be seen in middle distance to the south, its taller buildings distinct; its immense emanation of light reflecting on the underside of clouds.

It is a great city, Chicago — a considerable evidence of human enterprise. And yet, for all that, not even a visible feature on a small planet which, itself, in the infinite sea of space would surely escape notice.

I could not help envying, then, a man who had chosen to pass a career with his eye fixed on faint stars, measuring distances in years and adding up the years in multiples of millions. Time has a different meaning for him — different and less personal. In some odd way it seems to have lost its power over him and left him young.

In theory, to travel at the speed of light would be to defeat time altogether. Cosmic journeys of the imagination may have a similar effect. If I had it to do again, I would consider being an astronomer.

Flea's Vanity

Upon a continent there is a plain, upon the plain a city, within the city a neighborhood, in that neighborhood a street of houses, in one of the houses a dog, upon the dog a flea, and making its parasitic home among the bristles of the flea there creeps a mite, smaller, by far, than your eye or mine can see.

What does the mite comprehend of the continent?

And what lives on the mite?

These considerations of scale were brought to mind the other day by the news of a new theoretical model of the universe. The theory, which was arrived at concurrently by an American physicist and a colleague in the Soviet Union, postulates that the universe, exploding from that superheated node of primal matter no larger than a baseball, has expanded into a vastness of time and distance incredibly greater even than previously supposed.

Indeed, if their notion is correct, the "new" universe — larger by a factor of 10 to the one hundredth power than the "old" one — is of a dimension for all practical purposes ungraspable by the ordinary intellect.

An astronomer friend once drew a word picture of the cosmos to help my daughter better understand her place in nature's order. If New York and Los Angeles were taken to represent the boundaries of the *then*-known universe, he said, somewhere at approximate midpoint between would lie not a pebble, not a grain of sand, not even a wind-blown dust mote, but a submicroscopic particle invisible to even the most powerful instruments of magnification.

And that would be the planet on which my daughter dwelt, our planet Earth. She received that information with proper humility.

But now we are invited to another, more prodigious gymnastic of the mind. For if the scientists in Philadelphia and Moscow have rightly done their sums, the size relationship of the old universe to the new one is nearly as insignificant as was Earth's to the previously imagined cosmos.

A friend and I were afield one day last week, his dog with us. And this friend was speaking, apropos of nothing in particular, about how a chemically treated collar helped rid his pet of fleas. Why, he had wondered, would a band about the neck serve to exterminate unwanted guests over the animal's entire body? Then someone had told him — it's not a pleasant subject, exactly — that fleas are drawn to the moisture around the creature's eyes. In undertaking their ambitious migration from the dog's nether parts, they are obliged to pass across the killing zone of the treated collar. And thus, in time, the host is purged of them entirely.

That may be poppycock. Maybe flea collars work that way and maybe they don't. I can't say. But it sounds plausible enough and makes a good story in any case. And it set me to thinking about the relationship in size between the flea and the dog, a very large dog, upon whose vast and furry mass the former lived out its life, an inconsequential citizen.

What can the flea understand of the whole geography of a dog? Much less of the universe of yards and streets and stairways the dog traverses. Much less, still, of the larger universe the dog inhabits but does not comprehend. The universe, that is, which the physicists newly describe.

Nothing at all, most likely. Yet, for the mite that dwells upon him, the distance from the front of a flea to the back of one may be a day's march. And upon that incontrovertible evidence of his grandness, it is possible that the flea, too, is insufferably vain.

C . W .   G U S E W E L L E

Debauchery in the Wild

These remarks concern hunting — a subject which I gather from what I read does not provoke indifference. Many of my fellow writers periodically are seized, as one, by a compulsion to unburden themselves about the blood sport. No special reason for these outbursts can be detected. They are pure mystery, like the occasional rushes of lemmings to the sea. But since I am part of the herd, there is no choice except to run along with the others down to the deadly shore of controversy.

Surely your own opinion on this matter already is formed. Either you hunt and enjoy it, or else you have decided that hunters are a savage and depraved breed. Either way, nothing said here would be apt to change your mind.

What follow, then, with no aim at persuasion either way, are only some minor tales, full of the gore and vainglory of the brutal chase.

*   *   *

We were camped, three of us, in snow above nine thousand feet in late November at the edge of a high meadow in the San Juan range of Colorado, hunting deer or elk or possibly bear or, failing those, stray cattle or anything that moved. And on the fifth day someone spoke of doughnuts.

"What would you give right now for a box of doughnuts?" he asked.

Hunger had not plagued us. Besides the dried foods in our provision box, we'd had bits of venison tenderloin skewered on sticks over the fire and abundant speckled trout caught from an ice-rimmed beaver pond near the camp. But the mention of doughnuts was a mistake. Several more days remained, and from that moment our thoughts were on nothing else. Doughnuts became a fixation. We discussed them day and night — the various flavors of them, their texture, the way they broke apart and crumbled in the mouth.

The inaccessibility of doughnuts finally crazed us. Our eyes welled with emotion when we thought of them. In a kind of masochistic game — snowbound there, a day's climb down through drifts to the town and another day's climb back — we bid up the price we would pay.

Twenty dollars for a dozen, I think it was, when finally we broke camp and went down the mountain. We met a man carrying the edible parts of an elk on the backs of two pack mules. He wanted to talk about his elk, but we were talking about doughnuts. And at the first chance he broke away from us and took another trail.

There was a bakery in the town. We bought four dozen doughnuts and two quarts of milk. Those were for two of us. The third bought a whole German chocolate cake and a half-gallon of chocolate milk. We ate all this off the hood of the car in about three minutes, the one with the cake breaking the thing apart and bringing pieces of it to his mouth with both hands. And after that we went to the public showers of the town and, paying 25 cents, stood a long time under the nozzles fully dressed to cleanse ourselves of the smeared pastry and crusted milk of that incredible debauch.

We have gone different ways. The one with the cake became an executive in industry, the other an editor in California. We never speak about what went on at the curb outside that bakery. But even now, after 15 years, there is no desire ever again to hunt the mountains of southwestern Colorado.

*   *   *

I had been married not quite five months, living with my bride in a cottage beside a railroad track at the far edge of the city, when at 3 o'clock in the morning the clock-radio announced the maiden hunt of the teal season.

The first words of the radio announcer: *"The search continues for six men, dangerous and probably armed, who escaped early today from the county jail . . ."*

I looked at my bride and she looked back at me — a level sort of look.

"They'll go the other way," I told her. "They won't come this way, toward the city. They'll head for open country."

"Sure," was all she said.

I drove out the lane and found, where it met the highway, a great constellation of sheriff's deputies in cars with flashing lights. I explained my problem to one of the deputies. "It's the opening day of duck season," I told him. "Those fellows will go the other way, right?" But the deputy was uncooperative and mean-spirited.

"Buddy," he said, "it's your wife."

I went. No ducks flew that day. My bride was perfectly safe, although, as it turned out, the six prisoners — showing very poor judgment — had struck directly toward the city; had in fact walked along the very railroad track beside the cottage where she slept.

To the best of my knowledge this has not disfigured our marriage in any important way. Though I have had the feeling that sometimes, in small things, she is not as trusting as she might be.

* * *

Perhaps you have run out of patience with these tales of bloody pursuit.

I will not bother you with accounts of all those times, on the last evenings of failed deer hunts, when we have had to send a member of the party to a country store after some creatures whose flesh to rend and bones to pick beside the fire. It is an awkward mission. Invariably there are locals lounging in the store, all of them talking about hunting. The order is whispered to the storekeeper, but he is without sympathy.

"A *what?*" he demands to know. Faces turn. A mutter of derision fills the place. They refuse to believe that anyone would mount an elaborate expedition and drive hundreds of miles for no better purpose than to camp out and cook chickens.

And still there are worse things than a chicken hunt. Once, living a winter in the woods, I prepared an eight-rabbit stew for friends who were coming for a visit. Into the stew I put a jar of tomatoes given me by a relative. They turned out to be tomato preserves. An ice storm came. The friends canceled their trip. The stew pot boiled down to a sweet, pink substance the consistency of taffy.

Try subsisting a fortnight sometime on rabbit candy.

These are some of my memories of the uncivilized business of hunting. As its critics charge, and as I have confessed here, there is indeed much shame in it and much that is outright disgusting. Probably, if you do not hunt already, you will not now be tempted to take it up.

Corrupted Young

I seldom even pause to wonder, anymore, what strange turn of mind condemns me to a love of bleak dawns and cutting winds, with only a screen of bundled reeds or dry oak branches to deflect the winter's advance. The mystery is unfathomable, as it always was.

Again the other morning, at an hour when sensible folk are only just well settled into sleep, the alarm beside me spoke and it was necessary to creep out groaning from the bed — groaning with pain, but not complaint — and go to sit for several hours in a wet, cramped place, listening for the whisper of wild wings in the dark.

Waterfowling is a vice from which the young ought strenuously to be steered away, as from tobacco and gambling and foppish manners. For, if it can be avoided in the impressionable years, probably one is safe for a lifetime. Unguided and unwarned, I was corrupted 30 winters or more ago. The memories now are very many and nearly all uncomfortable.

Of a frozen December day in a green wheat field, and of three of us crouched together, burning cardboard shell casings in a can on the floor of the blind to stay alive, faces chapped raw, hands aching, feet without sensation, while all that day the geese kept coming, wave after wave of them, riding straight down the wind-tumbled sky to our decoys as if sliding down a wire — hundreds of them, hundreds of hundreds, from first light until the day was a pale memory in the west.

Of standing hip-deep in a marsh, a friend and I, hidden inside contraptions we had built — fiber barrels with the bottoms cut out and legs affixed to them, sheaves of dry cattail leaves fastened to the sides for decoration — the still water turning ice-mushy, as we stood praying that the ducks would come, and praying much more earnestly that some misstep would not invite the marsh in over the tops of our rubber wading boots.

Of a blind some other friends and I constructed once in nine feet of water on an oxbow lake the bluebills used, an elegant edifice with a covered boat shed behind and shelves and cupboards inside, with two stoves for heat and for cooking breakfast on. I remember the smell of bacon frying in the last darkness, and the disembodied muttering of ducks unseen above. And remember, too, how a late-winter shift of the lake ice, after the season had closed, ripped the blind from its moorings and then ground it into shards and splinters too small for fireplace kindling.

It's a fool's business, waterfowling. Often as not one comes home without game, without anything to show for the ordeal but windburn and a shaking chill and eyes half blinded by staring too long and deep into an empty sky. And yet . . .

If once, just once, you've seen the great geese come beating slowly toward you low against the wind, or a flock of half a hundred mallards all shining silver underneath as they bank and turn back to the call, then you risk being affected in a way that will change that season of all your years.

My daughters had such moments first at ages 9 and 10. Sometimes I wonder if I have done them a terrible disservice. But then I think of their great-uncle, whose way to his newspaper job took him each morning along a river road. And if the sky happened to be low and a gale was whining out of the north and the ducks were moving, sometimes he would turn the car around and go home to change his clothes. And the pursuit of publishable truths would have to wait another day.

He was a young man then. Fifty years and more afterward, when he had gotten old, he would sit looking out across a lake and his eyes would dust over with the contented look of someone full of more fine memories than he could ever hope to tell. Someday, a long time from now, if the years have filled them up that way, my daughters may forgive me the strange hours of rising and all the cramped, cold mornings their lives will hold.

But forgiveness is for later. For now, I'm afraid, the damage is done.

The Warming Cold

The house dark. The street dark. The hum of the furnace stilled. All of us — the dog, the cats, the people — struck motionless as statues by the sudden failing of the light.

Somewhere a cable had shorted. All along the block, and several other blocks, the drafts of a frozen night came fingering under the doors and prying at the window cracks of rooms where, only a moment earlier, comfort had been. It is astonishing how quickly a dwelling place goes cold, once the dark has claimed it. The walls we build to separate ourselves from nature are very costly. But they are very thin.

Once, years ago, when we were new in our house, the ice of a winter storm dragged down the wires and interrupted life for most of four days. The first night we slept under blankets in our own beds, only a little chilly. In the morning, we supposed, the problem would be fixed. It wasn't, though. We built a fireplace fire and soon burned all the dry wood on hand. The rest was in a stack in the yard, some of it left by the last occupant, old wood full of bugs and beginning to go punky. The stack was sheathed under an inch of ice. The pieces had to be chopped out singly and carried in to drain beside the hearth.

The thermometer in the hall recorded our progressive losses.

At first the fire warmed the whole room and part of the room beyond. Then the comfort zone grew smaller, until finally it had shrunk to a semicircle extending out two steps, no more, from the fireplace itself. By afternoon of the second day the indoor thermometer stood at 50 degrees. By morning of the next, it registered only a little more than 40.

People of some neighborhoods went off to rest warm in hotel beds, and the empty houses of some of them were burgled meantime. In others, the pipes froze and broke. Under our roof there was nothing to interest a discriminating thief. And having lived there only three months, we were too stubborn to let ourselves be driven out.

Our daughters were small then. Small enough that the four of us could fit together, crowded only close enough for common warmth, inside a double sleeping bag. By day we wore all our heaviest sweaters and coats and tended the fire and observed the thermometer, commenting on its steady fall. The kitchen stove was gas, so we were able to cook and keep warm cups in hand. By night we lighted our central room with candles, and read by a camping lantern, and told winter stories — storm stories — that were told us by the generation before.

And when fatigue drugged us all, which was early in that temperature, we stoked up the fire with dry wood, unrolled our bag in front of it, crept inside and went quickly, deliciously off to sleep, all closely touching.

I can't say how long we might have held out against the cold. Although I like to think now that, given food enough and firewood enough, we could have made it through to spring. In any case, that wasn't necessary. The fourth morning, at some small hour, we awoke in a frightful sweat, the fire burning high, the furnace throbbing and radiators hot to the touch, every light bulb in the house ablaze.

And as quickly as this telling of it, almost without any comment, life resumed its safe and uneventful march.

Then, several evenings ago, the lights went out again, though only briefly — only for a couple of hours. And the cold came probing. One of the cats passed through the room where we sat. The creature stopped and stretched, and the candlelight flung its shadow large against the wall. And all those memories came back.

I have been astonished by the clarity of the girls' recollection of those nights, for their ages then were only 2 years and 3. They remember it all: the sense of fine adventure, the dark hours occupied with stories, the minding of the fire, the nearness as we slept. Whenever the lights have flickered on a night of a winter storm, I have sensed in them — even when sometimes they have not spoken it — the yearning that we might need to draw so closely together, to amuse and attend and comfort one another that way again.

Rarely do we have to. The comfort around us is wonderfully reliable. Almost always we are safe, and that's the pity.

First Snow

The year's first snow arrived in flakes as big as butterflies, as big as birds. And it fell as if it never meant to stop. Streets disappeared entirely, all level white between the curbs. Grown people spoke of inconvenience, but children spoke of answered dreams.

I cannot remember much of childhood. But I do recall one snow in later years, which, because there were no appointments I had to keep, I could enjoy with the unencumbered happiness of a childish heart. I was staying the season alone in a country place. One afternoon a bank of gray rode up in the west, with a warmish wind ahead of it. Then the wind turned round to the north. And by first light of the next morning the clearing beside my cabin was a trackless pool of white.

There were other things I could have done that day. But none I had to do. So I put on my highest boots and took down my heaviest coat, and put an apple and a leftover piece of fried rabbit in my pocket, and filled and banked the stove. Then set out, bound for anywhere or nowhere, to put some footprints in the snow.

Nearly knee-deep it was, but light as air. Every branch and twig was limed with it. White of snow, black of barren trees — those were the only colors in the woods. I cannot say, now, how many miles I walked. I only remember the fine aimlessness of that day. It was a trek without a destination, with no schedule except to be back warm in the cabin at dark. That was more than 20 years ago, and in my stretch of woods there were fewer fences then. Also, younger legs were strangers to fatigue. The hills rolled away in an uninterrupted march. The starkness of light and dark gave the patterns of the land a clearer logic.

As far as I could see ahead, the snow was unbroken. Behind, mine were the only tracks. No one wondered where I was. No one cared where I was going. No one waited for me to arrive there. If by some odd chance a walker on that day were to have stepped too near a ravine's steep edge, or slipped and fallen into some crevice in the rock, his absence might have gone a long time unremarked. But the day had a friendly feel. There was no thought of that.

Rabbits crouched singly in little caves made by the bending of rank grasses under snow. The sun appeared, and struck that winter sea a blinding white. Sometime in middle day I stopped to gnaw my cold lunch, and a squirrel warming on his limb barked annoyance at the trespass.

My way was a long, long circle.

Against the rough bark of a tree I saw a scrap of brownish patterned cloth, like tweed. And put my hand over it, and felt a movement. And when I took my hand away the tweedy scrap flew off — a two-inch bird, like none I'd seen in any book. Later, just as the afternoon faded to pale lemon behind a timbered ridge, a flight of crows passed over, perhaps half a hundred of them, bound for the roost but traveling silently as crows rarely do, quick shadows cast between sky and snow.

Then the clearing and the cabin appeared. The day was spent.

Small things, all of those. But remembering them now — remembering the splendid aimlessness of that walk — it is possible to understand again, as in a child's dreaming, the surpassing glory of such a snow, and all its possibilities.

Then the memory recedes. The moment passes. I am thrust forward again 20-some years in time. And peering from the window with the ignorance of age, see only inconvenience after all.

A Definition

Our younger daughter has come of an age to have emphatic tastes of her own. Thus she denounced us at the table the other evening for placing before her something she refused to classify as real food.

The offending object was a turkey roll, conveniently prepackaged in its own foil cooking vessel and bought from the freezer shelf at the grocery for a price only slightly less than that of precious metals. She eyed the thing a moment with revulsion and naked contempt, then sank back in her chair and refused sustenance.

We did not press her. Just then my own head was light and my tongue numb from several days of severe foodlessness — one of the extreme diets that my wife from time to time prescribes. To me, that turkey roll looked exquisite. Small whining noises rose in my throat and my facial muscles jerked involuntarily as I contemplated it there on the platter. I did not mind that my daughter rejected it. Secretly I was pleased to see any of the competition withdraw. But I was curious all the same to know what it was about it she found so repellent.

"It's not real food," she said. "I like real food to eat — hot dogs and frozen pizzas and things like that."

"What the devil do you mean?" I demanded to know. "It's turkey. You always like turkey. You knew we were having turkey."

"It's not *real,*" she insisted. Scornfully, as if that much ought to be self-evident. She stuck to her position and could not be moved.

Presently the facts came out. A real turkey has legs and wings. It has bones to give it definition. It is not bred to the shape of the pan. Plainly this monstrosity before her was not a turkey. Or if it ever had been, something unnatural had been done to it. She would suffer not one bite to pass her lips. She sulked.

As I say, we did not oblige her to eat. Her mother ate, though. And so did I — heartily, with appreciative smackings of the lips and now and then a stifled sob of bliss at being allowed to break the fast. Her sister had gone elsewhere for dinner. But had she been there, you may be sure she would have eaten, too.

In the end, these coarse displays were more telling than any argument. She stole a taste while we pretended not to look. And then another. Except aesthetically, the thing was not so bad. The look of it still was wrong — unpardonably wrong. But the flavor was familiar. She decided she would accept nourishment, after all.

I sensed in this a valuable lesson for dealing with a daughter of distinct preferences and a rigid will. Threats and ultimatums are not the way.

She is, even at 11, a comely child. It will not be much longer before oafish boys with racing bikes and pompadours will be seen loitering in my yard. And soon after that — by the time she's no more than 25 or 30 — I probably will have consented to drive her and one or another of those louts to the movies together in my car.

Some of those ardent callers I will find more objectionable than others. But will I rage and issue commands? Not a bit of it! In a civil but effective way, I will simply make my position clear and without further comment withhold her 50-cent weekly allowance.

Sooner or later, I have no doubt, she and I will come to agree on what is a turkey and what is not.

Time to Get Even

Christmas day requires of a newspaper writer some small seasonal observation, and knowing it is mandatory gives one 52 weeks to get one's cliches in order. Ideally the commentary should be intimate, heartwarming and brief. It need not be inspired, but it must be inoffensive.

On every count except brevity, this little piece is doomed before it begins. Because what I am moved to speak about is the contemptibility of reindeer.

For at least a fortnight, now, the record player in the

children's room has piped the songs of Christmas. Como crooning. The Chipmunks cheeping. Hundred-voice choirs resonating along halls and through the door into the room where I have tried manfully to work. One of these songs is about a reindeer with a red nose. You know that song, of course. It is thought to be very charming and sweet.

Yesterday, on perhaps the thousandth playing of it, I happened for the first time to listen to the words. And the fact is that it is not sweet at all. It really is quite a terrible song that tells a disgusting story about creatures with wretched values.

The tale, as I get it, goes like this. Correct me if I am wrong.

There once was this runt of a reindeer whose bulbous nose had unexplained properties of luminescence. The other reindeer — *all of them;* the lyric is very specific on that point — seized upon his differentness for their own vicious amusement. They jeered and laughed at him and made him the butt of their tasteless japes. He was called names and excluded from the play of his fellows. He was made a pariah — all this because of the small matter of his nose.

Then his luck turned.

As happens with hundred-pound jockeys and seven-foot basketball players, his oddity was found to have exploitable value. The night was foggy. The journey would be long. The company's deliveries were in jeopardy. So it was that after years of being shunned and ridiculed, this runt reindeer came to the attention of the boss and became instantly the darling of the herd.

Until then, you might note, during his prior torment, the boss had shown no interest or sympathy at all. But now he was the favorite. A celebrity. The change in his social standing was dramatic.

"Then how the reindeer loved him . . . " the song relates.

Loved him, indeed! Rest assured that, inside, they were seething with envy. Backslappers and lickspittles were all they were. And it wasn't him they loved. Just the smell of success.

Now that's what I make of the song. Call it a charming story, if you like. I find it a cynical little tale — of behavior as repellent in reindeer as when observed in other species. The persecuted have long memories, though. And the runt reindeer still has accounts to settle.

There will be other foggy Christmas eves. It pleases me to think of the boss elf laying his finger alongside his nose and bounding from his sleigh with a hearty *Ho! Ho!* — only to find himself perched atop a minaret in Iraq or on a two-foot ledge outside a locked window on the 109th floor of the World Trade Center in New York.

But that will be a different tune, won't it?

Christmas Company

Ours is an old house that has known many previous Christmases. It has been warmed and mellowed by them, and their memories have permeated its walls — memories we do not have access to, but which are still no doubt very much alive for some of those who made them.

There are times — and especially in this season — when I am struck suddenly by the odd sensation that I am living in a crowd. The crowd includes the man who built the house and occupied it first, and the ones who followed, as young people with their family starting, and the daughter of that family through all her years from infancy until, in grown womanhood, she delivered the place into our stewardship.

They are there, all of them, in all the ages of their lives.

The first man — the builder — left the house itself and an

early photograph of it, but nothing more. The next, a dentist, left what may have been the first set of tools of his profession: boxes of silver-handled probes and pincers and tiny saws. His daughter after him left a doll from her childhood — a soft and nearly shapeless thing made from a white stocking stuffed and sewn shut. Discovered in a basement storage room, it immediately took its place in our own daughters' pantheon of strange and speechless friends.

In all our years in the house I have not found it in me yet to discard any of these relics — these and many more — of previous tenancy.

The day we moved in, I came upon a trove of old phonograph records, mostly from the 1950s and before, in a cabinet under a bookcase. They still are there. I take one of them out from time to time and put it on the machine. The worn grooves make a scratchy sound but the music is wonderfully evocative. It calls up perfectly the sense of that time when other people lived here and I lived in a different house and all of us were young — or at any rate younger.

As any architect knows, the way a house is made in large part commands the habits of its dwellers. Thus I suppose our Christmas tree stands in the exact corner where trees have always stood. And that children have always dreamed their dreams of innocent acquisitiveness in the same upstairs room where ours abide. And that the carpet before the fireplace has always been where gifts were opened. And that the breakfast tables to which those families afterward retired invariably stood where ours does now.

People may be as unalike as ducks and guineas, but there is little discretion in our use of space.

Yesterday evening, after all our Christmas energies had crested and been spent and the hours were winding down in a kind of reflective silence, one daughter spoke wistfully of the speed with which the day always seemed to pass. Specifically she meant that first dizzying hour of packages given and gotten, but I took her to be speaking of the rest of the day as well. And possibly, without even knowing it, her regret had to do with the brevity of childhood itself. For she and her sister sense already, though they resist it fiercely, the beginning of the end of their belief in childish things.

"You wish it could just last forever," she said. *"You try to slow down, but it's over so quickly."*

I almost imagined, then, that I could see all those others we share the house with — whose lives its walls also contained and shaped — nodding agreement at her statement of savage truth.

Quickly. So quickly.

The words set the records chattering in the cabinet and the silver-handled instruments chinking in their box, and passed like a chilly draft over a frayed stocking doll asleep on a playroom shelf.

Wind Drift

O ne recent afternoon, on the street outside the office, I saw a man coming from the bank, his shoulders drawn up inside his coat, leaning into a chilly spit of wind. An old man, he looked to be — but then I recognized him. He was a colleague of mine, someone I know from days when I was younger and he was nearly still a boy.

Somehow it startled me to meet him suddenly on that raw day, just come from taking the teller's receipt for another fortnight of his life, and to notice him for the first time well on in middle age. To watch the young grow old around oneself is the surest proof and also one of the saddest penalties of one's own march of years.

And the speed of that march is amazing. I speak of this too much, I know. But, beyond a certain point in life, it becomes one of the two or three personal discoveries most worth remarking.

For example, I write these words while sitting at a table in the country cabin in which I lived a winter a long time ago and which since has been but superficially changed. The wood stove two steps from my elbow still creaks and mutters, warming me as it did then. The table is the same one at which I sat to write so many tens of thousands of other words, most of them clumsy and useless as first utterances often are.

In that winter I was only a little more than half my present age. The table and its chair were among the first pieces of furniture my parents owned together, when they were even younger than I was then.

The porch of the cabin my father and I built together during a balmy week of one autumn. By the time he died, the porch already had begun to be old and to need repair. My mother, too, is gone, although certain of her favored spices still are on the shelf, and rugs she braided still on the floor — the rugs that received my feet on those long-past frozen mornings of my winter sojourn.

Alone here now in this silent hour of the evening, I almost can imagine the years not to have fled at all.

The December wind probes at a window corner as it used to. The voiceless quiet is a bit forbidding, as it was on all those other still nights — a silence no lock can keep out. Besides the creak of the stove there is only one sound. Faintly can be heard the baying of a hound as he courses across the timbered hills. And it is reasonable to assume that he is far descended from some creature who was a contemporary of mine.

How much all the things about me here are as they were in

that distant year! But not myself. The hands that hold the pen and tablet have changed. They have begun to be an old man's hands. Never mind the worse testimony a mirror might give.

The winter that this was my home, I kept above my cooking table a gallon glass jar of yellow cornmeal, and also a paper carton with a hole in the side from which hung an end of twine. The jar still is one-quarter full. Last summer I used from it in preparing fish my daughters had caught. The contents were perfectly fine, in no way stale or spoiled.

My daughters are about to be young women. And they are assembling their own memories of this place. Among those, perhaps, the memory of the use of that jar of meal in the cooking of their fish. Just as I remember my father one time putting into the carton that ball of string and drawing its end through the hole. Deliberately now I do not look inside to see what remains of the twine. I do not care to know.

A moment ago I stepped outside to search the sky and found the clouds had passed. The stars were very brittle, very near. The hound's voice has passed to silence. The stove's exertions have abated. Inside, the cabin cools.

And what has any of this to do with the young colleague mentioned at the start — the one seen marching bent into the wind of a raw day? Well, I could have told him that the wind in his face was hardly worth the notice. In case he has not guessed it yet, a greater gale is blowing at his back.

Colder than he can yet imagine, it is bearing him before it with astonishing haste.

VI

Counting Losses

When he was new in this world, and had no wisdom, a blown leaf in the park was his mortal enemy.

For the first six years he had one apartment window of sun. And waited warm on the sill through the silent afternoons of his mistress's working bachelorhood. The darting birds, too, alarmed him.

The second six years he prowled the larger kingdom of a house — shared it with a heavy-footed man, the man's three dogs, two creeping infants in their time. Survived the barkings-at and the intemperate huggings. Dispensed justice with a paw whose claws he kept sheathed. Mastered them all.

Caught a basement mouse, once. Brought it up in the morning to display. Then, not knowing how to kill it — or maybe why to kill it — let it get away. His one trophy.

Grew old, more patient. Let dogs and children touch noses with him. Slept a lot.

Watched the new cat come, a shaggy fugitive from the homeless cold of winter — and must have read in that the first sign of things ending, others beginning. But made his peace yet again. Slipped away one whole night with that new cat, that outdoor cat. Saw things he'd never dreamed of, and came back smelling of the jungle, eyes narrowed to slits of ancient triumph.

Moved slower now. Slept more. Remembered it all — the leaf, the darting birds, his mouse, that stolen night. Was full of years.

Lay down at last on a friendly rug.

Did not wake up.

Still prowls sometimes, at the eye's corner in a certain fall of sunlight in an empty room.

The Year of the Rat

The Junk Food Rat and I have passed into this new year with mutually unattractive prospects. The rat's name is Munch or Crunch, or something onomatopoetic like that. He is the subject of an experiment in my daughter's classroom, designed to prove that it is impossible to thrive on cookies, potato chips and chocolate bars. Munch is offered such stuff exclusively, and his weight and general condition are daily compared to those of a fellow rat who is receiving a conventionally wholesome diet.

My problem is the exact reverse of Munch's.

I am soon to be the subject of yet another of my wife's experiments designed to prove that a moderately dissipated middle-aged man who rarely exercises can be transformed, through some bizarre dietary regimen, into the clone of a young Burt Lancaster or Mikhail Baryshnikov. What it is about the turn of a calendar's page that triggers this reforming zeal I can't say, but it makes of January a disciplined and fiercely cheerless month, a sad beginning for a year.

The ordeal my wife has prescribed for me — for my figure, or whatever — was devised by that New York doctor who afterward was shot to death in a lovers' quarrel at nearly 70. It involves eating tonnages of celery and grapefruit and is guaranteed, if followed to the letter, to cause the waist to become wasplike, the backside knotty and lean and the stomach flat as an oaken board. A friend of ours recently endured this diet. It is reported that she shed pounds at an amazing rate and is now a gaunt shadow of her former self. Splendid as she is said to look, I have deliberately avoided her. After two weeks of celery, she must have the disposition of a she-wolf with pups the year the caribou forgot to migrate. Come anywhere close to her with a shaving cut or the least trace of a limp and your number would be up.

Food, as you may have guessed, is of some importance to me. It has figured large in the chronology of my life.

I cannot, for example, smell fish frying without being transported instantly to a high mountain glade among the pines and aspens many winters ago. One of our small party had stayed in camp to fish for trout in the ice-rimmed beaver ponds near the tents. When we others came back, the fire was snapping and fish were browning in the skillet. We built a reflector oven and baked biscuits to eat with the trout and squares of deer's liver spitted and broiled on sticks.

The mountains lay silver-blue at our feet and the morning sparkled. The snow slid off the low boughs of the pines as the day warmed. Birds chittered and begged at the rim of our camp. We were immensely contented and 30 years old, give or take a little, and the boiled coffee was as strong as battery acid. All of that the smell of frying fish brings back as plain as yesterday.

Other foods evoke other ages, other scenes, with potent effect.

A bowl of tomato soup with a pat of butter pooling yellow at the center and a dish of a certain brand of crackers at the side puts me immediately at the table of the house in which I was a boy. The school is a short block away, across my yard and a neighbor's. At age 9 or so I have come breathless over a fence and across those yards for lunch, lucky to live so near. I am speaking some complaint of the morning to my mother, but the pains of nine are small and transient, and we are pleased to sit together, she and I.

Recently I took advantage of an out-of-season evening to grill meat outdoors for what I imagine will be one of my last respectable meals. And as it always does, that smell — of the cooking meat brushed with a particular sauce — evoked the cramp and the creative clutter of the apartment of a writing friend and his wife, an artist.

In memory, their marriage is new, and they are still young, and I am the bachelor fed often out of compassion. There is in their house a yeasty, noisy confusion of things beginning. Of lives beginning, and careers. We are all older now. Their marriage long ago ended, and they have gone different ways — to different families, different work. What seemed so safe and certain then has been exchanged for other certainties. And, still, the smell of sauce glazing on meat over an open fire reassembles the pattern of that distant year. It is only illusion, but entirely persuasive.

So you see that food and history are, for me, inseparably intertwined.

Now I am asked to exchange all these memories of where and what I've been for the hope of the slender, marginally less repulsive middle-aged man I might yet, with luck, become. And am asked this by a wife who evidently has forgotten that our courtship was conducted over a succession of restaurant tables.

Probably I will obey. But I do not have to like it.

May Munch, the Junk Food Rat, prosper. May he grow sleek and glossy while his more regimented colleague unaccountably becomes sickly and slow-witted and dull of eye. And may it be recorded, at autopsy, that what finally brought me down was not my years of sloth and indiscipline after all. But rather, at the very end, an excess of celery and grapefruit.

Expendable Again

We love most intensely that creature or that thing which we fear may soon be lost to us. The thing itself has not changed at all, but the imminence of its loss has made it priceless. Consider the example of snail darters and pupfish and the whooping crane.

Probably not one person in a thousand — or in 100,000 — had heard of the snail darter until a few years ago. Whole generations had gone to their graves without ever speaking its name, and so might ours have. Except that the damming of a certain river was proposed. The snail darter was found to live in that river and, worse yet, was determined to be rare. And as with all the other creatures we have driven to survival's edge, that small fish became immediately the object of fierce and quite widespread devotion.

Now the snail darter has entered into the popular vocabulary and become a part of our national consciousness. As the minnow goes, so goes public morality. If the snail darter perishes, ring down the long twilight of ruin.

In the same way, I have known people to drive several hundred miles round-trip on the chance — an outside chance at that — of seeing a whooping crane in the wild. And an authenticated report of a particular variety of pupfish observed gasping in some fetid desert puddle has been known to cause ecstasy of the sort usually inspired by the rose window in the Cathedral of Chartres.

Beauty is not the point. Probably the same passion would develop for cockroaches and dung beetles if there were known to be only seven of them left on earth. But love is fickle. Let it be discovered that the snail darter is not endangered after all, that in fact there are whole river systems in which he teems in inestimable numbers, and our ardor for him will quickly cool. Let the whooping crane multiply beyond a certain point and you will hear him mentioned, if at all, only in terms of the fitness of his meat for the table.

All this is prologue.

A cat of ours became ill not long ago. The ailment wasn't serious but we did not know that at the time. The symptoms were ominous. Now this particular cat had a bad habit or two. Never mind just what those were — suffice that they were bad. But with the onset of the illness, it was amazing how these faults of his were brushed aside by our sudden new appreciation of his general excellence.

He became, for several days, the central figure in our household. He was endlessly held and comforted and stroked. His name was being spoken constantly and his virtues recited. He could do no wrong. There even was talk of letting him outdoors. Because of the hazard of dogs and street, he had been until then mostly an inside cat. But he crouched at the crack of the door with an awful longing, and now guilt assailed us. What was the use of confining him? What were were protecting him from — except life itself? And if his days were short, what use, what mercy, was caution now?

In due course he was examined. The results were inconclusive, and our concern mounted. He was taken to another city for tests of a more elaborate and more expensive sort. By this time cost did not matter, so great was his surpassing fineness as a cat.

Then the news was received, along with the bill.

The news was that he was not sick at all. Never had been. The symptom that so alarmed us had been just one of those things that happens from time to time with cats — a minor indisposition that has, and needs, no explanation.

You would not believe the change of attitudes. He must

wonder again why his name is so rarely spoken, except when linked with a curse at his old habits. If he mews at the crack of the door, a shoe toe moves him brusquely and pitilessly aside. He is just a cat again. A cat that cost a lot. His symptoms have disappeared entirely. Gone, too, is any memory of the lesson we might have learned. We have become indifferent and unforgiving again.

That's how it goes with snail darters and cats and all the other things and creatures in our lives — even the people in them — when we imagine they will last forever.

On the River

Daily I am filled with admiration for the fortitude with which most people manage to reel onward under the baggage of their apprehensions and their private griefs.

To meet and speak casually with them, one might imagine that all the pieces of their lives were in perfect place. There is in this something different, something finer, than mere pretense. It is an expression of the fundamental optimism which, against all logic, enables human beings to transcend — or at least to look beyond — the evil of the moment.

Of all the characteristics of our kind, many of them distinctly unattractive, this capacity for faith, for unreasoning hope, must surely be counted among the most appealing.

Yesterday I happened to speak with a man whose professional life was in the process of coming apart. Hard economic times had overtaken the company in which he held a responsible place. This had resulted in the laying off of several workers in his department — men and women he knew not only as employees but also as colleagues and friends. What is more, rumors of the company's sale were in the wind. So this man's own future and his position, which represented the investment of a career, were clouded by doubt.

But was he white-eyed and trembling with anxiety? Not at all. What thoughts may overtake him in the stillness of his nights, I can't say. But in talking about these matters, he was quite composed. The uncertainty, he confessed, was distressing. Mainly he was eager to see the future defined, so that whatever it held could be met and dealt with. In one fashion or other, he intended to survive.

The list of potential misfortunes is practically endless, and most of those are more punishing than his.

People who are important in our lives are lost to death or distance. We ourselves begin to exhibit the abuse and corrosion of years. Marriages go cold. Children go wrong. Ambition's goals recede before our grasp. But are these the things we talk about when we are together? Listen, and what you will hear oftener than anything is the expectant talk of more tomorrows. Pleasure in the moment we freely share. Disappointments are a private matter.

Whenever I am reminded of this habit of human nature, I think of a man I met once, years ago, who had set himself the challenge of descending the whole length of the Missouri River, from its headwaters to its joining with the Mississippi and thence to the Gulf of Mexico, alone in a small boat. The man was a foreigner, and the passion to attempt that mythic journey had been born in him while reading of the history of this continent as a boy in his distant native land.

At the time I met him, he had been more than two years on the river. The task he had undertaken was only half complete, but his vision of the majesty of it was, if anything, clearer than when he had begun. Along the way his boat had been several times wrecked, his provisions lost. Each time he had taken work only long enough to re-equip himself for the river.

In one of those accidents he had lost a foot. But that was a fact he had not bothered to mention — I learned of it from someone else — and he seemed surprised when I questioned him about it. Yes, that had happened. It had been a delay and an inconvenience. But he had been supplied with a new and perfectly serviceable foot, a manufactured one. It worked quite well, he said — and danced a little jig there on the river bank to prove the point.

Anyway, did anyone imagine that so magnificent a journey as that one could be undertaken without some price? With that, he got back in his boat and turned its prow downriver toward the next disaster.

There is something of that man's spirit in nearly everyone I know. The stream that carries us along is capricious and sometimes cruel. Wrecks are guaranteed. Yet crazy dreams give the passage purpose. And blind hope gives it grace.

A Sly Affair

Our relationship — well, why not finally just be forthright about it? In a word, our relationship is clandestine.

To friends and others who may be shocked or saddened by this revelation I can only say that I am sorry and ask their understanding. I did not mean for things between us to turn out this way. But it has gone too far and I am in too deeply now. I would not turn back, even if I could.

Sometimes it is she who telephones, and sometimes I. (Who

takes the initiative is not important. In an affair such as ours, where moments together must be stolen as they can, there is no time for little protocols.) Mostly we meet for lunch. We prefer some quiet place with cloth napkins where wine is served and where, at an out-of-the-way table or in a corner booth, there is less chance of being seen by anyone we know.

There, in what privacy is available to us, we open to one another our feelings and our most secret thoughts. For that hour or two we shut out the world.

Somehow I exist between these meetings, but it is painful. And then, when we do contrive to be together, the time goes past with such cruel speed that, afterward, I am left always with a rueful aftertaste of emptiness, almost resentment. I look around us at the other people, other men and women, so at ease, taking companionship so much for granted. And I am filled with envy for what I imagine their lives to be.

This is no way for anyone to have to live, we sometimes tell ourselves. *Can it be that these furtive hours are all we'll ever share together?* But even as we ask, we know the answer. We are not children, after all. That is the nature of an affair, and we should have known it from the start.

I have considered taking an apartment — some modest little midtown place where we could be alone together for longer than a meal. It would not need to be elaborate, so long as it was not actually depressing. Some simple furnishings. No telephone. A view, if possible. I've thought of it, but have hesitated to make the proposal. Because she is, in spite of any conclusions you have drawn, a proper sort of girl. The suggestion might even offend her.

So there you have it, and I hope you will excuse my burdening you with so personal a matter. There is nothing more to tell. We are trapped, both of us, and as far as I can see there is no help for it.

We both have our responsibilities.

And sometimes in the course of one of our trysts, the recollection of those responsibilities will intrude. *"Good heavens,"* she will cry out. *"I almost forgot it's my afternoon for the car pool. And there's a Brownie meeting after that. Then there's a man coming to fix the basement drain."*

And I will remember that the dry cleaning is ready and the bank is overdrawn, that the dog needs vaccinating and the neighborhood association has been writing nasty letters about my refusal to rake my leaves.

So we will leap up, then, the wine undrunk in our glasses, and flee out of there still crying out to one another our grim itineraries. Our meetings are wonderful and tender. But our partings, as you can see, are not the stuff of literature.

The house she goes home to and the one I go home to — where sometimes we pass briefly and almost wordlessly between errands — is the same house. In case I neglected to mention it, we are married, that girl and I. But home, as Robert Frost said, is only the place where, when you go there, they have to take you in. And marriage is a logistical exercise, like getting the troops ashore in Normandy or the coals to Newcastle.

Romance is different. Romance is something you look for over lunch.

Expert Counsel

In the space of a single week we received the news of four marriages among our friends either ended or in the process of ending.

There was, in every case, the usual quotient of misunderstanding and bafflement and hurt. But in none of them did there seem to be any dominant or compelling passion at the root — no rage over some grave wounding, no ungovernable lust for a lover, no argument over the dog.

No word of blame was spoken. Matters were proceeding with the utmost civility. Nor was there any talk of failure. In fact the parties all were going about the business of dissolution with such composure and evident good will as to give the impression their marriages had not amounted to much in the first place.

That is the pose which one is expected to strike, now that these private catastrophes have become a commonplace of our times. It is no longer thought remarkable if, out of a vague restlessness or boredom or simple curiosity, we decide to dismantle and rearrange our lives. There is even an attempt — mainly by those who have themselves experienced it — to invest separation with a kind of virtue all its own.

Far from being a cause for sympathy, they say, it actually is a splendid new milestone of personal growth. If that notion consoles them, I'll not debate the point. There are books about how to positively enjoy a good divorce. One almost gets the idea that one should try it on general principle, even if the notion had not occurred before.

That is the fashionable rhetoric. Behind it, of course, the fact remains that these shipwrecks generally are productive of a great deal of pain, and not only for those directly involved. Bystanders cannot help being affected, too.

So many pieces of such news, arriving as they did in so short a time, evoked not only surprise and sorrow but also a little shudder of alarm. One finds oneself glancing uneasily over the shoulder, wondering if one's own life is shadowed by some great sadness not yet known or even suspected. Because, you see, those friends' relationships were not as inconsequential as they now pretend. All of them were decent and caring people. They had been together most of their adult lives, from a dozen years to more than 20 — had striven and sacrificed and raised families together, or at least begun them.

And when they seem to say that none of that counts for anything, I simply do not believe them. It is what they think they are expected to say, what others will find more comfortable to hear.

Increasingly I am persuaded that a great deal of the ferment and disorder in our personal lives comes from listening too much to people who pass themselves off as experts but who are in truth little more than theoretical quacks. I have in hand a tract by a professor of child and family studies at a noted university, in which he unequivocally forecasts the growing popularity of cohabitation and a concurrent — possibly consequent — further decline in the institution of marriage. More women, he says, will come to see their husbands as "a barrier to their personal growth and development." And more men will want out of marriage in order to have a fling, or because they will become "sensitized to the heavy burden of what it means to be a man — economically, psychologically, physically and sexually."

I am amazed and proud to think that I am somehow more burdened by my manhood than were those men who survived danger and nameless disease, who drove and dragged themselves and their oxen and wagons across great rivers and hostile prairies and untracked forest, who huddled under sod shelters in the white howl of winter, who did all this to push back the frontiers of a continent — and who still considered family to be the center, the purpose of a life.

It is remarkable, isn't it? But that is what the learned professor says. People actually are paid to write and lecture such pap.

Women are told endlessly that their lives are empty, that their men have diminished and enslaved them, that the bearing and nurture of children is a meaningless vocation. And men are told that their mannish and assertive wives are emasculating them and sending them to early graves, worn out by anxiety and joyless labor. If the polemicists on both sides are right, then obviously there is very little incentive for men and women to live together. That might be how they would prefer it turned out.

We are all of us, in some degree, the creatures of other people's expectations. So the great danger, it seems to me, is in listening to these quacks and allowing their tormented view of the world to gain too much popular currency.

I recall a gathering I attended several years back. It was a sort of *salon* given by mutual friends for a visiting luminary from the West Coast. He, too, was associated with a famous university. And he had made a considerable reputation teaching and counseling in his specialty, which was marriage and the family. Had published books I believe. His wife, a charming and intelligent woman, was with him.

I was struck most, as he spoke, by his absolute certainty of everything he said. His tone and manner left no room for argument or doubt. Sometime during the evening I learned the reason for his confidence. It was because he had not neglected his research. That wife was his fifth one, or maybe his seventh. Anyway, some impressive number.

I never saw the man again, so can't say how his continuing research goes. But I do know that, not too long after his visit, his hosts, our friends, divorced.

The Arts of Exploitation

The letter came in last week's mail, but still lies unopened on the desk. Its envelope bore foreign stamps and the hand in which it was addressed seemed familiar. Inspection of the postmark confirmed my suspicion. The face of the writer rose immediately to mind.

He used to be a friend, years ago, before we understood the dimensions of his faithlessness.

In one of those early years he and I took a canoe down a fast little river and camped the night on a gravel bar and caught many fish. That much is a fine memory. Later, on a business trip, I visited him in New York where he was posted in his government's service. He lived with his wife, three children and a monkey in an old house in a village on Long Island, commuting to the city by train. His wife was a pale, Nordic woman, cold in her manner and full of what seemed to be a kind of brittle, unspoken fury, which mystified me at the time, but whose reasons I now quite understand.

Soon his assignment in this country ended and he returned to his own land. For the next decade, then, the mails and the international telephone lines brought us occasional bulletins about his life.

He wrote that they had bought a house. And from the desk where he sat at that moment, on a summer evening, he could look across a great distance to some escarpment blue in the failing light. While, nearer, bats turned and darted after insects against the amber sky. He was happy, he wrote, and for the first time in his memory fully at peace. He had left government service over a matter of principle. He and his wife were again very much in love.

The next word, several months later, was that she had left

him. And that, being unable to live alone, he had quickly married again — a much younger woman, a country child, wholly devoted to him and forgiving of his age.

Then, the next year, the news that this successor bride had gone tragically and hopelessly insane and, for the good of everyone concerned, had had to be divorced. How much of that was truth I cannot now say, but agony cried out convincingly from his every pen stroke.

More time passed — a year or two. The telephone rang. His voice came indistinctly from half a world away. That matter of principle which had caused him to leave the government had now become a source of danger. Friends had been arrested, and one of them had died mysteriously in the custody of the police. Warnings had been passed to him from contacts in high places. The ring was closing. It might soon be necessary to flee — to take up permanent exile.

Would I do him the huge favor of telephoning a certain woman at a number in New York? Tell her of his peril. Assure her of his devotion and of his need for her faith in him in these hazardous times. I telephoned the number he gave me. The woman's husband answered. Mercifully, however, they were estranged and she was in California. Finally I located her there and delivered the message, which moved her greatly. She wept on the phone.

He arrived, then. At our house. I remember that it was the Christmas season. He had not come directly but had stopped over some days or weeks at the loft in Greenwich Village of still another woman, an artist, who by his account kept owls and was dying of some incurable disease, and whose devotion to him had become oppressive and degrading. Anyhow, he was here, installed in one of our bedrooms, playing uncle to our children. But clung over by the sadness of the political emigre, the man without a country — a plight all the more poignant because of the gaiety of the holiday at hand.

Foolishly we believed it all, or nearly all. Even now, at some level, I am not sure how much to disbelieve. We took him with us to the homes of friends. At dinner, over wine, he would hold forth. He had an insatiable need for self-dramatization, and a remarkable gift for it. For he was as charming as he was brilliant, and a vivid story-teller as well.

As he spoke, the others at the table would acquire a sense of personal involvement in his predicament. They would feel the danger which pursued him. They would share his loss. They would become filled with inexpressible pity and admiration.

His effect on women — mostly, but not always, unmarried women — was astonishing. He was on the smallish side and not conventionally handsome. And yet, at parties, they would gather around while he spoke and before the evening ended one or more of them would be seen handing him their addresses on folded bits of paper.

The rest I will compress.

A man in exile must have employment, or else go back to face the political inquisitors. The newspaper for which I work was prepared to take him on in some capacity — to invent a place, if necessary — to spare him that. Instead, an acquaintance of mine took him into the family business. This happened because of a meeting between them for which I was wholly responsible, and about which I feel such regret and humiliation that even now, years later, it is painful to pass that man on the street.

He was given credit cards and money and airline tickets and dispatched around the country and the world on the company's behalf. It was a splendid opportunity, suitable to his talents, which were considerable.

Between trips he sometimes lodged with us. He was incessantly telephoning somewhere or being called. Calls to and from the dying artist with the owls and the separated woman in

California, who once traveled briefly to stay with him — and us — and then went away again. This lasted several weeks or months, I cannot remember exactly. Then, abruptly, it ended.

There was a cryptic telephone call from New York. He was leaving, he said, and would explain by letter. The letter, much later, was no more revealing. He had gone back to his homeland, after all — not to the dungeon of his tormentors but to take some position in the military intelligence apparatus of the very regime which he had professed to loathe and fear.

We paid his considerable phone bill and dealt a last time or two with the furious owl lady. We could not — or at any rate did not — deal with the vastly more sizable debts incurred through abuse of his company's trust and the misuse of its credit cards.

A year passed, possibly two. Then there came an urgent cablegram from that distant capital. *"There's been a terrible tragedy,"* it said, or words to that effect. *"Cannot bear to say more. Send telegram soonest."*

I wrote my reply on a single sheet and posted it by boat mail, the slowest way. *"Much sympathy,"* I wrote. *"Need details."*

Another year, then. And now this letter. It is fat and heavy. It gives the impression of bearing momentous news. But news of what? Surely some turn of fate or further personal crisis which I cannot even imagine, but into whose web it is planned that I and many others will be drawn.

Betrayal teaches its lessons too late, but it teaches them well. The contents of that envelope, however plaintive or eloquent, would have no more meaning for me now than a page from some stranger's dossier.

Maybe I will sometime open it. And maybe I will not.

And a Plainer Art

The notion of personal principle as the controlling factor in human relationships is so archaic as to have lost practically all meaning and, indeed, almost to invite ridicule. Loyalty, honor, forthrightness, the sense of fair play — qualities which used to combine to guide behavior in the way of fundamental decency — still are remembered by their names. But in practice they are increasingly rare.

Their place has largely been taken, in business and in private lives, by very different considerations of style and technique and ambition and sharp dealing which, put to the service of formulas that may be found in the instructional manuals on nearly every subject, are supposed to ensure our success and happiness.

If you think this assessment unduly bleak, count up on the fingers of one hand the number of wholly honorable, wholly principled people with whom you lately have had some dealings. Leave out your own family members and your friends of years. What was your reaction on those occasions when you realized you had been met with absolute fairness and consideration? If what you felt was gratitude and even some small surprise, then my point is made.

In business, success is defined by one's place on the ladder of power. And in the course of their advancement, many managers view their subordinates — in the same way they view their style of dress and the mannerisms they cultivate — as mere tools in the service of their ambition. When, afterward, this disloyalty is reciprocated, they respond with anger and incomprehension.

Corporations are not moral entities, and it is fatuous to think that they should be. They routinely deceive and cheat one another and the public, making restitution only when ordered to, and then without remorse. Products shown to contain defects which injure or kill the buyer continue to be manufactured and sold until, after an eternity of legal resistance, some court finally commands a halt. Although corporations, as such, are without soul, corporate decisions in these matters are made by men — men who are hurt and amazed to find themselves cheated by their own employees.

Institutional immorality spills over into private affairs. Transactions between individuals no longer can be conducted upon any general assumptions of trust.

Even in our most personal relationships, the rules seem to have lost force. Faithlessness, if not yet quite approved, has become a commonplace, the subject more often of humor than of dismay or outrage. The promises that people make to one another seldom are absolute, but rather they are qualified — qualified above all by the concern for something called *self-realization,* which is not to be confused with *self-indulgence,* though in appearance and in effect the two may be indistinguishable.

This seems to me to be the current state of affairs. But of course there are exceptions to be found, and the exceptions can be glorious.

Ten years or so ago I found myself thrown by pure chance into a business relationship with a man in another city. Or, more precisely, on a farm outside that city. We were strangers to one another, but, over time, we have defined the relationship and learned as much about each other's instincts and characters as it is necessary to know.

And it has become plain that his dealings are governed absolutely by an old-fashioned brand of honor.

If ever he confronts the choice between looking to my interests or his own, his will be slighted. He attempts by his skill and resourcefulness to avoid such conflicts, and mostly he is able to. But if the decision presents itself, it is, for him, not even a decision to make. And this is not peculiar to his transactions with me. Those are simply the terms upon which he has chosen to proceed through the world.

As you may well imagine, what began as a business acquaintance has become a friendship. His wife is a wonderful woman — generous, proud, much talented in her own right, believing in the same set of values. During these years I have watched their children grow into straight, clear-eyed young adults. And, as surely as I know anything, I know the decency that will direct them through their lives.

There are people who live by different rules, or by no rules at all. We meet those people daily, in nearly everything we do, and many of them give the appearance of having made great successes. My friend has met them, too. And he has decided — decided long back — that he wants no part of anything that success of that sort will buy.

He is a man traveling from the beginning of his days to the end with his face browned by the weather, a pipe in his shirt pocket and the difference between right and wrong, fairness and unfairness, decency and sly dealing clear before him. His eyes look squarely at you when he speaks. *I am exactly what I seem to be,* his manner declares. *There's nothing to hide. There are things I can do. And there are others I can't, or won't, do. I know my worth, and I know what is important in a life. I am my own advertisement. What you see is what you get.*

Several times a year I am privileged to sit at their table, drinking lemonade or iced tea and talking first about business, then about family and other affairs in common. And when the hour comes, finally, when I must draw on the armor of caution and go back to the world at large, I leave there refreshed — by something more and better than was in my glass.

The Monopolist

My daughters have become the owners of a Monopoly set, and playing the game has laid all our characters bare. The set has come west with us to the mountains — to the Front Range of the Rockies. At night, after we have returned from vigorous excursions in the snow and wolfed a hasty supper, we draw up chairs around the board.

The cabin curtains are closed. A log fire smokes and hisses on the hearth. As the dice roll and we bend to our work, the healthy ruddiness of the day drains from our faces, which become pinched and squinty with greed.

I cannot say that what we find in the game is pleasure, exactly. There are terrible rages. There are sullen disappointments. Occasionally there are tears of hurt and bitter humiliation. Still, the playing of it has come to engross us all. You might almost say to monopolize us.

The contest never really ends; it is only adjourned from one evening to the next. Betweentimes the board, the paper money, the plastic houses and hotels and the neat arrangements of our title deeds remain in place on the table. This obliges us to take our meals standing up, or from plates held in our laps, which we gladly do. What is important is the game.

I am, besides being a player, also the Banker — a role which entitles me to handle bills of important denomination. I disburse the payments for passing *Go*. I am the custodian of unbought properties and the issuer of mortgages. I interpret the rules and preside over the woes of the bankrupt.

It happens that I also have the middle-aged disease of early rising. Often, awake alone in the still morning, I examine the last night's board and the relative fragility of my situation. The bank's assets are on the chair next to my own. What if my problems are grave? Is not their solution readily at hand? A property or two retrieved from mortgage . . . a sheaf of currency moved from one stack onto another — *to be repaid later in full, of course.*

I do not act on these thoughts, but they pass through my mind. And I cannot help wondering, then, if real-life bankers, astir in some quiet hour ahead of their clerks and colleagues, are not from time to time assailed by these same dangerous notions. They must be. You occasionally read about them in the newspaper.

My wife plays cautiously, is prudent in her acquisitions and favors a robust cash position. During the game's early stages the stacks of bills mount impressively before her. Her voice is crisp and polite as she collects her tidy rents. Then, later, after Boardwalk or some other high-priced parcel has been developed with hotels, she lands on one of those, her hoard of cash disappears in a stroke, her holdings are disbursed among her creditors and she stumbles demoralized away from the table to write post cards or numbly turn the pages of an old magazine.

One daughter's pattern of play is much like her mother's, although she is noticeably luckier. Bankruptcy is longer coming.

The other is a hopeless plunger. She buys real estate with reckless joy. On the very brink of insolvency, she mortgages what she owns to buy more. Her cash reserve shrinks and is nearly exhausted. *"Buy!"* she can be heard to cry, as her empire sags toward apparent ruin. *"Build!"* she commands relentlessly, mortgaging her last railroad to put one more house on Ventnor Avenue.

We try to give her the benefit of our mature counsel, but she persists in this madness. And, in the end, she always wins. Worse, she wins graciously — manages to do so in spite of her handicaps of generosity and tenderness of heart.

Two nights ago, before the evening's last throw of the dice, she risked all to save her sister from collapse, buying some worthless tract for an inflated sum. When we left the table she was mired in debt, without liquidity, her borrowing power used up. She had done it, she explained, for no other purpose than to be kind.

To be kind?

Doggedly I followed her to her room. Kindness, I explained carefully, was not the point of the game. The point was to crush and impoverish one's adversaries and to acquire their holdings for one's own. Further, Monopoly was more than just a game. It had lessons to teach about the world — lessons she'd be well advised to learn. In commerce, there was little place for kindness.

All the same, she said, she would sleep better for having done it.

Never mind, I thought, as I left her and went back to survey the suspended game. Her sin of decency had been a fatal one. Her plight clearly was beyond remedy and the lesson would be learned soon enough.

By rights, the game should have been mine. My luck is better than my wife's and my nature is right for it. I am sensible, yet not opposed to risk if the occasion warrants. I have the killer instinct. But within minutes after beginning the next session of play, the tide turned.

My reckless daughter received a windfall. Her properties were redeemed from mortgage and more houses were erected on them. Followed by hotels. Each roll of the dice brought new tribute pouring into her accounts. Presently all the real estate was hers, and all the money. She had won again, in spite of kindness. And, with some gentle word of sympathy for the fallen, she went off to dream her dreams of untroubled conscience.

Something has gone wrong — grotesquely wrong.

In the book of rules there is no mention of decency and compassion. That is not how Monopoly is supposed to be played. That is not how the game is played in life. As far as I can tell, the lessons she is learning about the world are all the wrong ones.

High-Country Dawn

We find ourselves, in these years, in almost frantic need of periodic change, preferably frequent change. Not because our lives are arid and unsatisfactory, but because the daily marches of them are so familiar that we have become insensitive to their stimuli, blind to their meaning.

Possibly the fault is ours. Or perhaps it lies in the relentless — the inescapable — busyness which is a hallmark of these neurotic and complicated times. Whatever the reason, we feel an irresistible longing to escape, to withdraw together to some simple and silent place where reflection is possible and where we can come to know and value one another afresh.

I believe this desire must be, if not universally felt, at least a very common one. The means of satisfying it need not be elaborate. The essential requirement is a change of place. A day's walk in the country can suffice. A weekend in totally strange surroundings is even finer. A short vacation is the best of all. But as energy resources continue to shrink, travel will become progressively more difficult and more expensive — maybe even prohibitively so.

I can imagine the rise of a considerable new service industry, brokering the temporary exchange of houses between families in the same community who would find it entertaining and refreshing to step briefly out of the trappings of their own lives and into someone else's.

The setting is not important, except that it must impart a feeling of remove. What is essential is the sense of refuge. And for our family, while the gasoline lasts, these mountains one day's hard drive west from home have become that refuge. As I write this, it is the hour just before dawn of a gray morning. The air still is smoky blue and the temperature has dropped further in the night. Among the high peaks a storm is raging, and the crags are veiled by it.

A bitter wind comes raking down the mountains' flanks and whines at the corners of the cabin. New snow has fallen — still is coming, blown horizontal on the gale. As I watch, snow devils as tall as a house, taller, swirl up on the wind and go striding off between the pines outside the window.

Except for the wind and the hiss of the coffee pot coming to boil, all about is stillness. And the stillness is penetrating; it is inside me, as well.

For a little time — just now — writing seems not a task but once again the easy act of conversation it was meant to be. Presently I will lay and light a fire. The snap and mutter of the logs will take the cold edge from the wind's voice keening at the door. And the cabin will come awake — the children and their mother creeping from their beds, the day beginning.

I cannot say how we will pass the hours from now to night. Two small gray-breasted birds, juncos possibly, have come to fluff and huddle on the bannister of the porch. That is the first event to be remarked. We will watch the blowing snow. Probably we will eat — but only in response to our stomachs' wants, not on the signal of some school bell or factory whistle. Most of all we will talk. Of things that interest and are of importance to us all. Not, if we can help it, of any of those matters about which we ought to speak. We will observe one another in repose, and remember that we are not frantic, driven creatures, after all.

And in this slow speaking (or the absence of it), in these slow hours, the stillness inside all of us will expand and deepen. We will listen to the sound of it — the healing sound of hearts at rest. And even after the long road has carried us back to our lives, it may be hoped that some of that stillness will remain to blunt our desperation and prevent us, for a while again, from becoming strangers in our haste.

The Walking Wounded

Two middle-aged men were talking across breakfast.
Both of them were very full of pain. I didn't mean to
eavesdrop, but our tables in the crowded coffee shop were
only inches apart and I could not help overhearing. It was
soon clear that they were divorced men, fathers of children
with whom they had lost or were losing touch. Men who
lived alone.

One of them — the larger one, athletic-looking but a little
gone to overweight — was just back from Texas where he had
been in a hospital for tests. Something wrong with his blood, he
said, but the doctors couldn't find anything so he had said to hell
with it and come back home.

"How do you feel?" his friend asked. The second man was
slighter, grayer. "Feel OK now?"

"Great," the big man said. "Never felt better." But there was
preoccupation and a little edge of worry in his voice.

"Are you seeing anybody?"

"Naw, not much," he said. "I don't make friends easy, you
know what I mean? I've got a girlfriend — in Chicago. It's not
love or anything, but we have some good times. She's honest with
me and I'm honest with her and I think it's good for me. To tell
the truth, she's what saves me. But I don't want to get real close to
anybody, if you know what I mean. I don't want to get hurt
anymore."

The confession struck them both silent. It was strange to hear
so large a man speak of hurt.

"So how are *you* doing?"

"I don't know," the smaller one said. "I've got a problem."

"Yeah?"

"I sent my daughter a birthday present and I didn't even hear back from her."

The big man nodded in understanding and sympathy.

"I sent her a $20 gift certificate. And nothing — not a word. In a few months now she'll be ready to graduate, and I just don't know."

"Send her a present," the big man said. But his friend was dispirited and unsure.

"I don't want to seem like I'm trying to buy her love. I'm finished with that."

"Send her a present. I mean it."

"You think so?" Brightening.

"Damned right! Send her something real nice. Fifty bucks or a hundred bucks or whatever you can afford."

"I just don't know . . ."

"Look, she's going to grow up, you know what I mean? She's going to mature, and she'll look at things different. And you'll be glad you did it."

"Maybe."

"Believe me, she's going to grow up. And she'll want to have a relationship with you again. She'll change. She's bound to."

"Maybe," the friend said again, but without much conviction. "What if she doesn't, though? What if I send it and it's just like her birthday — I never hear anything back? I hate to just throw it down a rat hole."

"Well, yeah. That's true."

Silence overcame them again. The smaller man sighed. "I don't know," he said finally. "Maybe I'll send a card."

"Sure," said the other. "Hell, it's mostly the thought, anyway. Or how about this? Open an account for her — you know, a savings account. Put a couple hundred bucks in it and don't tell her. Send her a card, but don't say anything about the money. Then if things change and you've got a relationship again you can say, *'Look here. Here's what I did when you graduated.'* And if it doesn't work out . . ."

The big man, you could tell, had a lot of practice at hedging losses of the heart.

I'm not an expert in these matters. We are all just struggling to hold together the tissue of our own lives, and no one gets to be an expert except when it's too late. But I am by nature a meddlesome man. Don't send money, I longed to turn and say to him. Go yourself, and take something — something unexpected and improbable. A book of poems, tenderly inscribed. Or better still, take something warm and alive. A kitten, if her heart ever leaned to those — if you can remember. Maybe it will be all wrong. Maybe she will despise you for it. And surely it will not brush away the hurt of years. But what possibly can be the harm of having tried? What losses have you left to cut?

That's what I would have blurted out, unbidden. But I held my tongue.

The two of them pushed back their cups and stood together.

"Maybe I'll just send a card," the man said.

"Sure, that's nice. Why not?"

They went out, then, saying to one another, "Take care of yourself" — though neither had the vaguest notion how. And I sat thinking, as the waitress cleared their places, how rarely it is one hears people speak so directly of love over breakfast, and that it must be a habit peculiar to the ones who are without.

Roosevelt

It is a sunlit morning in the bedroom, and the gray kitten, Roosevelt, is playing with an inflated balloon. I expect you know the nature of kittens — feisty, inventive, unquenchably optimistic.

The brilliance of winter light falls in bars through the window, drawing sharp patterns on walls and floor. Past those and through them, large-eyed and untiring, Roosevelt pursues her pink balloon, pausing only to chew a string of glass beads, her other toy, or to investigate her tail.

But it is the balloon she prefers. It is of respectable size for an adversary, but altogether helpless. It tumbles away foolishly when batted. The balloon has a painted face, a laughing one, that is about as large as Roosevelt's own. The laugh remains, even when the kitten snatches up the balloon near its stem and carries it with her teeth — though the eventual result of that is easy enough to guess.

She does not know the thing will sooner or later explode. Such an event is not in the limited range of her experience. Nor can she see, as I do, that inside the first balloon there is another, and inside that one perhaps another still. Not even I can see those faces, to know if they are laughing.

What Roosevelt cannot know, either — has no way of suspecting — is that within the hour she is to be put in a box and taken away to the veterinarian's for surgery. It will be an operation of the female sort, necessary if the cats of a household are not to increase their numbers exponentially. All the same, this experience ahead will be her first acquaintance with the unhappy fact of pain. To this moment she has known nothing except food and fondling and the nearness of children's noses. This afternoon she will discover there is more — and worse. She will be baffled by it. To the extent she is able to think in such terms, she may feel in some way betrayed.

I have been touched by this, watching her play here in the sun on the floor in the perfect trust of what is, in a sense, one of her last hours of kittenhood. Will she come back changed in ways never intended? Changed in heart? There is no helping that, I suppose.

But somehow, observing Roosevelt and her pink balloon, I cannot put out of mind the odd notion that I am seeing a metaphor for all our lives. Gently it begins, or usually so. Life shows a laughing face. Then, like the balloon, it explodes unaccountably at our touch and reveals another face — endlessly, one face inside the other, some smiling and some not.

Perhaps a marriage ends, and in that unexplained catastrophe a child's world is disassembled and rearranged. And so through all our years: careers blossoming and then, in some moment, gone wrong or shunted in a new direction; a friendship ended, but another gloriously made. Great losses and great gains. And all of it — the good as well as the capricious hurt — visited on us in a fashion we no more understand than the kitten, Roosevelt, understands the principle of balloons or the reason for the painful journey she is about to take.

Yet there happens a curious and touching thing.

Between these events it becomes possible to remember how to trust again. Never quite as freely, it is true. Never without a coin of caution in the shoe. But it does happen. Kittens manage it, and so, almost always, do we. Being able to imagine our tomorrows requires it.

The Dark of the Year

Spring mints the green currency of hope and expectation.
Summer spends it in stifling labor. The autumn walks in cool
serenity. But now — now is the season of long consideration.

The sense of that is clearest in the country where, from the
steamy windows of winterbound farmsteads, people consider
their fields — tan and empty between hedgerows drawn against
a slaty morning. Already they imagine how those fields will lie in
June and what will grow in them. Here sorghum, there beans.
But that is an age away. For now, they consider the woodpile
and its sufficiency.

Cattle on a nearby pasture consider the house; stand facing
it. They consider the man who will come out its door, and when,
and what he will bring to them, and how much of it. That is the
event of all their days.

Birds, small on their frozen branch, attentively consider the
hawk.

The hawk, death in repose on his fence post, considers the
mouse.

The mouse in the grass considers a seed.

And the seed is perhaps considering — vainly and too soon
— the future it contains.

All that is winter's business. There is not a great deal else.

The city we somehow imagine to be different, a place, if not
without seasons, at least less subject to them. But is it, really?
There were, last spring, fresh beaver cuttings among the poplar

brakes at the river's edge, not 20 minutes by foot from the central commercial district. The creatures still are there, lodged in some eddy beside their changeless thickets to watch the Dakota ice come grinding down.

On higher ground behind, the buildings make a cold geometry of steel and glass. But they are only shelters after all, like the farmhouse, although grander and more complicated. The people in them dream the season past and send their eyes far out from walls into the pale immensity beyond the river, looking to spy the hawk.

The bird on a utility wire considers the empty feeder and its litter of sunflower husks and sings a curse to hunger.

The cat on his sill puts his face against the glass and considers the tree in which that bird will nest. Calculates angles and windage. Decides even now, long months beforehand, the precise spot where he must wait to meet the nestlings at the end of their maiden flight.

No one ever promised that it would be a gentle world.

The mouse will eat the seed that meant to be a plant. The hawk will kill the mouse. And then, broken in some gale, will fall in turn and be plucked to feathers by a fox. Cattle stumble in the drifts and some do not get up. Or maybe it is the man who falls. His fields go back to berry tangles and broom sedge.

Even now, a century late, someone will come to trap the beaver out. You may be sure of it. The city's buildings, too, will pass one way or other — in settling and slow rust or in the blind, white bursting of some sun that men have made.

All these are winter notions, risen out of the season's stillness *and its long — too long — considerations.*

We must admit they are truths on their way to becoming. And still, for a little longer, there is in all of us — the seed, the hawk, the mouse and the man — a splendid vitality. While it remains, until another spring and maybe much beyond, there will be other, easier truths to light the winter's dark.

Cruel Birthings

Spring calving has begun untimely at the farm. The month and the weather are not favorable for it, but the animals cannot be blamed for that. It's the farmer who must be held accountable. If he errs in June — fails somehow to keep the cows and bull apart — someone will pay for it in February.

The winter calf understands nothing of this, of course. It only knows that, one moment, it is suspended in a tropic dream upon the perfection of the amniotic sea. The next moment it has been expelled gasping and mewing into a place of awful cold — some snowy, brush-girded ravine a bit out of the rake of the wind, if its dam has been lucky or provident enough to find such a place for birthing.

That sudden it is, and that unkind.

The wonder is that such winter calves ever manage to stay alive. But they do — most of them. They are hardy little creatures, and they were arriving in snow, or their distant forebears were, for many thousands of years before men came to regulate their seasons.

Having no previous experience at being born, it cannot possibly occur to them that they are arriving at a wrong and dangerous time. They must assume the winter world is the only world there is — always and everywhere a torment of sleet and quaking cold. They do not imagine any other circumstance, any gentler season, for being born in. And so, uncomplaining because complaint is not in them, they suffer themselves to be cleaned with a rough tongue and nudged up on trembling legs.

If they are quick enough and strong enough, they find the place to nurse — and live. If not, they stagger and fall and the coldness numbs and claims them. Either way the farmer discovers them in the frozen morning. Bounding with their dams among the herd. Or small and stiff somewhere in the brush, in a trampled place of snow where their one terrible hour or so of life began and ended.

Last night, sitting warm beside the window of my house, I watched the silver dinner plate of a moon come riding up over the trees. The light threw the trees' shadows across the snow. Brilliance without any warmth. Light as cold as polished bone. I got to thinking, then, of winter calves, and wondering what agonies before morning might be credited to my account as a careless farmer.

And after that, oddly, I found myself thinking of children, and of how alike is the experience of the newborn of any species. They cannot imagine a world any different than the one into which they have arrived. The Cambodian child does not know there is any landscape in which hunger is not the principle feature. The child of a Calcutta slum does not complain of filth. A refugee child must surely believe all humanity to be contained in a hut of corrugated tin or a canvas tent. Probably a child born to the survivors of a nuclear holocaust would be able to conceive of no civilization, no parent race, except in terms of the terror and disfigurement it saw at every hand.

So the perspective of a human infant is as narrow as a just-born calf's. Pain and milk are understood, but not injustice. Never mind that it is a winter world — never consider that, or even know it. One survives if one can, and if not, one dies in the drift.

But that is the end of the similarity.

For the calf, if it lives, does not remember those first nightmare hours in the dark of winter. Or, if it does remember, does not blame the careless farmer — just plods dumbly and unreasoning through the circle of its years.

But the winter children of the world are different. They come eventually to understand what exactly was done to them, and by whose fault. They do not forget. And sooner or later, because of that, there is a heavy account to be paid.

Deer's World

We sat on an icy log, my friend and I, in mid-afternoon of a dead-of-winter day, a bottle of wine in the rucksack along with a block of sharp cheese and some hard little red apples collected in an orchard the October before. The brilliance of sun reflecting off snow made 20 degrees seem nearer 40. Moisture rose straight up like steam from our wet trouser legs.

A long time we sat there resting, hardly speaking, before we ate. We had spent a half-day in the world of the deer and were finding it hard, now, to come back to the other world of ideas and obligations.

There are experiences in nature that take you entirely out of yourself — out of your man-like habits of feeling and thought into some different and more elemental mode. That happened to me one night in late autumn on a ridge in the high mountains when, waking in darkness and feeling the weight of new snow on the tarpaulin that wrapped me, what I experienced, instead of uneasiness, was exhilaration and a sense of fine self-sufficiency. I had with me all the things I required — food, the means of making fire, a weapon. And I believed (wrongly, perhaps, though in the moment it seemed beyond doubt) that I could cross a thousand miles of that country, given time.

The feeling comes sometimes in the presence of a great flight of waterfowl, on one of those blustery mornings when they come spilling down out of the north ahead of the wind, filling the sky from edge to edge and speaking their cry of wildness directly to your heart.

At times like those you are put in touch again with a part of yourself that has been crusted over by habit and affectation. You are, if only for that instant, nothing less or more than a creature alive among other creatures in your time.

Our purpose that day had been to learn how the deer traveled in that particular stretch of woods — to understand what routes they moved by, and why, and if possible their destinations. To that end we had put the farmhouse and the sounds of the barn lot and the plodding tracks of cattle behind and, laboring in unbroken snow halfway to the knee, had obliged ourselves for several hours to enter as nearly as possible into a deer's mind, think a deer's thoughts.

Here, where a slender tongue of brushy ravine ran up from the river bottom to connect with the larger woods, would be a way to pass in cover to higher ground, with only brief exposure while crossing the cleared line of a fence. And there, in fact, the trail began. But soon divided. An obstacle had presented itself — a graded pipeline right of way. Thirty open yards of terrible danger.

But see, a shallow ditch bisects it. And several hundred feet beyond, another. Moving low, in the faulty light before dawn or just past sunset, the place could be crossable.

Exactly so. The band of deer had divided into two groups, according perhaps to age or temperament. The bolder had used the nearer ditch and the rest, hesitating, had passed farther on to use the other. Their tracks told that story plainly. Beyond there, the route was quite direct. Across a hillside in the safety of crowding trees. Down into the bed of a frozen stream. The stream — its steep banks five feet high and more in places — curving through a jungle of dry blackberry canes along the bottom of a small, wild meadow.

The trail has led here, and with evident purpose. But what purpose, exactly? *In the meadow's lower corner can be seen an appealing place, grown up in sumac, with a cluster of yellow birches behind. It is a place neither very exposed nor very confined — with any danger visible as it enters the meadow from the top, and with the deep escape route of the stream reassuringly near behind. One might choose such a place if one were a deer.*

We stood looking down at them, my friend and I. Six oval nests of birch leaves, each one the size of the folded body of a sleeping deer — with snow a foot deep all around but the nests themselves dry to the touch. Through all the nights of blinding storm the six had bedded there. Even if deliberately looking, it is with some amazement you come upon a thing like that in the woods, as upon a miracle revealed.

We found our icy log, then, and opened the rucksack and sat half-dreaming in the brilliance of the afternoon, taking a long time to come back from where we'd been. We should have been hurrying. My friend was supposed to be on an airplane that night, bound for another city on business.

But there was no haste in us. We drank the wine, instead, and ate our cheese and apples. "Never mind," my friend said finally. "I'm not going to go after all. I'll telephone. Someone else can handle it."

That is the peril of such excursions outside oneself. Experienced too often or too intensely, they might have the power to change our very natures. Which must be why, in almost every generation, there have been people who have journeyed into wilderness and who have not, by choice, returned.

The First Flowers

In the dark of the year, which also can be a dark season of the heart, we have profited from a visitation of elves.

They came in the night, as elves usually do, and laid the downstairs table for a festive breakfast. They spread a flowered tablecloth, then searched until they found the brightest yellow place mats and arranged on those the company china. And on the chance these happy preparations might somehow have gone unnoticed, they also left a message. *"The Eleves,"* it said, *"were here!"* They have, these elves, a better eye for decoration than for spelling — but that is of no importance.

All this happened while we were sleeping. So that in the morning, when we went down the stair, we found the breakfast room transformed. That blossoming of flowers, that explosion of color, had swept the season's grayness quite away. And in that instant — not a bit too soon for our spirits' sake — thoughts turned from the cheerless march through winter to the expectation, suddenly made close and keen, of an easier and brighter time.

Much is said about the nurturing skills of parents. But I have been struck sometimes by children's innate sensitivity to our needs and to the nuances of mood around them. Their accomplishments of reason may be less. But being animals in nature, their antennae are acute, and like the dog that trembles on a cloudless day they sense the storm before it comes.

Just what the crisis in the household was — what impending storm of the spirit — I have forgotten. Nothing specific, I expect. Likely we had all been too long indoors, our temperaments drawn thin by too much cold and too much talk of politics and inflation and tragedy in Africa and all the other craziness abroad in the world. Conversations moved in circles and ended with sighs. Food had become tasteless. Friends were all occupied, and work a tedium. In our war against winter's darkness, the dark had won.

The elves were not entirely selfless in their errand. They had in mind the ritual breakfast — French toast, sausage, the full production. And they sensed that strong measures would be needed to rouse the listless keepers of the house to such exertions. But whatever the reason, the effect was immediate and great.

The sunlight falling through the window on that flowered cloth seemed unexplainably less cold. And then the weather did in fact change, breathing a balmy foretaste of winter's end. Suddenly I began noticing seed packets on the racks of stores. And I began thinking of yard work — with distaste, of course, but at least thinking of it. Whatever had oppressed us passed from mind and even out of memory. Laughter reclaimed its place among the noises of the house.

It is the lot of parents to be awake at many strange hours, exchanging quarters for shed teeth under pillows, gnawing the carrots left for the Easter rabbit, drinking Santa's glass of milk with queasy stomach and doing the duties of elves in other seasons. But we have proof that all this nurturing is not one-sided.

For, thanks to those smaller elves of ours, we are certain now to make it through the dark tunnel of another month or two, our way lighted by that bouquet arranged for us in the creeping stillness of a winter night. And the cloth will remain on the table until there are real flowers outside the window to take its place.

Design for Living

The archaeologists of some future age will be amazed when their shovels lay bare the crumbled remains of the house I intend to build. Whoever he was and whatever gods or devils he prayed to, the good scientists will say to one another, here lived a man of parts. Because in my mansion there will be many rooms.

Self-aggrandizement and ostentation will not be its purpose, though. Looking closer, the archaeologists will notice a strange thing. Most of the rooms will be bathrooms. Probably they will draw from that all sorts of elaborate and wacky conclusions.

They will postulate a culture scatalogically preoccupied. Or a civilization whose light flickered out ingloriously after a long pandemic of dysentery. Scholarly monographs will be published in support of one or another of these theses. Experts will line up for and against the scenario of terminal flux. Theologians may even become involved. They all will be wrong.

The truth of the matter, which is not really complicated at all, is that I mean to build such a house — a house with five bathrooms at a minimum and maybe six or seven — because I live in a family of three women. That is not a sexist observation. It is a statement of absolute fact. Three of them, I repeat — one wife, two daughters, the daughters just entering now upon an age of exceeding concern about their grooming.

In the course of the year I come under occasional pressure to rise early on weekend mornings to go with them to church or to other events of indisputable benefit. Generally, and increasingly, I am unresponsive. I lie abed, pretending sleep or sickness. This is not because I take lightly the needs of my spirit. It is because, if I do happen to get up, I am soon made to feel a nuisance and an obstruction.

Just the other Sunday, for example, aflame with loving kindness, I threw back the bedcovers and announced that I would appear with them at the early service. Did this inspire any happiness? Not that you could notice. The bathroom happened at that moment to be unoccupied, and I made the mistake of going in there. Even a backslider's teeth occasionally need brushing. Instantly a current of outrage and impatience spread through the house. Angry talk could be heard through the door.

He's in the bathroom! Oh, no, not now! Tell him to pass out the hair dryer. Ask him if the curlers are plugged in. How long? How much longer?

I live for the hunting season. My wife is mystified by this passion. She wonders where I find the stamina to rise morning after morning, in the smallest hours, to go afield after creatures I seldom catch. But the chase is not the point. If you consistently get out of bed and dress at half past 3 o'clock, sooner or later you are going to find a bathroom free. As I see it, the choice is either to be a hunter or live in a house next to a filling station.

When the girls were younger this was no burning issue. But now there is their hair. Soon there will be rouge and eye shadow to apply, toenails to paint and other, more arcane functions of adornment. So I total up our requirements. One bathroom for each of the females of the house, making three to start. My daughters have begun having friends in for the night. And the friends' hair is no less demanding of attention. Separate facilities will have to be provided for their morning convenience. Which puts us at five.

And what of the potted plants? There was a time when I naively thought that plants lived on window ledges and in hanging baskets. They do not — ours don't, at any rate. They spend the greater part of their time draining in wash basins and bathtubs. That makes six.

It might also happen that once in a while we would have an

adult visitor. And I am not going to be put in the position of having to say that, although I am the owner of six bathrooms, none of them is available for the visitor's use. So the guest facility makes seven.

And if my own lamentable situation is to be in any way bettered — if I am to be able to give up hunting and topping off my gas tank and making trips at strange hours to all-night convenience stores — then the final installation will be mine. Bringing the grand total to eight bathrooms.

That is the central feature around which the plan of my house will be arranged. We will be a happier family. Probably my health will improve. Those archaeologists of the future may make of it what they will. But if they themselves happen to be the fathers of daughters, it is possible that the cry of my great need will ring out to them from the mute dust and tumbled stones of another time.

Awaited Calls

The old cat sleeps beside the telephone and has never had a call. Has never had a friend. She was a lady of the streets for as long as age was on her side. But she waddles now. Her tattered hair skirts drag the snow. Her beauty mark, a notched ear, is wasted on the prowling toms.

Other cats have come and gone — undone by years or by the wheels of some indifferent car. The old cat stays, cautious and durable, nested safely amid the clutter of books and papers on the telephone table from which, with slitted eye, she observes life passing.

None in all that procession of other creatures has cared

much for her. The dog waits for her around the corner of the stair. The cats, allies of the dog for purposes of ambush, crouch atop and under and behind the furniture. Returning from some small excursion the old cat — the friendless one — peers into the darkness of the open doorway and considers the gantlet to be run, measures the distance to her perch. Then makes a dash for it.

Out the others come then, erupting from the shadows in hot pursuit. It's all for sport. They've never caught her and do not mean to catch her. They only want to make her scurry and scramble humiliatingly. Something about her must invite torment. Does her manner betray the insecurity, the shame, of having once been a winter stray? Whatever the reason, her entries all are the same, all noisy and harried. Even the smallest, clumsiest kitten new to the household soon joins the baying rabble at her heels.

She has perfected the art of being inconspicuous. If it were not for our using the telephone we might forget she lived with us at all. She sleeps a lot, as old cats do. When stroked, or scratched behind an ear, she seems surprised and a bit uneasy. She objects to being held. One could almost suppose that she had achieved so final a state of wariness or disillusionment that affection no longer figured in her plans.

But twice in these years there have been periods when, through some sequence of sad misfortune, the old cat was the only creature remaining to us. The losses left empty places in our house and in our hearts — deficits which the strange, shaggy, reticent survivor moved promptly to rectify. She left her station beside the phone and found the courage to strop herself against a trouser leg. At night she curled at the foot of the bed where one or more of the others had previously slept.

It was not so much that her nature had changed. The caution still was there. After having passed so many solitary hours she had no sense of how to be a lap cat, nor do I think she wanted to be. Her purpose in those times seemed to be less in receiving attention than in giving it. It was as if, responding to our need, she played the pet as best her misshapen temperament would let her.

After several weeks, then, the replacement cats would begin arriving. And immediately — though with no show of pique or resentment — the old girl would return to her accustomed habits, taking up her place beside the phone again, waiting for that call that never comes. And soon the new cats would learn to devil her and lurk beside the door.

These other ones I value for their glossiness or grace or other virtues. The old cat I value for the goodness of her heart.

I remember those times when she was not just kept, when she was needed. And I am led to think that there must be a great deal of unknown and unsuspected tenderness about, like the consideration in that old cat, waiting only for space and reason to be noticed.

The Homely Table

By some process too unspecific to describe or even clearly to remember, one particular place to eat takes on the character of home. Nearly everyone has such a place. You take meals in other restaurants — in some of them more often. Never, though, with quite the same comfort or satisfaction. Those establishments are agreeable enough, but one is not family there. One is only a patron, and always will be, whatever the unctuous pretense to the contrary.

A place that used to be my eating home is a parking lot now.

Its owner presided there for a generation. Then he retired and, as so often happens, the magic was gone. Under the new owner, the business fell away into insolvency and the building was razed. Another such place closed when the proprietress moved to another city. It has since become a discotheque — a watering spot for the gaudy debs and dandies who congregate at its remodeled entrance like a flock of preening peafowl.

These are losses one does not easily sustain. With much effort a new base can be found and the sense of easy familiarity recreated there. But it is a matter of years in the doing.

My present headquarters is more than just a restaurant. It is a kind of talisman. I go there on those days when there is absolutely nothing to write and no realistic hope of ever writing anything again. Winter light filters soft through the windows. Seductive odors pass outward from the kitchen. A lively company comes and goes. And invariably in that hour or so an idea presents itself, or several do. Fairly thin little ideas, some of them. But in an emergency, one does not cavil about details.

The catalyst of this — the psychic energizer — seems to be the salad, a vast bowl of leafy greens laced with surprising ingredients but containing, as far as I know, no controlled substances. So inspiring has been this salad that, in more than four years, I have explored the menu no further. There are wonderful things on it, no doubt. But as a creature of habit I will never know. Merely to think of ever having to do without that salad brings on panic and a momentary giddiness. I would not relish having to go so late in life into another line of work.

The other noon I happened to run into friends at this favorite place, also habitues and also, as it happened, having salad. So we shared a table.

The establishment justly prides itself on the freshness of its greens. And on this day the freshness was indisputable. For one of my companions, upon lifting a crisp leaf to mouth, exposed a small but perky worm that was making a beeline across the plate toward the shelter of a heart of palm.

What passed through my friend's mind I can't say. But he seemed perfectly composed.

"Look here!" he said. "Do you see it?"

We bent for a closer inspection. It seemed to be an uncommonly clean little worm, hardly more than one-quarter inch long — of a pale beige color, shading to green at the tail.

The people at the next table had taken an interest.

"What have you got there?" they asked.

"A worm."

"Oh, a worm." They continued eating their own salads, quite undismayed. Evidently they, too, were regulars there. And not about to be put off by so small an event as the discovery of the *worm du jour.* It was, after all, nothing more than the certain promise of an eventual spring.

Now if that had happened in some pretentious beanery with brocaded walls there might have been an ugly scene — curses and shouted threats and the rest. It's different in a place you consider home. If a worm appears you either eat it or pass it up, but either way you do it quietly.

I count the owner of that restaurant my friend. He is interested in my work, and I in his. Without his hospitality, I sometimes could not work at all. Best of all, he is my own age or a bit younger. I wish him much prosperity and a long life and no retirement ever. Continuity is essential to human happiness, and the notion of starting over at some new man's table does not appeal.

So long as he promises to keep his door open and that salad on his menu, I will promise not to examine its contents too critically for their length or speed afoot.

Captiva Island: Sea Sense

Young eyes are the best for seeing wonders. Afterwards, except in odd and accidental moments, impressions rarely strike with such transforming force again. I was 21 before I saw an ocean. Just last evening, at more than twice that age, as I was walking at the water's edge the sense of that first revelation came briefly but powerfully back.

The swollen, softened orange ball of sun had declined to a point just above the watery horizon. A moderate surf was rolling, and a chevroned squad of sandpipers was retreating and advancing quick-legged with the subsiding waves. The rising night wind blew a chill through the coat. Suddenly, then, I remembered that old moment exactly.

There'd been a curious sensation not of strangeness but of return — almost of homecoming, to that place of ancestral nurture whose chemistry we carry still.

Also a sense, for the first time, of actually living on a planet, whose curve the eye could see and whose defining features were larger and more enduring than buildings or paved roads.

And an appreciation of history as something grander than simply words printed on a page. An intimation of the vast narrative flow of it — the ancient, frail voyages undertaken; the romance and greed and questing courage of the hopeless dreamers who first turned their ships toward the uncharted edge.

I felt the certainty of adventure waiting out past vision's reach. Of countries to be known about, and people unlike any met before; of a thousand languages falling strangely on the ear.

It took my heart away, the ocean did. There are certain experiences by which each of us marks his life, and for me that was one. Since then I have crossed the ocean by ship, with great whales spouting just off the rail and gulls coming out from unseen land to announce the journey's end. And many times, by plane, with the reefs and shoals and drowned mountains shading lighter the endless blue below. I suppose, in fact, that I have seen — from one altitude or other — all of the world's largest waters and a good many of the lesser ones as well. Never, though, with the intensity of feeling of that first visit to the shore.

Until last night, that is, when, for no reason I can name, it came washing over me again for just an instant.

The mingled smell of salt and living matter filled the air with a terrific pungency. The waves rose up, and in the smooth fronts of them, just before they curled and crashed, could be seen a suspended freight of strange and broken things. The water was a presence — full of mystery, vast and old and fecund and powerful beyond imagining.

Then the globe of sun dropped from sight, the evening shaded darker, the sense of it was gone. And the sea, instead of being a wonder, was once more only a fact in nature, pleasant to stand beside while waiting for dinner to be called.

Captiva Island: The Bloom

The sea's changes are swift, its economies harsh.

One afternoon the waves tumble in joyfully to scour the sandy margin of the island's western side. By next daybreak the Gulf lies glassy as a midlands pond. And becalmed upon it like an armada of small, ungainly ships are the pelicans — many hundreds of them — rafted away as far as the eye can see, all swollen with prosperity.

From a great way down the beach the figures of two men can

be seen slowly to approach, stopping and bending as they come, dragging something large between them. The two men draw nearer. They are employees of the inn. What they are dragging is an enormous plastic sack. And what they are putting into it are fish, dead fish, cast up during the night in truly inestimable numbers at the water's edge.

Can you imagine being asked to gather and bag and cart away all the fish from several miles of the Gulf of Mexico? The job has no end. More fish are coming in. Far out, beyond the pelicans, the new sun strikes to a white sparkle the upturned stomachs of an infinitude of dead fish, all of them surely destined to lodge finally on that beach.

Ordinarily, pelicans have to work a little for a meal. But here a table has been laid for them. These pelicans do not fly. They only have to wait, and presently a ripe morsel will float by in easy reach. It is a spectacle of gluttony, and yet only an inconsiderable fraction of the fish are eaten. Most find their way to the edge of sand. Bending, bagging, the men with the sack go slowly past. Glazed of eye, they are, and heavy of heart. One of them speaks of having sinned greatly in the bar the night before. He is performing, therefore, a labor of contrition — but without much hope that it will leave him cleansed.

What occupies the pelicans and the men is a consequence of something called the *red tide,* an intermittent occurrence in nature that has again plagued the Gulf coastal waters for the last several months.

The blame for it rests with a one-celled aquatic creature whose name is *Gymnodiniun breve,* present usually in unnoticeable numbers but apt suddenly to multiply, for reasons not perfectly known, until a single quart of sea water may contain as many as sixty million of the organisms. Such a bloom, as it is called, can actually turn the sea a deep maroon over a considerable area. A poison is released, able not only to harm other aquatic life but even to cause people ashore to experience smarting eyes and a choking sensation.

Here we have been spared the worst of these effects. The tide apparently occurred some miles southward. What we have received is only the drifting result of it. But the fishing has gone sour, even in the sound to the island's landward side. Fish still can be found, the guides insist, but only at a greater distance and then not readily.

In the afternoon, when the charter boats come in, the resident pelicans do not congregate as usual at the dock, below the fish-cleaning table. Scraps have lost all charm. They are out with their fellows at the larger, fouler banquet. Nor do the lodgers from the inn — the sunbathers and shell-gatherers — find the beach so congenial a place to be. Except where the two men with the sack have newly passed.

Unmindful of any of this, the vast water goes through its endless processes.

The inn is built at a place where the island pinches down to a ribbon of land hardly more than a hundred yards across. When the next hurricane comes, long-timers here say, it all will go — that bit of land and everything that's on it. Whether they are right or wrong, who can for a moment doubt that the sea's indifference is at least as fathomless as it's beauty?

Gymnodinium breve prospers. Vacationers complain. A million fishes die. Pelicans wax sleek and lazy.

And it is all the same.

Captiva Island:
Vacation Friends

Vacation friends are easy friends to keep. There are no demands, no expectations, no old debts or long loyalties. It is a friendship unencumbered.

The family from Cincinnati is here again, and it is the fifth or sixth year running. School vacations in our city and theirs coincide. So we have become, for one another, fixtures of this place. We have watched each other's children grow. We leave our chillier latitudes and bear south to this island, where the sun warms and the breeze is never still. And meeting here by pure repeated accident, for a fortnight we are as close as most friends are apt to be.

Sometimes we take a meal together at a restaurant. Sometimes our daughters trade overnights at our two cottages standing 20 steps apart. The son of that family, who is 8, seeks me out for consultation about his fishing, and I am very full of authoritative advice — although, in strict fact, my own fishing luck is usually rather slight.

We take, for this little time, the keenest interest in one another's lives. One recent night we sat together at a table in the darkness outdoors and talked two hours or more. Talked about our children getting older, and about the seasons of a life. And also, with some regret, about that day when — in our children's growing away — the habit of coming to this place will surely change. Our values, we have found, are much the same. The details about us are significantly different, but the longer purposes that impel us — our hopes, our apprehensions, our private griefs — are quite alike.

Shortly we will go away from here, the two families of us, back north to where we hope our absence will have tempted the spring to flower. Maybe we will come again next year, and maybe not. The very uncertainty is, itself, appealing. But if we do come, we will surely meet.

I do not remember, when I was young, my family having any such vacation friends. Possibly you encountered someone somewhere beside a lake. Then, after the briefest time, you made a last pleasantry and the world swallowed those people up. There was no use investing much in acquaintances so insubstantial.

I think that our children's view must, on account of the Cincinnati people, be different and more secure. Distance means less. A year is just an interval like any other, no more final or forbidding. Our daughters go away. They come again. There is a continuity to that. The friends are here — as surely as the tide brings shells from many places tumbling up onto the same stretch of sand.

All can be reassembled as it was the year before. No separations are certain. No griefs terminal. No change past the hope of remedy, and no loss past our power somehow to recover. That is not altogether or always true, of course. But it is a fine illusion to nourish in the young, and a harmless enough deceit at any age.

Northbound by Air:
Clay Memories

Paradise recedes. Beneath a speckle of low clouds, the
geometric groves and coiling tidal rivers of the Florida
coast fall rapidly behind. I can see them still, but they have
lost the persuasiveness of fact and have passed into the
murk of things remembered or imagined.

Two hours ago we sat for breakfast in a breezy room whose
open windows fronted through palms and silky Casuarina trees
upon the Gulf, lying slick and still as a lake. Other guests of the
inn — only a few of them at that late hour — shared the dining
room. But a barrier had come between us. We no longer had
anything in common.

For they were dressed for their adventures of the day; for
prowling the beach or riding off in boats to where shells waited
on the unmarked sand of empty islands. While we, by contrast,
were in our traveling clothes. The mark of despair was on us. The
others noticed that and, it seemed to me, took care to look the
other way, as if the sight of us might bring bad luck and cause
their own holidays to end.

Only the Clay Lady was sympathetic.

She comes from Maine, with a suggestion of that chilly coast
in her inflection, and sits for half the year beside warmer waters.
Her station is on the deck of the marina, where she may be found
each clement day from midmorning until almost the supper
hour. Boats arrive and leave. Tall masts sway at the moorings.
There is a marina society, made up of children casting bits of
shrimp for sugar trout or dangling fish parts after crabs; a woman
reading in the sun; two anthropologists hotly disputing some
issue of chronology in the long story of the species.

Later the fishing guides come in with their catch and throw

the leavings to the pelicans that pace the dock, knowing all the day's events in order. The Clay Lady may notice these fine distractions or at least must sense them, but she gives no sign of it. All day she sits at her potter's wheel, in smock and apron, entirely devoted to her work — the sun glancing silver from her hair and from the moist clay as it takes form under her pliant hands.

It is a great piece of luck to be potter-in-residence at such a languid meeting place between land and sea. Often, in her joy, she manufactures objects without either name or known purpose. Possibly their function later will be found. No matter; the shapes please her. They may please someone else.

Daily my daughters called on the Clay Lady and watched her at her wheel, while she spoke with them about such incidental matters as the shapes their lives might take — lives that are still, for a little longer, as plastic and full of possibilities as clay itself.

This morning she saw us coming from our last meal and knew by the look of us, by our heavy step, that we were bound away from there. "Do you have a moment?" she asked. We consulted the watch. *Well, yes. A moment.* She led us past a line of palms and shrubs in flower to the storage room where, beside her kiln, she kept her works in progress.

"So that you won't forget," she said simply. And took down from the shelf some small pieces. Rejects, she called them — to excuse the giving. But, if flawed, wonderfully flawed.

It has seemed to me that a seaside inn with a resident potter might acquire further tone by having a writer-in-residence as well. He could sit at one of the tables on the marina deck and smoke and spill ashes on himself and look disheveled, while typing out flawed paragraphs to present to the guests as mementos of their visit. In fact, at a social hour the other evening, I made some suggestion along that line to the managing director, who replied obliquely with a comment about the weather and quickly moved away into the crowd.

Now the island is behind. The clouds have thinned and, far below, the plane's shadow is scuttling north across Georgia. But the Clay Lady's gifts ride with us. In the year between now and going back again, I will keep them near at hand. Her happiness — the happiness of that place — is caught in a glaze that is suggestive of water and sand.

And if, in the next dark season, one of those little pots is held against the ear, I have no doubt that, like a shell, it will give back across great distance the windy rustle of the sea.

Between Seasons

Outside the window a tree was budded. There was no explaining it. But neither was there any mistaking what met the eye. The tree, a soft maple, had begun to reach in ancient faith toward a season that you and I could not yet see.

The punishment of ice and polar nights was fresh in mind. In the basement the old furnace throbbed and rumbled. An arctic wind still whined at the window corners. Birds hunkered on the branch and the squirrels had resorted to eating roof shingles. The turn to a gentler season was unimaginably remote. One foot set deliberately ahead of the next, like cattle plodding in blind file toward the comfort of a far-off barn, we marched dutifully on but could not notice the distance shortening at all.

Daily it did shorten, though. And there, outside the window, was the proof.

There is nothing about winter that any of us can usefully tell a tree. The tree — that one, or the one from whose seed it grew, or the one that struck its root in colder earth than those — remembers them all. The hardest winters and the longest. The winters upon the edge of the vast, advancing ice; winters whose duration no calendar could measure. Winters that carved and forever changed the land. The memory of that is written in the behavior of the descendant tree.

What it tells is that spring always comes, or always has. Not necessarily soon. But sometime — always. Against that certainty the tree prepares. Hence those out-of-season buds.

A freezing rain had fallen overnight, and ice sheathed every branch and twig. The buds were of a deep maroon color, and folded very tight, each the size of half a grain of popped corn. Unaffected by the cold, they waited their time.

In winter's agony, the bird remembers the stirring bug, the greening seed.

The squirrel gnaws the bitter roof and imagines better fare.

The cattle plod grayly on, and so do we.

In all things alive, even in the hardest times, the tide of expectation is very patient, very strong.

Jeopardy

A life is experienced most painlessly, if that's the word, when it is lived in unbroken continuity. Given a choice, I do not think I would much care to resume mine again after too long an interruption.

That odd thought occurred the other day upon returning from a mere two weeks away from the claims of the world, away from the press of obligations and the addictive stridency of the news, out of reach of all but the most urgent messages. Two weeks only. And what met us on return?

A note, first of all, written in sorrow by the young woman who was caring for them, that one of our cats had died. The oldest one — the woolly possumcat, the notched-eared stray who slept in her box beside the telephone, waiting for that call that never came. Never mind that we have a lot of cats. We have none to spare. And that one had been with us since the time of our children's first memories.

After the note, the mail. Ordinarily I love to sort and open the mail. If I happen to be at home, I rush to snatch it from the box as soon as the postman's footfalls have receded down the drive. But out of the fortnight's collected stack of it, the first letter, as it happened, bore bad news. In the second envelope was another and unrelated disappointment. So it went — the accumulation of ill tidings more than canceling out the half-dozen or so enticements to enter some sweepstake or other and become forever rich.

And there was more.

Among our friends, a relationship had been overtaken and contorted by distress. A telephone call to the farm elicited word of several crises, none catastrophic but all demanding to be resolved at once. The small yellow car — the Asian instrument of my torment and financial ruin — when started up after two weeks' rest, gave out the unmistakable whinnies and thunkings of its imminent next collapse.

Now, the point is not that our despairs were any worse or more numerous than anyone else's. Of course they aren't. Occurring in the normal course of things, one or two a day over the span of two weeks, they would have taken their normal place in the uneven pattern of events. The bad mixed with the good. Wounds still, but with healing time between.

The trouble was in the concentration of them, received all at once.

I considered, then, with greater understanding, all those people whose affairs have been interrupted in far worse and longer ways than by any vacation — by being held prisoners of war, say, or hostages of some terrorist, or by suffering any other involuntary absence of great duration. Naturally they yearn to come back to the world they knew. Their every thought is fixed on that. But, in the actual moment of homegoing, how their eagerness must be qualified and confused by the dread of all they will find altered about that world. And the dread is well grounded. For the changes are sure to be many and large.

The current of change is irresistible. Some is felicitous, some wretched. This mixture, lived day to day, can be easily enough endured and may even be described as happiness. But the weight of it, thrust upon one collectively, may be insupportable. At least, in a much smaller way, that was our experience.

It all has been dealt with. The farm needs have been met. The unpleasant letters have been answered. The old cat sleeps the end of winter through under a bush in the backyard, a little clutch of frostbitten flowers marking the place.

The children vow they'll take no more trips, ever. They cannot bear such hurts of coming back. The memory will soften, and that will change. But the experience has put them in touch with a somber truth, which is that the only people who are ever really safe are those with nothing and no one much to leave, and therefore nothing much to come back to.

The rest of us are forever exposed.

The End of Privacy

I saw a man with a bullhorn on a street corner at noon and the combination of those two — the man and the machine — was deeply unsettling. He had a look of rapt craziness on his face. All around him the offices and store buildings loomed up, discharging their occupants into the lunch-hour crowd. Streams of chilly people hurried along the sidewalk. Mostly they parted and went on past the man at the corner but a few hesitated, then joined the little circle around him.

I can't say what his message was — what creed or cause he argued for. I was going by in my car. Through the open window I saw him with his face uplifted and his eyes rolled white in transport and I heard an unconnected gabble of urgency, amplified many times by the battery-powered speaker he held to his mouth.

But in the time it took to find a place to park he already had moved on. Followed by his collection of disciples or the merely curious, he had taken up new station at a different and more distant corner. So I never caught up with him and will never know what news he may have had for me.

I have wondered, since, why it was I found so small an event disturbing. The reason, I believe, is because that man and his machine seemed somehow to represent the degree to which technology has exposed us all to unasked-for and unwanted intrusions on our lives. There is hardly a human being alive — at least in an advanced industrialized society such as ours — who is not in some way a perpetual hostage to the craziness of his fellows.

The telephone is the most obvious and most commonly decried implement of these intrusions. The damned thing rings. And because it rings it must be answered. (By uncanny happenstance, mine rang just now. When I answered there was silence and then, unspeaking, the caller hung up. That happens at least a dozen times each day. My telephone number, it seems, is different by only a digit from the one the public can call to receive the last night's sports scores — and I will suffer a lifetime for that.)

Utter strangers telephone for no evident reason except that they are lonely.

Some call to rant and ramble, counting on the element of sheer surprise to ensure them at least a few minutes' hearing. Deviants choose numbers at random from the directory and whisper obscenities and invitations. Racial and ideological fanatics call to mutter cowardly threats. Zealots telephone to ask if our souls are in order.

Now there are machines able to deliver recorded messages of solicitation, automatically, to thousands of telephone numbers in succession. And surely that is as awful a form of craziness as any mentioned above. It is as if a television advertiser were empowered by remote control, to turn on your set at any hour of day or night when he wanted his message heard. Probably that, too, is coming and will be a standard feature, not an option, on the TVs of the future.

In political campaign seasons, sound cars patrol the streets and proclaim the virtues of the candidate whether we are interested to hear or not.

In the theater the other evening, a pocket paging device suddenly crackled out. Some physician or salesman was receiving a reedy-voiced communique from his office. Several hundred faces turned and the play was disrupted, though the startled actors carried on. Probably it did not even occur to the man to be embarrassed.

These are some of the odd things that came troublingly to mind when I saw that strange, disordered fellow shouting out something or other on a street corner in the noon hour crowd. We have invented machines for convenience. Too late, we have discovered that they can as easily be used to amplify lunacy and give fresh scope to arrogance and inconsideration.

There is a good deal of craziness promulgated — and has been for as long as anyone remembers — from Speakers Corner in Hyde Park of London. Much of it is extravagant and seditious. But it is spoken from stepladders by means of the unaided voice. So you can choose your lunatic or you can ignore them all.

Poets are rather widely thought to be mad and a little dangerous. But by the time they are heard of, most of them already are dead and safely shut away between covers in dusty libraries.

And what of newspapers and newspaper writers?

No one can make you read. No one can prevent you from turning the page. As wrong-headed or crazy as we may be, it must be admitted that we do not telephone you at home or follow after you with a bullhorn on your way from the office to lunch. Not yet, at any rate. In these days of strident thoughtlessness, who can promise what tomorrow will bring?

Fire One! Fire Two!

It is a commentary either on the onrush of science or the debasement of spoken language that civilization has come to be imperiled by a danger which many of our public leaders are unable to pronounce.

They appear on the television in these troubled days to speak of what they seem determined to call the *Newk-yuh-ler* threat. And the awful thought intrudes: *My God, if they can't even say it right, how can they possibly protect us from it?*

Presidents say it that way, and men who would be president. Generals and rural newscasters say it that way. So do almost all children under the age of 12. There is hardly anything more chilling than to hear a Southern senator expound on the risks of a *Newk-yuh-lah Tack* and the possible wisdom of deterring it with something known as a *Pre-eminent Strack*.

This is one of the things I believe has brought a special and arcane terror into the nuclear age. Not so much the fear that we will all be blown up as the suspicion that we may gradually be losing the power to speak. A danger that is unpronounceable becomes alarming in a way altogether greater and different than the one describable by a word we have safely mastered. Being unspeakable, it must surely be worse.

A high official of civil defense came on the air the other night to advise us of the ways in which we might contrive to live through a *Newk-yuh-ler* bombardment. He was clearly rattled, as one generally is in the face of hazards one cannot accurately name, much less understand. And he inspired about the same confidence you would feel in an orthopedist who diagnosed a backache as rising from some maladjustment of your *spiral* cord. I looked into the face of that earnest, uncomprehending man and realized immediately that, if Armageddon comes, we are all going to be entirely on our own. And probably better for that.

This imprecision of language is a sin often attributed to the young, and it is true that their capacity for speech does seem to be declining

An experiment with drugs which happens to send some adolescent gibbering and shrieking off to an asylum for a year or two is described in the flat, post-pubescent vernacular as a *bad trip.*

A newspaper story not long ago described the vexation of property owners whose homes fronted on a certain fashionable park. One of them stepped out the door in the evening and inquired of a young lady why she was relieving herself on the lawn: The girl-child's reply was, *"Tell me about it."* That's not eloquence, perhaps. But it is, to my mind, one of the more arresting fragments of dialogue to be found anywhere in the whole body of modern literature.

If an earthquake were to send the city of San Francisco slipping off into the Pacific, it is possible that the contemporaneous generation of Angelenos might find it in themselves to utter a toneless *Wow* or *Outasight.*

My purpose here, however, is not to indict the young. For if the national fathers cannot be bothered to learn to say correctly the most dangerous word of these times, then surely the decline of speech has earlier roots — as demonstrably it does.

I once worked for a man who, during my two years in his employ, never got beyond the first syllable of my last name. Admittedly it is a troublesome name. My own father changed its pronunciation to accommodate his friends at the office.

Whole tribes and nations have come to be wrongly described for generations simply because, when it came to phonetics, their discoverers and conquerors happened to have tin ears. Seemingly trivial imprecisions can have large meaning. Ask an African cleric, for example, if there is any difference between being canonized and being colonized. Or a Frenchman if there is a difference between a *voila* and a viola.

There are, for a fact, certain words that dare not be written in the newspaper out of fear that a slight typographical error might turn that sentence into a howling public nuisance or cause for litigation.

Such uneasy thoughts rise when I hear men of careless mind, some of our leaders among them, discuss the problems of the *Newk-yuh-ler* age. They are men whose ear may not detect — and who may not be interested to know — the difference, say, between a missile and a missive. And who, if advised that they were about to receive one of the latter from some enemy, rather than summon a translator might press a red button instead.

Farfetched, perhaps. But all that separates the boobs from the bombs is the one small letter "o" — and maybe less than that.

The Road to Sudbury

The mathematics teacher does not look like a fiend. In fact, she is a strikingly handsome young woman, clear of eye, wholesome of manner — an unlikely candidate for the devil's work.

Each week in this teacher's class there is written on the blackboard or distributed on a ditto sheet a problem the students may undertake to solve for extra credit. These exercises are not, strictly speaking, mathematical. Rather, their purpose is to expand the logical power of young minds.

They go like this:

The first customer buys half the rabbits in a pet store. The second customer buys 13 rabbits. The third customer would like to buy nine rabbits, but he wants all-white rabbits, and two-thirds of the remaining ones are spotted. Then the first customer brings back one-fourth of the rabbits he initially bought. Three of those are spotted and seven are all-white.

And so forth. I work here from memory of what I saw on the chalkboard the night of open house, and probably my memory is inexact. But you get the idea. Applying logic to the information that is supplied, you are supposed to be able to know many ducklings were in the cage next to the rabbits.

A full week is allowed to find the answer. The involvement of parents in these exertions is not only permitted, it is encouraged. One isn't *required* to participate, you understand. It depends entirely on whether you love your children and want them to succeed scholastically and in their later lives.

The extra-credit problem for the current week is a map of 23 cities connected by a network of roads. One town is designated as the starting point of the journey, another as the destination. The object is to proceed from start to finish, visiting each town only once and never passing twice along any stretch of road.

The map seems very innocent and straightforward. But, like the gentle manner of the teacher, it is deceiving. That piece of paper is an instrument of Satan. The trip it proposes cannot be made.

We tried all one evening, my daughter and I, until I whined and wept with frustration and she turned away from me in disgust. I had scribbled on the map until it was hardly legible, and had to do a tracing of it on another paper against the light. In the morning I rose early and bent over the map until it was time to go to work. Then I brought the resources of industry into play, turning out 50 copies of the tracing on the office Xerox machine. One by one I spoiled those.

I have come to hate the towns on that map, all of which have cute New England-ish names like Barre and Putney — all self-consciously quaint. And I have sworn never to go to New England on the chance that I might come upon a real village bearing one of those names and lose my self-control, maybe run amok.

The right-hand side of the map can be traveled easily enough. The towns there are farther apart, and there are clues. The left-hand side, however, is a web of roads and a cluster of hateful habitations. With unremitting effort and $25 worth of photocopying, it is possible to visit all of those — except one. You can get to Sudbury, missing Manchester. Or Manchester can be reached by leaving Sudbury out. To arrive at both of them, one short segment of roadway must be traveled twice.

Who wants to go to Sudbury in the first place? I wonder. Probably it is some wretched hamlet whose cheerless inhabitants still practice the burning of witches. God forbid that I should ever have to go there. If I do, it will be for the single purpose of delivering the mathematics teacher into their hands.

The week will be up at midnight. After that it will be useless to go either to Manchester or Sudbury. But it is Friday for a few more hours yet, and we still have a dozen or so copies of the map. So I bend again to the damnable paper.

My heartbeat is irregular with anxiety and fatigue. The roads shift and blur before me. But in my devotion to mathematics and my child, I stumble on, passing through Manchester for perhaps the five hundredth time, Sudbury, like true wisdom, forever unreachable ahead.

Aerosol Pollution

I have long taken a layman's interest in graffiti — and not only, or even especially, the kind to be found on lavatory walls and running mainly to limericks, telephone numbers and deviant invitations.

While I cannot claim to have made any real study of public scribblings, I have traveled some and, like nearly everyone, have spent some time in train and bus station washrooms. Also, my life's occupation has required a degree of concern for language and its uses, of which graffiti indisputably are one.

The Oppression Must End!

I saw that pronouncement the other day, written in strident five-foot-high script on a windowless building wall. Technology is a wonder. What the printing press did for the advancement of literature, the spray paint can has done for graffiti. That same day, but from a different wall on a different street, another declaration cried out.

Humanity Is One, it said.

Worthy enough sentiments, both of those. Why, yes, of course, oppression must end. Who is against that? As for humanity being one, it is a truth not only of philosophy but of biology. Oddly, though, when scrawled large across public walls, the words failed to inspire. What I immediately felt, instead of admiration for the ideas, was contempt — even anger — toward the unknown writers of them. And in attempting to understand this reaction, I have come to the following conclusion.

There are societies in the world in which the free commerce in written ideas is forbidden by law or by practice — societies where public discussion is difficult and where the content of newspapers, books and all other written matter is controlled absolutely by the ruling authorities.

Thus the citizens of the People's Republic of China have had to depend periodically upon wall writings for the conduct of political debate. Similarly, in Poland during martial law, the message on the walls from the people to the regime read: *The winter was yours. The spring belongs to us.*

In such circumstances, the resort to graffiti is not a question of choice but of necessity. The people are communicating with one another and with their rulers by one of the few means left to them, and the meaning of what they write has immediate and unmistakable substance. In our society, however, irrespective of its many other faults, no such obstacles to political or moral arguments are raised. Any proposition, however lofty or outrageous, can receive a full hearing.

The power of unfettered language is immense, which is, of course, why tyrannies fear it so. Whoever abases language squanders one of the principal resources of freedom — his own, mine, yours.

The Oppression Must End! Which oppression? Perpetrated by whom? What practical steps may be taken to end it? *Humanity is One.* Well and good. But what follows from that? How ought the appreciation of humanity's oneness influence the conduct of individuals and nations? These are large concepts. Men and women have committed years, whole careers, to formulating reasoned arguments and putting forward specific programs on their behalf.

Comes now some yahoo to reduce it all to a wall slogan.

That, I believe, is what so annoyed me about those spray-painted graffiti. They trivialize ideas. They devalue language. They are the work of posturing and lazy minds, gratified by gestures but too muddy or too feckless to bother with the arguments.

By contrast, the limericks and invitations on the lavatory wall are wonderfully innocent. They may offend. But they do not harm.

Sufficient Sounds

The piano exercise they are mastering now is a simple piece by Beethoven, called "Ode to Joy." The tune is aptly named, for the lilt of it sweetly fills the house during most idle minutes of the day. And though some of the chords still confound them, the music — even such imperfect music — comes as a miracle to one whose own fingers at that age were like great, numb loaves of sausage on the keys.

The instrument they play is an ancient upright, painted black. I shuddered when it came into our lives, fearing there might not be room enough under one roof for me and the hymns of discord, endlessly repeated.

That concern was unnecessary. For the capacity of a house is not absolute. Within reason, the space has a way of expanding to accommodate whatever new creature or activity is introduced. Very soon, then, as always happens, the notes of the piano had merged into the larger and indiscriminate sound of our lives together. That sound is like a tapestry, and it is composed of many threads which are detected singly only if one deliberately commands the ear to separate them out.

Just now, for example, besides the "Ode to Joy," a rhythmic thumping can be heard. I do not know how long it has been going on, since I grew used to it months ago and it seldom registers any more. It is the sound of a tennis ball striking the door of the garage. My daughter — the one not seated at the piano — is playing some solitary game outside there on a chilly afternoon.

From a different quarter of the house comes, more faintly, the whistle of the tea kettle. I know its meaning exactly. My wife intends to pour a cup and sit a few quiet moments — well, not quiet, exactly, but private ones — with the day's paper before shouldering again the millstone of our punctual hunger.

Nearer at hand there is an insistent scratching. What possibly could be making such a racket? Why, it's the dog, of course! An hour or so ago a peal of 'tween-seasons thunder sounded, and in her fatness she has gotten wedged under the bed where she fled to escape her terror of a storm that never came.

As for me, I produce a typewriter's clicking which the others, except for the stuck dog, are not close enough to hear. But even if they were, probably they would not notice it, since that is my customary background noise.

These are the threads which, taken all together — these and numberless routine sounds like them — provide the subtle announcement that the fabric is intact, that we are still, for a while longer, all together.

One recent weekend morning I found myself, shortly after waking, unaccountably depressed. There was nothing, no sadness or distress, that I could put a name to. Only a curious sense of loss and vacancy as I made ready to set out upon the day. Then I realized that something was indeed missing. Not *something*. Someone. One of the girls had spent the night at a friend's house. And in her absence, her sister, too, was sleeping late.

The stillness was deeply affecting. The lack of their sounds — the empty place where their voices and their morning rustlings should have been — left a cavity that the traffic on the street outside and the barkings of early dogs could not begin to fill. And I was struck by how much I have come to depend on the accidental noises of them about — the percussion of garage door, the splash of water in tub or sink, even the cannon fire of their occasional wars — for proof that my world is in order and the household complete.

These separations still are rare. Soon, though, they will

increase in frequency. Then become habit. Until finally, depending on geography and circumstances and the turns that lives can take, this apartness becomes more or less a permanent condition.

The black piano will fall voiceless. That is as it should be. It is the same for all creatures that raise their young, invariably to give them up. I do not rail against it, but neither would I care to hurry it. And I could not pretend, that recent silent morning, to have at all enjoyed the rehearsal.

Shameful Ups and Downs

Different things embarrass different people.

The very rich are embarrassed by the subject of money. They rarely speak about it. Some of them decline to carry it. The talk of stock options and blocks of real estate is permissible. But mere money — the grubby stuff that you and I pass back and forth between us — is unfit to enter into discreet conversation.

The English are embarrassed by eating. The public taking of nourishment fills them with an agony of humiliation. An English hotel dining room is the quietest place I know of, outside a cemetery. Care is taken that fork does not make a chinking sound against plate. No one says a word. Eyes do not meet. Food is brought to mouth with furtiveness and regret. The diners give the impression of having been caught in a shameful act.

The Germans are embarrassed by too much talk of history. The Russians by the discussion of elections. The editors of *The Washington Post*, after Janet Cooke's "Jimmy" story, by any mention of Pulitzer Prizes for fiction.

And Americans in general, as you may have noticed, are

embarrassed by riding in elevators. This oddity, as far as I know, never has been examined or explained. But the fact of it is indisputable. Notice, the next time you get on an elevator, the strange deportment of your fellow passengers.

Conversations stop. Faces become empty of expression and eyes go blank. Roughly one-half of the riders stare rigidly ahead, their gaze riveted with fascination on the inner elevator door. The rest incline their heads upward to peer, with equal absorption, at the winking lights of the floor indicator. It is not that they are afraid of getting off at the wrong stop, for the behavior is the same even in an elevator going from ground to second floor in a building of only two stories. Rather, it is as if they believe that only the power of concentration can assure the machine will operate.

American elevator riders also have an aversion to touching. In a nearly empty elevator, they press themselves tightly against the rear and side walls. If necessary, they will let a partly loaded elevator go past and wait several minutes for the next one in order to lessen the unutterable hazard of contact.

Set these idiosyncrasies alongside the conduct of people in other countries, where elevator riding is considered an adventure and an opportunity for high sport. In Spain, for example, though the posted limit of the machine may be 20 persons, it is not regarded as being fully occupied unless 35 have been gotten aboard. The doors are held forcibly open while, with communal cries of advice and encouragement, newcomers are seized by the arms and dragged into the ruck of bodies. Sometimes the cable breaks and the machine plummets to the basement. But that is a risk that has to be accepted. Spaniards set a high value on grace in the presence of great danger. In riding the elevator, as in passing the bull with a cape, the beauty is in the nearness of death.

In Rome, on the other hand, the elevator is a place for

celebrating life. Italian men are especially fond of elevators. When the door slides closed, the journey between floors is enlivened by sudden, sharp female shrieks of astonishment and reproach. In the crush, it is impossible to fix blame for these small trespasses. Anyway, to forgive is divine.

I do not know what to make of this distinctly American embarrassment about riding in elevators. Any more than I know why the rich are disgusted by talk of money. Or the English are ashamed to be seen eating.

Yesterday I put the question to several people riding with me from the first-floor change machine to the third-floor employee canteen.

"Why doesn't somebody say something?" I asked. *"No one knows we're in here but us."*

They were staring straight ahead at the doors, or up at the numbered lights, fingering their lunch sacks nervously.

"It's our little secret," I said. But it was like shouting into a cave. Not one of them answered, or even made a sign.

The Bicentenarians

It looked for all the world like one of those paths that cattle carve across a pasture, plodding in solemn file between barn trough and pond. Cattle neither improvise nor consider. Theirs is a mindless march. They will travel that same path for all their days, unless some barrier is presented to deflect them.

In time, the trail becomes a shallow groove, beaten under their hooves until the earth is as bare and smooth as bone. Seeds fall uselessly there, and nothing — not even weeds — can any longer grow. Years may pass, then. The pasture may stand empty, the cattle having long since gone off to some other farm, or gone to hamburger. But the path remains, a record of those creatures' habits and a metaphor for the rote monotony of their unexamined lives.

I came across a path like that the other day, but in an unlikely place. It was in the city's heart, where no livestock ought to be. Straight as a wire the beaten groove stretched away along the boulevard median, telling its terrible story of some creature's sad routine. But what sort of animal had made it?

I bent to examine the trail for spoor. No prints could be found. And no droppings. If no more imaginative than cattle, at least this beast was more sanitary. Crouched there, I heard the sudden near drumming of approaching hooves, and sprang aside in time for it to pass.

Blue shorts, it wore, with notches at the side. And shoes with the name of a guided missile. No shirt. A brass ornament on a chain around its neck. Sweat bands about its forehead and wrists And, on its face, an expression of the most exquisite pain. I took closer notice, and far behind that one — strung out at intervals along the dun ribbon of habit and despair — came others of the herd, both males and females of the species.

Those eventually drew near, too, and could be seen to be an ill-sorted and irregular lot: some lean, some ponderous, some nimbly prancing and others putting foot in front of foot as gingerly as Indian fakirs traversing a bed of broken glass. The look on all the faces was the same, however. Eyes glassy and a little sunken; veins throbbing; nostrils flared; dry mouths agape, like carp left too long on the bank of a stream.

It dawned on me then what they were pursuing. They were after immortality. Just as the path across the pasture speaks of a cow's need for grain and water, this path cut deep into the boulevard median told of certain people's wish to live forever. Although, so huge was their obvious agony, it was necessary to wonder if living forever would be worth the trouble.

Once the meaning of the trail had been discovered, I realized that some of the makers of it — or of trails exactly like it — live on my street. Sometimes in the blue morning, before the alarm goes off, I hear them pass. Whole families of them, the sire and the dam and even, in some instances, their young. The slap of their feet against the earth rises up to where I lie inside the crack of the bedroom window. And I feel a moment's bite of envy at the thought of them progressing ensemble — perfectly fit and not at all aged — on toward the 22nd Century.

They will see things and know marvels that I scarcely can imagine. They will live to watch their children turn 100 years old in beauty and vigor. They will watch starships come back from far galaxies and hear the astronauts tell of finding no one there. They will live to see the earth turn green again under its mantle of nuclear ash.

They will see the Middle East pumped empty of oil, and the commerce of the desert returned to camels' hair blankets and glass beads. They will see the $50 bill become the minimum denomination of exchange, like today's copper penny. If they are very, very lucky, they might even live to see an Equal Rights Amendment ratified and Social Security made solvent.

All that would be something to see, I have to admit, lying there warm under my electric blanket. But then I hear the hooves of the returning herd. Under the window they pass again. Their gait is less regular than it was. They can be heard to stumble now, and, when stumbling, sometimes to whimper softly. There is a rank moistness in the slap and jostle of their approach. The breath is torn from them in ragged sobs.

The look of those faces along the beaten path is freshly remembered. That and the nature of cattle. And purged of envy, drawing the covers closer around me, I concede immortality to those who care to pay its price.

The Arch Ladies

I do not suppose for a minute that the Caldwell eyebrow ever will take its place in literature and medical history alongside the lisps, clawed hands and hemophilia of certain of the European royal families. But it is a trait as pronounced as any of those. And for whatever small credit it may be worth, I can claim to be the first to have observed and described it.

There hangs on our bedroom wall a photograph of several women of the last century — seven sisters of the Caldwell side of my wife's family, arranged three in front and four behind for a formal portrait. At various times the picture has been stored under beds and in closets. But for the last two or three years it has been displayed, mainly, as I remember, because of the attractiveness of the carved frame.

When the photograph was made I cannot say. Although, counting back three generations, it must have been in the late 1860s or early 1870s.

The look of these seven sisters is not — how to say this delicately — either very warm or winning. I would judge them to range in age between about 16 and 27 or 28, ordinarily soft and charming years. But they all have put on somewhat frozen expressions for the occasion. Perhaps that was the convention for photos of the day. Their hair styles, too, are severe, parted in the center and caught up in a bun behind. Nor is the period dress particularly becoming — puffed shoulders, balloon sleeves, high choker collars and stiff fronts, brocaded and starched. Four of the seven display some sort of identical watch or large locket affixed high on the bosom, just inside the shoulder.

The photograph once was richly tinted. But the artist's colors have faded over these hundred years and more, especially from the faces. So the immediate effect — the costumes, the sepulchral pallor of those features so grimly set — is of a picture that might be found hanging on a study wall in some unoccupied castle in Transylvania.

The girl on the left in the front row is my wife's grandmother. And the one on the right, behind, whom I would guess to be the youngest, can be seen at a closer look to be in fact quite beautiful, very tiny and wasp-waisted, although it is reported that she became elephantine in the later years of her life.

For some months I felt an indefinable unease in the presence of that picture. There was about it something subtly disturbing — something that challenged the idle viewer. It was as if the photograph had made a statement and was waiting now, had been waiting lifetimes, for a response.

Then one day I noticed. It was a quality in the faces of the ladies. Something about their eyes. No — their eyebrows. And specifically the right eyebrow. Either in fact or by some accident of shadow it appeared markedly more prominent than the left one. What's more — and this was no trick of light — that right brow was sharply arched.

Of the seven girls in the picture, six exhibited the characteristic quite strikingly, the seventh not at all. It was as though their brows had been drawn up and affixed with tape. To the affected ones it gave an oddly quizzical expression, a look of penetrating disdain. Or was it something else and worse?

In any event, this seemed to have been a common feature among the antique ladies of that line. One could imagine generations of Caldwell women scuttling through the gorse of the Scottish highlands and, later, along the first rude lanes of the New England colonies, the right brows of all of them asking the same silent question of the world.

Then I put it out of mind.

Until, several weeks later, I happened off-handedly to glance at another picture on that wall, this one a photo of my wife. The realization struck me like a fist, and what was amazing was that I had not noticed sooner. She had the Caldwell eyebrow. Quickly I got out the scrapbooks and searched through them for pictures of our younger daughter, the one who most favors her mother. I examined six years of school photographs. And is it necessary to tell you? Of course the feature was there.

My understanding of genetics is slight. But I seem to have read somewhere that the heritable tendencies a parent transmits to his child are not susceptible to compromise. That is, the genes pass intact — then manifest their results or not, depending on their dominance and the characteristics the other parent happens to bring to the union.

The Caldwell eyebrow, it appears, is carried by a very powerful gene. It does not cause the bearer to be locked away in the tower or disqualified for coronation, if coronation were the issue. But it will be loose among us until this affected branch of the Caldwell tree happens finally to wither away in barrenness. A very extensive branch it must now be, though. For there are seven sisters in that picture, and six are marked.

Coldly they stare out from behind the glass. Arch and sardonic, and wholly in control.

"Do you think he has noticed?" they are silently asking. That is the question in their eyes.

"Who can be sure?" answers my wife, from her frame beside them on the wall.

And then my daughter, from a page of the open scrapbook: *"I believe not yet."*

Oliver

The white cat, Oliver, has slipped off the edge and into his midlife crisis. I have been there, so I know what he is going through. Some of us announce the event by having nervous breakdowns. Others grow beards, or begin a sly affair. And some, like the stockbroker Paul Gauguin, give up job and family to answer the siren call of a different career.

These remedies are not available to a cat.

He has no way of knowing which of those other households along the street might greet him with a friendly hand, and which with a thrown shoe. He has grown accustomed to sleeping in upholstered chairs beside fires. He knows the exact placement of his food dish, and the sound of the can opener. It is no use to remember the odd mouse caught or bird eaten over the years. Oh, Oliver is good, all right; he is talented in these matters. But a cat on the lam has to be good *every day*. In a word, then, he is trapped.

There never is any telling exactly what triggers the midlife collapse. In women it sometimes is said to be caused by the fading of beauty's bloom. In men, by the decline of sexual vigor — although the veterinarian some years ago removed that from the list of Oliver's concerns. In his case, the crisis seems to have been provoked by the arrival in the house of yet another cat, this one a mere kitten. Several previous additions to the menagerie he has endured sullenly, but without violent display. He bears, I think, no special malice toward this small newcomer. But sheer numbers have begun to tell on him. He has finally snapped.

The personality change has been dramatic and appalling. He has become a street brawler, a common thug.

It is a Jekyll-and-Hyde existence that he leads. He does not abuse the kitten. He frowns a lot, but does not attack. And when invited to, he still curls softly in a lap and purrs as winningly as ever. But let a door stand ajar an instant and he is through it and outdoors instantly, lip curled and spoiling for a fight. Somewhere, evidently, he has located another misanthropic cat.

I don't know how the other fellow looks, but Oliver comes home a wreck. His ears, which used to be so silky-pink, are cut and punctured and crusted now. There is a patch of fur gone from his forehead and an ugly welt across his nose. He looks the way George Plimpton must have after three rounds in the ring with Archie Moore.

This has been going on for days — no, weeks — now, and still they haven't settled it. Or maybe there is nothing to settle. I can't say about that other cat, but Oliver, I believe, is fighting just because it feels good. Feels better, at any rate, than simply sitting and staring out windows, brooding on the crisis that has overtaken him in his middle years.

I tell him that he'll burn himself out.

He comes reeling home at meal time all bloody and moth-eaten. And hunkers down scowling in front of his food dish. And gives the new kitten a long, even look as if to say, *You see what's happened, don't you? You see what's become of me, all on account of you?*

Then, after eating and sulking a while, he makes his way to my lap for consolation and advice.

"The thing is," I tell him, "you've got to pace yourself. You're burning the candle at both ends and in the middle, too. Keep on this way and you'll wind up just another punched-out club fighter with funny eyes and headaches before you're eight."

Time is the great healer. One day, eventually, his rage will pass — it always does, with all of us. We accommodate to the changes in our lives and grow placid again. We shave off our beards and return to our families and ask for our old jobs back, deciding not to be painters — or, in Oliver's case, a mugger — after all.

It will happen, with patience. But for now, he lays his tattered ears back flat against his head and leaves my lap with a growl. He already is planning the next battle. He is not quite ready yet to be told about coming to terms with his own limitations and the world as it is. And I understand.

Neither, for a long time, was I.

IX

The Stirring

In legend, wolves have suckled human foundlings and reared them with their own cubs. Sailors overboard and at the edge of death have told of being supported and nudged ashore by considerate dolphins. But turtles? Surely turtles are the unlikeliest of heroes.

Not to the shipwrecked woman plucked to safety — "haggard and hysterical," as the description went — by a passing ship in the Philippines. Haggard she deserved to be — anyone would be — after having clung for life two full days to the back of a giant sea turtle. The end of the drama was witnessed by the ship's company. They threw the woman a life preserver and, according to one of them, "the moment she transferred her hold to the life ring" the great turtle slipped down and vanished in the ocean deeps.

A thing like that sets one to learning what he can about turtles. That they are long-lived we knew — but not that they are the longest-lived of all vertebrates on earth. Stupid beasts? That seems self-evident. Not so, say people who have tried to train them (for whatever purpose). Turtles, it seems, are reasonably bright. Concede, then, longevity and a certain degree of wit.

Compassion, though? One has to draw the line somewhere, and surely it is rather much to ask belief that these ancient reptiles, so little changed in any essential regard these last one hundred seventy-five million years or more, can be stirred to pity! Yet — how else . . . how else to explain why that mossy giant rose out of the South China or the Sulu Sea to bear a frail land creature on the surface of the waters?

And not for just a moment either — for more than 48 hours. Through sunrises and moonrises. Through the emptiness of nights and the blaze of noons. Imagine, if it is possible, that woman's terrible confusion of gratitude and revulsion, of terror, even perhaps of a kind of giddy exultation. Then into that strange universe came a ship, the faces of men, a flung life preserver. And the thing was gone as strangely as it arrived.

But why? Why? Why any of it? Somewhere here there's the presentiment of a primal riddle whose answer, even if it could be found, sane minds might not be able to contain. Look for that answer in your next bowl of turtle soup. Or at the jewelry counter, in the tortoise-shell ornaments made for a lady's hair.

The Oldest Maps

We have begun watching, as we drive, for turtles crossing. It is a bit early yet, but not by much — only days, perhaps; two weeks or three at most.

Why they march and where their spring journeys lead are questions of mystery. Someone must know the answers but I do not. Why especially they seem determined to cross country roads in such reckless numbers is unexplained. It may be that the places they are bound for are places that turtles have traveled to through all the springtimes of their ancient race.

A salmon raised from the egg in a hatchery and later released will one day return, out of all the sea, to the single small stream of its own wild parents' birth. Not always, but many more times than not that will happen. Possibly it is the same way with turtles. The route was established long before there were roads or automobiles or any other signs of us about. The map is written in their bones.

But all that is speculation. What is known is that, at a particular moment in the warming of every year, as if on the sounding of some signal, the march begins. The turtles come out of field and woodland and shoulder up through the grass of the road ditches, across the gravel margin and out finally onto the pavement itself — an alien terrain where none of the rules is known.

There is no information about roads in the genetic memory of turtles. And evidently they are without imagination. For if they notice a machine of terrible size and racket bearing down upon them, they do not hurry to get across or attempt clumsily to maneuver. Instead, they withdraw inside their shells — as, figuratively, other threatened creatures, including sometimes human beings, have been known to do — and wait for the danger to pass. Which is fine if the danger is a ferret or a fox, but now only spares them that final instant's vision of the tire.

I have seen drivers swerve their cars deliberately, even cross to the wrong lane of the road, for the small but savage pleasure of squashing a turtle. You know these drivers, too, although possibly not from turtle season. Their taste runs to flame decals on the sides of the car, hula dolls on springs in the rear window and vanity license plates that say *LUV* or *BOBBY RAY.*

They fly past you with a resonant *varooom!* — a blurred vision of pimples and wispy facial hair, the hula dancer shimmying in the window. The car lurches. Another turtle explodes. This is how they express *happiness.* One cannot help wondering what they do when they are feeling mean.

I wrote a small story once about a man for whom these cumulative springtime tragedies had become unbearable — who carried a shovel and bucket in his car so that he might clear away and give decent disposal to all this flindered wreckage of turtle lives. And who sometimes, at reason's outer edge, could be found standing with his shovel, the traffic whizzing past him on some road slippery with death, shouting out his crazy complaint against the feckless, unconsidered ruin for which the mashings of the turtles — and of opossums, dogs, cats, rabbits and finally even people — had come to stand.

In spirit, I was that man.

Not all the turtles make it to the road. They die in the woods, too, overtaken on their way to somewhere by fire or some other enemy in nature. But the character of what remains is vastly different and finer than what's left by a hurtling car. The olive, outer skin of the shell peels away to leave a chalk-white, empty helmet. And if you walk the woods much, sooner or later you will find one there among the leaves, likely chewed some at the edges by forest mice but still an article of beauty — wonderfully complicated in its jointing.

The turn of mind that would find joy in the exploding of a turtle is genuinely to be feared — caring, as it does, no more for the form or fine complexity of a society than for the life on the pavement ahead. What is complex cannot be understood. What cannot be understood must if possible be broken.

But eventually the vanity license plate goes to rust and the name of its owner is not spoken anymore, or even remembered. Then the next spring, as in all the springs before, something commands them and the turtles move, their numbers seemingly undiminished.

For all these millions of years, they have been doing that. And seeing it again, one is inclined sometimes to ask who has learned more about survival after all: the creatures careening mindlessly along the highway in their clever machines, or the smaller, simpler beasts met slowly crossing?

Socrates and Thee

Writers being paid as they are — mainly in disappointment and contributor's copies — I have often thought that the next most useful tool after the typewriter would be a well-developed talent for living off the land.

I do not speak here of the incidental sprig of watercress used to spice an otherwise tame salad, or the jar or two of autumn jelly refined from the squeezings of dusty blue fox grapes. No, I have in mind bellying up to the whole robust feast which we are told a benevolent Providence has prepared for us — but at which table, due to ignorance, I have never found a place laid for me.

Instruction in the subject ought to be supplied as a

mandatory adjunct to courses in literature and composition and creative writing. That would be a start, at least, toward relieving the very real moral and social problem of all those graduates who are spewed forth with their baccalaureates in English but no practical means of support, and who are soon hunger-driven into advertising, public relations, journalism and even shadier crafts.

A friend of mine who writes novels used to speak expansively about something he called Nature's Bounty. He claimed to be especially fond of the hearts of young cattail stalks, chilled and lightly salted. Then his wife took a professional degree and steady employment. And as far as I know he doesn't go into the woods much anymore — at least not to graze. He owns property, grows vegetables of the cultivated kind. His current encounters with raw survival have to do with rabbits in his green beans and grasshoppers on the zucchini. There is no point looking to him for advice.

My own wife's mother had wild cravings. On spring days in her later years, stirred perhaps by recollections from girlhood but also by an urge older than any specific memory, she would creep out to the hedge at the side of the yard and come back with an assortment of weeds in a pan. These she would simmer over a low fire until they were the color and consistency of fresh tar. And would pronounce that mess delicious, although I could not help noticing that the pan and its contents sometimes remained in the refrigerator until they had been grown over entirely by green fur.

Just what those weeds were I can't say. Somehow I was never inspired to ask.

There are books on the subject, but which of them do you trust? Take the matter of skunk cabbage — or, if you find that name unappetizing, the bastard-toadflax. A most offensive plant — stinks, contains a substance which, when eaten raw, causes the mouth to burn intensely. Has the sole virtue of being plentiful.

In one book I own, considered an early standard on wild edibles, the author tells of eating skunk cabbage boiled in several changes of water and seasoned with butter, pepper and salt and finding it, if not ambrosia, at least "pleasing." But lately a new field guide has appeared, advising that, unless one wants one's mouth set on fire, it is necessary first to dry young skunk cabbage leaves, then reconstitute them in soups or stews. *"Boiling,"* the book explicitly warns, *"does not remove this (painful) property — only thorough drying."*

So I am finished with bastard-toadflax before I even began.

Still, the idea of foraging remains attractive in principle. And only the other morning, putting books and amateur counsel aside, I arranged to further my education in the company of an expert. This new-found friend, who happens also to be a writer, has been eating wild plants for the best part of 95 years. If he has suffered from it, it can't be told from the quickness of his intellect or the sturdiness of his gait. You will never know a man more at home in the woods. He used to keep a lawn in which dandelions were welcome. ("I didn't eat very many of them — but then they didn't bother me much, either.") Now he lives at a retirement center on the edge of the city, so we drove a short way to a piece of hospitable woodland he knew of. He was speaking, as we left the car, of a particular fungus that can be found on the sides of logs.

"Smells like a pineapple," he was saying. "Just as juicy and nice as anything you'd want. Tastes wonderful!" I made hasty notes, meaning to be alert for one of those as we walked. "The only problem," he added, somewhat sadly, "is it *won't stay down."*

His eye missed nothing. The tip of his walking stick explored gently through the undergrowth. "You know the May apple, I'm sure. Fruit's good, but the root is a very powerful *cathartic."* Or, later, "Yes, that's a Red Haw. Are the berries edible? Oh, sure! As far as I know there's only one *poisonous* Red Haw."

You will perhaps understand why, as we pressed deeper along that woodland path, my note-taking grew less purposeful. One morning's walk would not suffice to clarify the menu. Nature's banquet includes too many surprises and ambiguities.

My hand, as we rested, had come to fall idly on some foliage beside the path.

"What do you have there?" my friend said, bending to see. "Oh, that's a good one — wild parsnip. I don't know whether its root is edible, though I think so. The trouble is . . ."

The inevitable qualifier. My hand already had begun recoiling involuntarily.

"*. . . it looks just a whole lot like the plant Socrates died of.*"

And with that my notebook's entries appear to have ended altogether.

A Thinking Man's Bird

People acquainted with my defect have asked how the turkey season went. I have not been asked about this a lot, you understand — the interest in turkeys being rather less universal than the abhorrence of hunting. But, yes, there has been an inquiry or two.

In fatigue and futility, that's how the season went.

We matched wits, the bird and I. Now, with my average-size brain of 1,400 cubic centimeters or maybe a bit less, I am back home, sleeping in my own bed. And the turkey, with his brain the size of an aspirin, is still out there uninjured in the woods.

Some naturalist with a nitpicking passion for detail will crawl out of the woodwork, complaining to the ombudsman of the newspaper that the turkey's brain is not the size of an aspirin. It is the size of a walnut. Corrections will appear in all editions. That is always the way of it. Turkeys ahead of writers every time.

But has the naturalist ever personally autopsied one, or is he taking somebody's word for it? I say the bird's brain is the size of an aspirin, or maybe an Extra-Strength Tylenol. If I ever get close to a turkey, I have something else in mind than whipping out calipers to measure its cranium.

That is for a future spring, however. Just now I am recovering from the ordeal of this one.

This morning I came awake in a panic in the dark bedroom with a sense of having tragically overslept. I turned on the light and peered at the clock — which said 4:30 a.m. The season was over, but habit is a relentless master. And that is the dominant aspect of the hunt. The hunter is not allowed to rest.

The turkey has all the best of it. He goes to his roost when the sun declines, nods off immediately and sleeps 10 hours at a minimum, perfectly unruffled there on his branch, his dreams disturbed by nothing except an occasional happy recollection that tomorrow will be another day of the breeding season.

Meantime, the hunter is hunkered exhausted in some cabin or tent, oiling his weapons, practicing his calling technique and drinking stimulants to keep him awake while he discusses with his fellow assassins the strategy they will employ when — before they have gotten comfortable in their bedrolls — the trumpeting of the alarm sends them forth to battle again. Several days of this and the body begins to waste, the hunter's razor senses are blunted. The advantage shifts increasingly to the side of the turkey, who greets each dawn perfectly refreshed and full of enthusiasm for his morning's duties.

The single mercy is that the season lasts only two weeks. By the end of it, the hunter, stumbling out of the nettles, mud-caked to the knees, eyes staring glassily from a face smeared with a fortnight's layers of camouflage grease, is alarming to see. The flame of hope has burned low. His legs do not carry him straight forward any more. The thought of a whole night between sheets fills him with ungovernable emotion. He has forgotten why he went to the woods.

That's the condition in which I returned home, reeling from car to house and fumbling with my key at the lock.

"Where is he?" my wife said.

"Where's who?" I let fall my burden of guns, duffel, laundry, crusted boots and the other detritus of my happy days away, but managed to keep my feet. That heap of things did not include a turkey.

"I thought you told me his brain was —"

"That's right," I mumbled. *"The size of an aspirin."*

Tired as I was, I could not help noticing that she was looking at me in a clinical way. And that what appeared to interest her was the distance between my ears.

The Truth-Givers

Primitive cultures transmitted the slender body of known facts about their world from one generation to the next verbally, in the form of myths and folk tales. Now we have libraries and computer memory banks and instructional television and great universities. And in spite of all this, our methods for informing the young really have progressed very little.

We still are the oral teachers of those who follow us, and it is truly remarkable that even a few of them manage to grow up with any sensible understanding of the planet on which they live. The event that brought this to mind was a nature walk the other

Saturday in a suburban park with a troop of Junior Girl Scouts —
a dozen little girls in credulous pursuit of some badge or other.

I went along meaning to be no more than a protective
presence on the fringes of the expedition. Instead, I found
myself pressed — *dragged* is the better word for it — into the role
of the shaman, the Truth-Giver, the Teller of Ancient Facts. It is a
role I have not sought and for which I am unequipped, as
became obvious the moment we embarked down a wooded trail,
my small proteges trailing attentively behind, waiting for the
book of nature's mysteries to be opened to them.

The subject was supposed to be the seasons — in this case the
spring.

I sifted frantically through the shallow midden of my
memory for information about spring, and found little there.
Something happens with the sap of the trees. Leaves unfold. It
turns warmer The days lengthen and mosquitoes appear.
Colorado ski reports stop being published in the newspaper.
That was the sum of it — pathetic scraps of knowledge you would
expect a child to bring home from preschool, at the latest. In
desperation, then, I elected to discourse upon nature in a more
general way.

A large white rock presented itself.

Do you see this? the Truth-Giver inquired. *You may not know
what kind of rock this is.*

"It's a sedimentary rock," came an instant reply.

*Yes, as a matter of fact. It's limestone. It is made of the shells of
thousands and thousands of tiny sea creatures.*

"You mean" — (one of the others) — "that this all used to be
covered by the ocean? How long ago was that?"

A very long time ago.

"Could it happen again? How soon will it be?"

*Actually, I don't know. That is — I suppose it could. But not
right away, I shouldn't think.*

Then the first one again, the precocious one: "Sedimentary rock is one kind. And igneous is the second, but I forget the third kind. What's the third kind of rock?"

"Let's get out of here!" said the one who was concerned about the ocean.

And we passed on, mercifully, to a bush. *Perhaps, said the Truth-Giver, you do not know how plants travel.*

"By their seeds. Some blow in the wind."

"And some stick to your clothes."

Yes, certainly. But how else? A respectful silence. That one stymied them. *Do you see these purple berries? Well, they taste good to animals. So the animals eat them and travel around.*

The Truth-Giver crushed a berry to reveal the seed in its purple ooze.

Then they pass the seeds.

"Pass them?"

Right. In their droppings.

The group, in unison, made a nasty sound with lips and tongues.

But the Truth-Giver pressed onward, flinging out whatever came to hand from his bag of myths. *This tree bears bumpy green balls called hedge apples. If you put one in your basement it will keep bugs out of the house. And here's an insect's egg case.* (Discovering, too late, that it was only some sort of woody deformation on the surface of the leaf.) *Anyway, see this moss? It always grows on the north side of the tree. Which means that this other trail will undoubtedly lead us back to . . . "*

We emerged from the forest into the parking lot of a subdivision. The lot was in the process of being enlarged.

That's called a bulldozer, said the Truth-Giver, recovering nimbly. *Seldom encountered in nature.*

They were, in fact, momentarily lost.

Remember, now. We started out along a stream, didn't we? And

they agreed. *So if we just make sure to walk downhill . . .*
"Look, that's the side of the tree the moss is on."
"Yuk! Here's a last-year's hedge apple all covered with bugs!"
. . . it is certain to be the right way home. Now isn't it?
And it was. The stream was where it was supposed to be. The Junior Girl Scouts raced ahead toward the cars, their heads no doubt whirling with all of that new, if not terribly useful, knowledge.

But driving back to the city, I got to reconsidering. And I realized then what sort of world I had presented to them. A world as Franz Kafka might have described it. A nightmare terrain, prowled by animals that left purple droppings from which bushes grew, in which it was advisable to hasten downhill, always headed north, in order to get home before the sea came rushing back again to cover the land.

They have qualified for their badges. But it will take gifted teachers the next 10 years or more to clarify their minds.

So I understand better how it was that primitive folk came to believe, on the word of their elders and shamans, that the earth was round, that toads did not give warts, that the moon was not the sun's paler sister and that tomatoes could safely be eaten.

We have our universities and computers today. But much of that same nonsense still is spoken by those of us who are supposed to know.

Fashion of the Village

It is fashion's ambition to rule us. We learn very early the conforming power of the group and the penalty for defiance. And later those are lessons which are hard — for some, impossible — to forget.

This sad truth was illustrated the other evening by a manic scramble to satisfy a school dress code for the following day. The code was not established by the teacher or the school authorities. It was an invention of the children themselves. It seemed they had agreed to uniform themselves in a special way: two-toned athletic jerseys, with a class slogan in letters on the front and the wearer's name on the back. Practically none of them had such shirts, but they could be obtained — at a price — and the place of their availability was made generally known.

I uttered resisting noises. It was an extravagance without any point. Just hunting the damned thing down and getting the required legend on it would be an imposition, likely to occupy the best part of the night.

How many in the class already possessed shirts like that? I demanded to know.

"A few," my daughter said. "Maybe three or four."

And how many planned to appear in them on the morrow?

"All of them," she said, with perfect certainty. True or not, it's what she expected would happen.

I remembered, then, how cruel that age can be to children passing through it. The failure to conform is a sin most fiercely punished. That is the process by which the group demonstrates its sovereign role. In the natural world of which we are a part — in the world of insects, say — mimicry has several uses, one being the avoidance of predators. The chief predators of children are their contemporaries.

To wear shoes of the wrong style or to turn up the bottoms of jeans in one-inch rolls when the fashion is three-inch is to invite ridicule of such savagery as to cause one to pass through the remaining 60 years or so of one's life thinking oneself a klutz.

That is the power the group holds. The terror of klutzdom is profound and lasting. It is sufficient to have sent generations of men away to the office wearing knotted around their throats an ornament, the necktie, which, besides being uncomfortable and restricting circulation to the brain, has no imaginable use and for which there is in fact no explanation at all, except the group's decree that it should be displayed.

I once had a friend who came from a village on an island in one of the great lakes of East Africa. Through some combination of luck and desire, he had made his way to America to be educated. Up to that time, he told me, he was the first boy of his village to grow to manhood without having his teeth filed to points. That, too, was a matter of luck. If he'd stayed at home a year or two longer, no doubt his smile would have been as alarming as his fellow villagers'.

He didn't stay, though. He came abroad and discovered the pleasures of eating apples and corn on the cob and other items for which regular dentition serves better than sharp pegs. He passed from adolescence to adulthood in this country and had gotten not only his college diploma but a master's degree and possibly a doctorate as well. He knew a lot. Among other things, he knew that he was finished for good with living where people filed their teeth to points.

I hope that, my daughters, too, will one day have the good sense — especially in the more important questions of a life — to perceive the stupidity of the group and its fashions, and to stand against those when they are mean or self-destructive.

But that is for the future. On the issue at hand, the crisis of the shirt, I shamelessly gave ground. The clerk at the store was dazed and irritable, having already affixed slogans and names to 18 shirts before ours during what she had expected would be a slow evening behind the counter.

My daughter went off to school that next day radiant with confidence. She was happy. The group was happy. I still was not especially happy, but that was beside the point.

All right, I asked her afterward, *how many didn't have shirts?*

"How many?" she said, surprised. "Why, we all had them." Score one for neckties and filed teeth. But the game is long, and not quite finished yet.

Custom of the Tribe

The Metal-Faced Ones come out singly and in pairs and groups from the school door to the car, and when they smile their spun-steel smiles the glare is blinding. My older daughter has joined the Metal-Faced Ones. Her sister, younger by a year, will follow presently.

This pleased them hugely. The wiring of their mouths is not merely a sign of social arrival. Current wisdom holds it to be indispensable to a normal girlhood, like fluids and nourishment and pierced ear lobes and the mastery of French.

Beyond doubt, society's standards of beauty have grown more exacting. When I was young, and all of us were less lovely, braces were for the remedy of gross deformities. Children whose teeth protruded so radically as to frighten dogs or be a hazard on a crowded bus were carted off to the orthodontist. Anyone able, with whatever difficulty, to whistle or eat an apple was spared.

How to account for the intensity of the present interest in dental correction? Is the national jaw deteriorating? Have dentistry's advances made possible the detection of problems earlier overlooked? Could it be that, as a group, orthodontists have cultivated more lavish tastes in foreign travel? Or that, there simply being more of them in practice now than formerly, it has become necessary, as a matter of practical economy to diagnose more alarming overbites?

Never mind the reason; the pressures have grown very strong. Whereas, when looking upon my daughters' faces, I have seen only surpassing charm, keener eyes evidently have observed shocking disfigurement. And as the number of Metal-Faced Ones has grown, teeth without wires have become the stigmata of cruel disadvantage.

So the appointment was duly made and the apparatus installed.

They hurt, braces do — at least for a while. But like the pain that immediately precedes sainthood, it is exquisite to endure. The newly beatified are immediately identifiable, mouths swollen and misshapen, cracked lips working and writhing over the wires. The Metal-Faced Ones receive supplies of wax, which may be packed over the teeth to lessen the abrasion. Globules of the wax fall to the floor, stick to the shoes, are trodden into the carpets.

When the lips are drawn back to expose that waxy oval in simulation of a smile, the effect is ghastly. There is only one other place I know where you see smiles like those. It is in the interior of the Cameroons, among a people who subsist their whole lives eating a gray paste called fufu and who have not yet received word of the invention of the toothbrush.

My daughter came home from her first appointment and I knew she was my daughter. I recognized her clothes. Now, in a surprisingly short time, I have forgotten how she used to look; have come to feel a certain affection for her new face; have learned to kiss with caution, lest she or I be cut; have grown used to the chinking and chiming of metal when she speaks. One day, months from now or years, all that iron will fall away and she will again be transformed. She may smile a stranger's smile, but it will be a smile of such perfection as to give young boys a sudden weakness in the knees.

Meantime, the orthodontist will travel well and widely. And my interests also will be served.

For her braces advertise me — along with other fathers of the Metal-Faced Ones — as someone to be reckoned with, to be taken seriously. Men of other cultures festoon their women with strands of cowrie shells or gold bangles, or put rubies in their noses. The whole sum of their worldly means may be exhibited so. Then, when they are seen to pass, others will say, *There is a man of substance.*

That is the aboriginal purpose of such displays, and people are the same the world over. It just happens to have become custom among men of my tribe to put their fortunes in their daughters' mouths.

The Burying Tree

Bur oak (Quercus macrocarpa) — a giant of its species.

Three hundred and more autumns ago an acorn fell from some parent tree whose majesty can only be guessed. And in the spring that followed, the acorn burst, sent up a switch. That may have been the very season the explorers Marquette and Jolliet came probing down the unmapped Mississippi. How else to say how long ago it was?

Louis XIV held forth in splendor at Versailles. In India, the stonemasons had just put down their chisels from building the

Taj Mahal. In Africa, Dutch traders had established an uneasy toehold on the Cape Peninsula and the first settlers had begun arriving there, but it would be another two hundred years before David Livingstone would perish in the interior in his search for the source of the Nile.

The acorn's switch became a sapling, which grew in time into a landmark for the convoys of settler wagons and the armies that later raged across the hills to decide the issue of union.

The land changed. A nation and its purposes changed, but not the tree. Much more than two centuries had passed when the first man came to build his house under the giant oak and keep his family in its shade. The man's name was Guy Middleton and he was my grandfather.

How else to say how long?

When I was very young (and he not too much older than I am now) it never occurred to me to ask his feelings about the tree. And then I grew beyond the age of speaking about such things, and so the chance was lost. But I will tell you a couple of memories. The first is of all our buryings among its roots.

After spring windstorms, birds were sometimes found killed by their fall from the nest. Or sometimes gravely hurt, to be nursed futilely a day or two. Or we might happen across a field mouse freshly dead, a mole pierced by the tines of the trap or a young rabbit struck by the plow. All these creatures we laid solemnly to rest — my cousins and I, and little friends from that country neighborhood — close against the base of the oak tree. Most everyone, of course, remembers such a burying tree from childhood. It's where we began our acquaintanceship with grief.

My other memory is of the family's in-gatherings on the Fourth of July. In the dusk after supper, while lightning bugs winked and hawk moths drank at the flower garden, we would be made to sit safely in the chalky-white wooden lawn chairs. And the men, at discreet distance, would set off the fountains and

Roman candles and other pyrotechnics which, in those late Depression years, must have been painfully bought. Finally the children would be allowed to bend sparkler wires into hooks and throw them up to lodge, showering light, in the lower branches of the oak. Nothing as small as those could harm so great a tree.

Most of those parents are gone now, and we children are far gone in age. I see a perfect image of my cousin, Barbara, at age 7 or 8, turning cartwheels in a white dress in the sparkler light. Her son was married just the other day. That's how suddenly it happens.

The Middletons lived there 35 years, then another family for 30. And I am told that family's children also nourished the old tree with their buryings and bereavements. Eventually a small subdivision came pressing close, and the shade of the oak fell on four houses instead of only one.

New people occupy the place now, and they have accepted good-naturedly the burden of being the custodians of so many strangers' memories. So when I heard the other day that a storm had taken the great tree I felt free to drive out uninvited to view the wreckage. The man was at his work, but his wife came out where I was standing and remembering. She is a straight, girlish sort of woman, and her daughter was with her — going on 12, no less straight or clear-eyed, certain to be as pretty as her mother. The daughter has a gerbil planted among the roots.

They had just spent money to try to keep the tree safe. Some years ago a central crack had opened, widening with each winter's freezes. The tree surgeon had tried with cables to draw it back together. But only days later the freak wind had come, breaking those cables like threads. It fell unheard, she said. Her husband had looked through the window during the storm's thrashing and announced simply, "It's gone."

After all those generations of friendship, however, it even had come down benignly — falling *against the wind* into the only space where it would cause no damage. Engineers with slide rules and winches could not have done it more exactly.

The lower trunk still stood. One day, she said, they hoped to square off its top and build a playhouse there. The idea was a consolation. In any case, the project would have to wait. For the daughter had discovered in one hollow snag a bird's nest that had survived the storm. It could not be molested until the young were fledged.

We joined hands, then — the mother, daughter and I — to see if together we could reach around, our faces pressing sideways against the rough bark as we stretched. But its girth, 15 1/2 feet, was much too great. The nearest hand could not even be seen, let alone touched.

Another generation of us was needed. And surely the great stump will be waiting, with all its years, when that generation comes. As quickly as time's river runs, it won't be long.

In Transit

Hotel porters stir awake. Hotel cashier waits sleepy in his cage. On floors above, all the suitcases snap shut at once. Elevators descend and taxicabs appear, then speed away, the fleet of them, to the common destination.

At the airport counter the men stand in line unspeaking — just show their tickets or wordlessly present their plastic, then give their bags, then stumble away down a corridor, briefcases in one hand, folded leather suit bags in the other.

In the terminal window, low above the tarmac and the parked planes, a suggestion of a sun appears, swollen pink as seen through prosperity's pollution. In the right window is the white disc of the unset moon.

The flight is called. One hundred twenty-four seats. Twenty-three riders. Numbed by the hour, all take their places, arranged at careful distances apart. No word passes. No sign of recognition, though all will be borne in risk together to the same city half an hour removed.

The machine shudders and whines. And in a rush they are levitated through the miasma, up through a pallid dawn that makes no warmth and gives no light through the windows. For illumination, there is the console above. Twenty-three arms go up to activate the switch. Twenty-three monogrammed leather briefcases make a chorus of declaratory clicks. Glazed eyes stare down at yellow-lined pads, groping for the sense of words scrawled there yesterday during the trajectories of different planes.

Breakfast is offered and refused. They all have eaten. Or misremember that they have. Or else have given up eating altogether in these hateful hours of their obligatory rising.

The vessel that carries them slows and labors down. The yellow pads, all scribbled over with mighty thoughts and powerful secrets, are put away. Seatback tray tables are returned to their original upright positions. Briefly, now — how long, three minutes, five? — the traveling men allow their eyes to close. Unsleeping, they imagine sleep. Then they are cast out of there, carrying their briefcases importantly, like men with satchel bombs, into the foulness of another thriving place.

Momentarily, they consider that the smoke in the air might be the product of the burning of themselves and of their years. Then taxicabs appear. And all these men are delivered away to someplace, inspecting their envelopes of airline tickets as they ride, to be certain tomorrow's flight is in order. The moon overhead still is brighter than the scarcely risen sun.

It is, they tell themselves, a life.

Or is it? some different voice, some voice outside themselves, inquires.

Always, for longer than they can remember, that has been the first conversation of the day.

Still in Transit

We are projected ahead into the sunrise atop six suitcases, a dozen indiscriminate boxes wrapped in brown paper, a crate of Rocky Ford cantaloupes and a metal cannister of frozen Beefalo semen.

Six, we are — seven including the driver. God knows how many more, if you count the sleeping sperm.

The driver has taken off his hat and settled to his work. The road unrolls to Memphis and points between. Aboard this ship of passage there is no seatback literature discussing the nomenclature of the machine in which we ride, or telling us what we must do if there is a sudden loss of cabin pressure or if we should all plunge together into some great water.

It is just a bus, of about the kind most buses tend to be. And we are safe in the knowledge that, if the pilot were stricken, any one of us could bring the craft safely in. Not all the way in to Memphis, maybe, but to some level place at roadside where crickets chirp among the thistles.

There are no babies aboard our coach. All of us are craning our necks over the seats, looking for the inevitable baby. But there isn't one. A bus ride is somehow deficient without the complaint of a baby, ceaseless and near at hand.

Once, years ago, I rode a bus across the country from New York beside a girl with a baby. The coach, like this one, was nearly empty. But she claimed the seat beside me. She was 19 or possibly 20 years old — long on babies but short on luck or money or husbands or anything else. She was tired, and needed something to do with the child. So she nursed the baby and then gave it to me to hold, who had never in conscious knowledge ever held one of the things before. And then she went to sleep.

She slept, if I remember right, from New Jersey to somewhere in the middle of Ohio. Slept very peacefully, with the side of her face against the window glass, while her offspring emitted ear-splitting howls from a face swollen red with fury and desolation. I did everything for that baby except suckle it myself. People kept looking over the seatbacks at me holding my noisy burden, and thinking to themselves, *"Jeez, guys like that really ought to be sterilized!"*

Dew sparkles on the long grass of the road shoulder. In the valleys, fog pools like smoke. The road unrolls and the country modulates but does not change. Cattle standing all with their backs to the new sun. A beekeeper's hives stacked in a meadow corner. Wading herons, mirrored by a glassy pond. Old houses painted white.

The riders are eating their breakfasts out of paper bags. They carry no briefcases, no sample kits. No urgent business calls them. The only errands they are on are the small, tender errands of their lives. Besides the six suitcases in the hold below, three more are on the overhead rack. And one of those is tied shut with twine.

The people finish eating and wad up their sacks and turn their faces sideways in sleep. Not, though, the driver, whose sunglasses are as large as saucers and whose head is held alertly and straight forward toward Memphis.

Could that have been a small cry I just heard?

And was that not another?

A young woman comes back along the aisle toward the

convenience at the rear. And, yes, she is carrying a baby. There
was one aboard after all, stowed away among us in the early dark.
I watch sidelong as the girl passes, careful that our eyes should
not meet. And I think I have seen her before, a long time ago.
On a bus somewhere in the East.

The coach hurtles on down the unrolling road. Inside, all is
stillness. The others all are asleep. I hear the snap of the door to
the convenience unlatching. And I sleep, too — or pretend to —
breathing deeply, mouth slightly agape. I hear her footsteps go
away up the aisle. This time she has passed without handing me
the baby.

The Loyal Tim

My name is Ozymandias,
king of kings;
Look on my works, ye Mighty,
and despair!
— Percy Bysshe Shelley

In my next incarnation, if it can be arranged, I will live in a
stone house behind a stone wall crept over by ivy and wear a satin
lounging coat and have a gardener.

The gardener will garden and I, in my coat, will lounge.
Within the wall, all will lie in perfect order. Wherever the eye falls
it will find discipline and, of course, great beauty. I don't mean to
say my garden will be excessively formal. But it will be rational
and deliberate. Nothing will grow there by accident.

We will pass our easy days there, my diligent gardener and I.
To him it will give usefulness and pride. To me, pure lazy

pleasure. It will be a small paradise into which outsiders will, from time to time, be privileged to come for visits.

Some people, as you may know, live that way already. I saw an advertisement in the paper the other day, placed by such a man, looking for such a gardener. The advertisement spoke of exotic trees and flowering shrubs. Scientific knowledge was required. References would be demanded. An extensive library of horticultural books was available for browsing during off-duty hours.

That's how I mean for it to be the next time around. But in this present life it is a different story. There hardly is any point in my placing an ad. What would there be to say?

Bindweed taking everything. Limbs from diseased elms a danger. Rampant honeysuckle prying at the boards of the house. Dandelions and chickweed warring on a terrain of beaten clay. Bushes of unknown variety advancing toward the porch. Roses blighted. Fissures opening in the earth. No sun at all. Help! Come soon! Wear protective clothing.

It is possible some gardener, thinking that a joke, would come to survey the job. And looking from the window of his car — getting no nearer than that — would cry out *"Faugh!"* and quickly drive away.

(Even while writing this, I have seen the man in the house behind interrupt some yard work of his own to peer across the fence into the fantastic rot and tangle of my grounds with an expression of fascination and naked disgust. He has never spoken to me about it. But he is there now, just his eyes and the top of his head visible over the bushes.)

In the spring of the year, when there are baseball gloves to be bought and other seasonal needs for money, boys of the neighborhood often appear looking for work. After they have been shown what lies in back of the house, some of them, too, have said *"Faugh!"* and not been seen again.

This year, though, there has come to me a lad who seems made of fiercer stuff. Tim is his name, and he lives on the next street. He is not the gardener I would engage for the next life's paradise behind the wall. He is small as a cricket and very slight, but he has staying power and raw courage and he works at a price I can afford.

We have been into the terrible jungle together several times now, this Tim and I, and have seen things there that neither of us much cared to speak about afterward. We have hacked and grubbed and driven back the threatening wall of greenery a little. We have dragged out of it and bagged and bundled matted stuff that trash collectors have refused on principle to handle or cart away.

It is the hottest, scratchiest, most unpleasant sort of work, to which there is no end in sight. And yet Tim keeps coming back, working it in between school and soccer practice — always cheerful, always optimistic, flinging himself at the dark edge of the wilderness. There is no quitter in him.

Just yesterday he arrived through the gate which, freed of vines, swings freely now, and announced, in a proprietary kind of way, "It's looking fantastic!" He must have noticed my jaw go slack. And being raised in a decent house, with respect for truth, he quickly amended that.

"Anyway," he said, "it looks a whole lot better." And possibly that is so. It's hard to say.

One day, no doubt, a voiceless wind will blow across this piece of ground, empty of house, empty of life, empty of all except the bushes and bindweed creeping out to cover everything with their unnatural vigor. What sort of yard I kept will no more matter then than the vanished wonders of a forgotten king on some stretch of desolate sand.

But in the meantime, Tim's fine enthusiasm drives me on.

Perspective

We want importance, all of us. But importance is a matter of setting and the moment.

Just now two wrens have come to occupy the balcony of the house where we are guests. It is an early hour. The first sun has just surmounted a far treeline to the left, the trees blue with morning. Directly to the front lies an expanse of cultivated land and, at the distant end of that — what, three miles, five? — is another margin of trees, nearly lost in fog the dawn has not yet burnt away.

All the others staying here are still asleep. The hour belongs to the wrens and me.

I am sitting in a chair just inside the sliding door that opens onto the balcony. But, while I am fully in view, the small birds do not appear to notice. Or, if they notice, are not alarmed. They weigh perhaps an ounce apiece, those wrens. Which means that I am something more than two thousand times their mass — or very large indeed. And am, in spite of that, unnoticed.

As compared to me, the house is very large. Beyond the house lie the vastly greater fields. And beyond those fields, a continent, a world. And then a universe. And beyond the universe, who's to say? On such a scale as that, the absurdity of wrens imagining themselves important surely is clear.

But wrens, unlike most of us, aren't given to somber considering. They do not, like us, calculate their place in the order of things — their smallness against the wrapping immensity.

If we were to leave the house, such a silence would come in after us as to make it unimaginable we ever had been here. If we were to walk out across that reach of field — not even to the far trees, just a fraction of the way there — we could not be noticed any more. And this is not even to speak of our place in the greater world. Or in the great clockwork of larger, fiercer worlds all spinning together through time and darkness on courses undiscerned.

Importance? The notion of being somehow important — of even being so much as worth a passing footnote . . . Why, surely that's a joke! And once that thought occurs to us, which may begin to happen sometime past the middle years, hope is apt to go cold in us. And the song dies in our throats.

We consider too much. We are rational to a fault. We appraise the dimensions of ourselves and find, in those calculations, much reason for despair.

Not so these wrens. They have come, the pair of them — an ounce or so each, two ounces of life in the aggregate — and with the day's first sun striking warm on their fawn backs, they have entirely taken over for their own the balcony of the house, beside this field, fronting on the greater distances of this planet. One of them has found a perch on the back of a chair. The other prefers the hood of the charcoal cooker. Bobbing and bowing formally to one another, they have passed several quiet minutes preening and fluffing away the memory of night.

Generations of their young may fall doomed from the nest. Winds may break them. They may be bound finally for the mouth of a fox. The end will not be kind. That much is fact.

But they know one song. And not caring much who listens, they sing it boldly. And in this still moment, this setting, for all their cosmic unimportance, they fill the world.

X

Summertide

A disquieting episode it was that Tass, the Soviet press agency, reported from the Kamchatka peninsula in far eastern Siberia. It seems that hares — thousands of them, whole phalanxes and legions of them in teeming formation — streamed out of the tundra and across the countryside in a singleminded passage to the sea.

Ordinarily among the timidest of creatures, the hares trooped in silent, fearless waves through the streets of Siberian settlements, mindless of the frenzied yapping of dogs. What prompted the bizarre expedition? Unlike the migrant lemmings of Scandinavia, theirs was no errand of mass self-destruction. No, it was food they sought — they were starving. Upon reaching the water's edge, according to the Tass account, the hares fell greedily to eating heaps of cabbage-like seaweed washed ashore by the tide. Then, having fed, they marched back together the way they had come and vanished again in the tundra.

There is terror in this little occurrence, for anyone who cares to consider it. For it only illustrates what becomes of a species — any species — whose numbers outstrip the food supply of its accustomed range. How pertinent the message for a world in which millions of human beings cry out with hunger in the night, whose population at the present rate will double in a mere five decades.

Suppose that another such mysterious trek of the Siberian hares were to occur a few years hence. Would the villagers again stand transfixed, watching the remarkable migration? Or would they be obliged to fall upon the hapless creatures with clubs and sickles, frantic to fill their own shrunken stomachs?

Suppose again that there should be still another, final march a century from now. It is not impossible to imagine that the hares might come out of the wasteland, the cool wind rippling the fur on their gaunt bodies, and pass down through strangely silent villages where no dogs barked and no eye marked their passage. And, coming finally to the ocean, might find only a doomsday emptiness of sand with all the seaweed eaten — mankind having been there first.

Fools and Foxes

S he lives alone in a house in a wooded valley, hemmed about by the relentless encroachments of the city — an island of wildness, a still and untrammeled place that is threatened as much by men's attitudes as by their actual works. She is an artist, a gifted and sensitive woman. Her house is shaded by old trees. Flowering foliage presses close around, some of it planted, most natural.

The house, its setting, express her and also nourish her.

I have said she lives alone, but that is not exactly so. Other creatures share her bit of woods and some of them, the foxes and opossums, she feeds. Probably she feeds the birds and squirrels as well, but it's the others she speaks of. Feeds them bagels gotten from the market. Or, lacking bagels, sometimes bakes them popovers.

Her father used to live in his own house a short distance down a path from hers in the woods. He began the practice and continued it for many years. And, though the father is gone now, she carries it on. Each day she leaves her bagels in the usual place, down near the stream. Each following morning they are gone.

The opossum has struck me as a fairly common sort of beast, with some mildly interesting characteristics but nothing that is apt to inspire lyricism. This friend says that, with acquaintance, they come to have a certain charm and individuality, and I will have to take her word for that. The red fox is another matter. If ever you have been lucky enough to see one near at hand in the wild, the moment will be with you always. I have had several such encounters, and each of those is as clear as yesterday.

Once, as I was scuffing along through the leaf litter of an old logging road, a fox stepped out boldly from the edge not many yards ahead and sat down directly facing me, in a patch of sunlight through the trees that struck his coat to flame. And curled his tail around his feet and examined me, perfectly doglike and unperturbed for several moments. Then, with great composure, got up and walked back unhurried the way he'd come.

Another time, one warm afternoon of late spring, my father and I were crossing an abandoned farm field of rank grass and nearly stepped on a fox. He had been basking there, asleep — putting to lie the legend about his cunning. He bounded up with a yip, so close we might have touched him if we'd been quick enough. The look of amazement and humiliation on that fox's face was comical to see.

The finest meeting, though, was on a summer morning in the high Rockies.

I'd been fishing for stream trout and, as the sun began to warm, climbed the bank of the little brook and started to step out through the fringe of bordering aspen when I saw the foxes playing in the mountain meadow very close by. There were four — two adults and their pair of young who then, in August, were nearly grown. They played as any family might, tumbling and bounding and good-naturedly boxing, entirely occupied with one another, full of the perishable joy of the summer not quite yet ended, the winter not yet quite come.

For a long time I watched them, a quarter-hour at least. And it was as fine as anything I have ever seen in nature.

Our friend, the artist, called the other day with a piece of unhappy news. Although on rare occasions over the years she has seen more, a single pair of foxes has been the likely stable population in her woods. The valley runs up beyond her property line to another house, in which new neighbors recently have come to live.

She'd had a brief conversation with the woman of that house.

"We got one of the foxes," the woman said cheerfully. Meaning by that they had managed to kill it.

Our friend was struck speechless, unable to reply.

With luck, the woman added, they'd soon get the other one. Then there'd be no more danger to her dog from foxes. Now, the dog is of a short, stout kind, meant for herding farm animals. A likable breed, I'm sure, though my taste has never run to them. Why it ever would occur to a seven-pound red fox to tackle such a dog as that, or how he'd hurt him if he tried, defies sensible explanation.

But sense is not the point. The point is that that woman and her family have come to share the woods and to strive, as soon as possible, to empty it of the disquieting trespass of anything they cannot fully tame.

By such predations does the lifeless desert advance.

Civil Wars

My younger daughter is beginning to compete. And in the clamorous flow of small bodies to and fro along the soccer field she will learn, sooner or later, to draw blood. From all indications, that will be later rather than sooner.

There already are a few — the precocious ones, and large for their years — who have the idea. They are able to accept a kicked ball full in the face and, after pausing briefly to determine that nose and teeth are still in place, to lurch back into the fray, meaning to give at least as good as they have gotten. Around these few the success of the Stallions will have to be built. (It is a peculiar name for a team of little girls, but you are mistaken to suspect a male chauvinist in the woodpile. They chose it themselves by democratic vote.)

For the others, of whom my daughter is one, there is a hollow place — a rotten spot of courtesy and deference — where the killer instinct ought to live.

They pay honor to a strong kick, not much noticing whether the kicker's shirt is blue, like theirs, or red. They find pleasure in the queer dexterity of anyone able to impart speed and approximate direction to the moving ball. It is an act of beauty which, by and large, they are seldom inclined to interrupt.

To them, the opponents' goal is not something into which one ever actually propels a shot. It is more in the nature of a mythic concept, a splendid abstraction, like romantic love or the ability to speak the language of the French. One does not dream of achieving the goal — else it would no longer be a goal. It is privilege enough simply to draw near.

Their own goal, however, the one they are defending, is another matter entirely. The distance between its net posts is at least a day's march. The net itself is like a great mouth gaping with hunger to receive the ball — a sort of logical and inevitable catchment into which everything must be funneled, either by sequential accidents or by the slope of the terrain itself.

When the enemy host comes bearing down, all savage and adept, bleating a barbarian cry, the Stallions — I mean my stallion and the ones of her nature — all stand transfixed, like birds before a snake. I do not know if it is terror that roots their feet in place. It may be pure admiration. In any case, when destiny shunts the ball into the net, as almost always happens, they evince no particular despair. Quite the contrary, they seem almost pleased to have been there to watch it happen.

At the half-time intermission there are quartered oranges to suck. And at the end of the match, cans of soda pop from the coach's ice chest.

This mentor of theirs is a huge bear of a man. They have

bought him a T-shirt with the legend "Great Coach" printed on the back. But I can tell that like many of the Stallions themselves he is flawed by gentleness. He allows them all to play. He does not rend his garments and assail the officials in the way a truly great coach is duty-bound to do. He is indiscriminate with praise. He speaks of mere effort as if it were a virtue, when what he should be speaking of are the more subtle ways to trip and gouge.

All of which is only to say that he does not put the importance of winning in its correct perspective.

In the latest match my daughter happened to be standing in the way of a cannon shot unleashed by some larger girl. It caromed off her side and left a considerable bruise, rewarding her with the character-building opportunity to play with pain. She smiled. And in my happiness for her, I smiled, too. She is making progress.

This is the team's first season, and so naturally a building year. With a good weight program, the proper use of steroids and a couple of decent drafts, I see the eventual makings of a contender. The involvement of a few concerned fathers like myself also undoubtedly would be helpful.

Meantime, the Stallions are either 0 and 4 or 0 and 5. About which there may be more to say another time.

Snapshot

Time, stand still.

Stop just here, just now — on this cool, green morning, with the early sun pale through new leaves and my small garden flourishing and the children awake in their rooms and the gray kitten, Roosevelt, marching along the top of the board fence.

My daughters have had a friend to spend the night. Theirs is a wonderful and peculiar age, an age it will be painful to watch them leave. They are at the threshold of much, and yet are childish still. A part of their lives does not include us any more, but only a part. And it is, for a little while longer, a bearable fraction.

They have wakened early with their friend. The three voices, light and melodic, come down from an upper window to where I sit here, walled in by greenery, watching the day begin. I cannot hear what they are saying, nor is it proper that I should. Their concerns, at this hour, are their own. They are entitled to secrets. But I do hear the general tone of the talk, which contains a kind of contentment that has to do with more than their just having crept from bed. They are full already of the inexpressible languor of summer coming on.

Who does not remember that feeling? There is victory in it — the anticipation of pure and perfect release. No segment of a life to be found later will ever unfold with a riper, more pungent hedonism than a child's summer. In the last days of school, as freedom nears, a kind of craziness starts to take hold, and all the rules lose force. Those days must be a hell for teachers, unless they are wise enough just to let go and be infected by it too.

So powerful is the recollection that even now, in middle age, though I go to the office as expected and keep up a pretense of devotion to my duties, I can feel that old start-of-summer craziness rise like a tide inside. If ever I do something unexplainable or punishable by law — immolate my typewriter or take to gamboling along public parkways like a *Playgirl* centerfold, garlanded with flowers — probably it will happen in this dangerous season of the year.

The children have noticed me out here and a cry has come down from the window. *"Is there any breakfast in this house?"* one of them demands to know — one of my own, their guest being much too polite.

Last night they watered my vegetable garden. Its dimensions are 6 feet by 15 feet, a tidy plot in which every leaf is counted. They watered it with the excessive passion of their present mood. An hour ago, in the early light, I found radishes beaten flat and tomatoes drooping and several branches of squash broken over at the joint. I looked on this damage with mild regret but without any anger at all. That's how this time of year commands that everything should be done — immoderately, beyond reason.

A sleek grackle has come wading with his iridescent mane of feathers to peck among my sodden plantings. May he find something of use or interest there. I'll leave him to it, and go now to answer that command about food.

By mid-morning the girls will be in swimming suits and demanding transport somewhere. By noon, this noon or another, the summer will have passed, and several other summers, too. And there will be boys — the sons of friends, suddenly become louts with predatory eyes and suspicious intent — hanging around the house.

By afternoon, all these children will be gone. Gone off to other places in the world. Waking in other houses of their own, faintly remembering how the tide of summer used to rise. Remembering perhaps, this very morning.

Time, stand still.

Games of the Hun

Faint across the morning there came a sound, a distant purr. Which became a snarl. Which became a small boy on a motor scooter, noisily trailing a plume of dust along my lane. Well, not my lane entirely. It served six other cottages besides the one where I was lodging. But because it passed so near my open door — steps only from where I sat — I had a proprietary interest in the traffic along it.

Like the cottages, the lane was built a long time ago. It was meant for occasional egress from the lakefront out to the highway and thence to town to get eggs and milk and newspapers and other sensible provisions. It was never intended for a raceway.

But came now this small boy in his crash helmet, blazing along the gravel strip — back and forth, endlessly — at the maximum speed and racket his machine could generate. I knew which cabin he came from. His father had a large and noisy boat, with an airhorn which he hooted as he sped around the perimeter of the lake. Sometimes he pulled water skiers behind. Other times he just took the boat out driving and hooting for the pure joy of it, swinging near the shore to shred weed beds and set fishermen's rowboats bouncing crazily on his wake.

When not nautically engaged, the father walked about his cottage grounds carrying a large battery-powered radio that emitted strident polkas, audible for a mile across the water. After dark, his habit was to set off strings of firecrackers and aerial bombs left over several weeks from the Fourth of July. From this man's loins had sprung the boy on the motor scooter, and the child was not accountable. Noise was in his genes.

I tried closing the cabin door on the side facing the lane. I looked out at the shifting patterns of cloud and water and, by an exercise of will, thought to empty my heart of hatred and view the motor scooter not as a torment but as a test of saintly patience and thus, perhaps, the instrument of my eventual beatification.

Then I went outside and stood in the lane.

The boy rode up and stopped directly in front of me, the machine idling. *"Shut it off,"* I told him. The helmet encased his whole head, except his eyes, which peered out alarmed. Something in my manner had gotten his attention. But I was not abusive.

"This is a tranquil place," I said. *"Or it used to be. People come here to be undisturbed. To hear birds singing and whatnot. That's my door..."* I pointed, and it was obvious that was the door I had come out of.

"I don't hear any birds singing. What I hear is your motor scooter going back and forth in front of my cottage. Time after time. Maybe you could ride somewhere else."

"Where?" he said.

"How about in front of your own cottage?"

The eyes looked back dumfounded from the slit in the helmet. I left him there and went back inside. Several minutes of blessed silence followed. I opened a book. Then I heard again a distant purr, which became the snarl not of one motor scooter but of two. The boy had a brother. The two of them, wearing identical helmets, were astride identical machines.

And marching behind them came the mother, the earth trembling under her great thighs, to stand with arms folded in plain view, defending the inalienable right of her spawn to foul the day.

I was tempted to go out there and appeal to reason — to discuss calmly the subject of inconsideration. There are now something over four billion of us on earth, I could have pointed out. But by the time her boys are grown there will be six billion.

And in their children's day, possibly ten billion. *Ten billion people!* In that crowded world, what did she imagine would be the result of the kind of inconsideration she was teaching?

People are going to be edgy, I might have warned her. Never mind motor scooters and aerial bombs. Hell, you'll get shot for sneezing! That's what I could have said, but didn't. I just eyed her cravenly through the window where she stood, legs planted like oaks, and resisted the brief temptation to go outside.

That evening the big boat bore down with a howl of its klaxon and sent my small craft heaving and spinning on its wave. The driver, the father, was grinning. I gestured to him across the dusk. He made a second pass, and returned my gesture.

"What's that mean?" asked my daughter, who was fishing with me.

"It's just a kind of salute," I told her. *"Like opposing generals give each other before the war quite begins."*

Autonomy

In the last week both daughters have rearranged their rooms and they are elated to discover that, in at least this small respect, they can control their world. In so many other things they are powerless.

Except occasionally in restaurants, and sometimes even there, they eat food that is chosen for them. They travel on holidays where we travel. As it happens, they love those places — and love them they must, in any case, or else stay home.

They are financially dependent, their allowance a dole whose amount and frequency are decided by someone else. And the dole is subject to threats of being withheld, although that has never happened.

Of real privacy they have little. We observe the small convention of knocking at their doors before entering. But we know, as they do, that there is no serious possibility we will be denied access for very long.

The law commands that they be educated. And, once they are delivered up to the school, the teachers dispose of their days and sometimes of their evenings as well.

The hour at which they must retire to sleep is fixed. Special circumstances and strenuous appeals may vary it some, but generally speaking it is a rule in whose making they had no part. So they lie down when told to and, whether rested or not, rise up again when commanded.

Life is unfair, a president of the republic has observed. He might have added that childhood is undemocratic.

In the matter of the arrangement of their rooms, however, our daughters have seized control. Not without some grumbling on my part, since I am the beast of burden — the lifter and carrier of beds, the mover of bureaus, the hanger of pictures and mirrors and the plugger of the nail holes where they hung before.

One of the girls, disabled by summer flu a day or two, and with too much time to think, mapped out the new floor plan in her mind. This small assertion of power inspired her sister to do the same. The plans were unworkable, I said. Logic and function dictated where the articles of furniture must go — logic which had governed the rooms' arrangements in the first place. There was no use tampering with the laws of geometry.

But they persisted. So for two nights the beast labored and at the end of that, stepping back to look at the result, it was obvious that major improvement had been wrought. The rooms seemed lighter, more spacious, even more functional. In every instance, without exception, their instincts had been borne out and mine shown to be dogmatic and uninspired.

I would not make so much of this, except that it clearly is one of the early steps in a process that will continue and gain greater force in the years immediately to come. For if they are competent now to control the space in which they live, will it not seem to them reasonable that they should exert autonomy in other things? And, eventually, in all things?

The power of parents is the power, first, of sheer size. And then of undoubting trust. And finally of wisdom. Then, on a certain day, in some matter perhaps as small as where a bed will fit, what passed for wisdom is seen suddenly to be capricious and flawed. From that moment, authority begins to come unraveled. And the process, once set in motion, cannot be reversed.

Among the subjects of a political tyrant, the result of that discovery is called revolution. On shipboard, it can end in mutiny.

For children, with any luck, it ends in whole adulthood.

Accidental Lives

The fate of all things alive, from the wind-borne seed to that most complicated vagabond of all, ourselves, turns on accidents and capricious luck.

My wife's mother used to speak of her memory from girlhood of traveling orphan shows that would from time to time visit her town. Brushed and combed, the children would be displayed, sitting on chairs under lights on a theater stage. Members of the audience would come forward — or not come forward — to choose from the merchandise and relieve charity of one or several of its wards.

There could be no knowing, in that moment, the reasons for the choosing. Some, surely, were taken for love's sake, to fill the place of a child earlier lost or to assuage some other terrible grief or loneliness. Others, no doubt, were selected for size and strength and their usefulness as unpaid field hands and chamber maids. Probably there were even worse purposes.

The point is that nothing was sure, nothing promised. For an hour or two, there under the stage lights, lives stood at the point of unfathomable turnings. Then the lights went out and the theater emptied and the children not taken, which is to say most of them, were loaded on wagons or on a train and carted away to be shown in the next place.

Such, in an exaggerated way, is the power of luck in all our lives.

A friend's daughter for some time had wanted a cat and, after some persuading, recently was told she could have one. As it happened, I knew a house in the country where kittens were available — among them several gray ones, which was the little girl's choice of color. I needed to go there for another reason, so my friend went with me. We were commissioned to come home with a gray kitten, but that turned out not to be so easy.

The mother cat was a creature of the barn crevices and the high grass. She had borne her litter under the floor of the smokehouse, in a safe, dry place reachable through a hole in a board. Reachable, that is, by her and them, but not by us. And she was teaching them her wild ways.

When we arrived, she had brought them — five of them, I think — out onto the grass at the entrance to her lair, where they wrestled and ate from the food dish and took the summer sun. They could be admired there, but they could not be touched. The first sign of near approach sent them back into the darkness of their hole under the floor. And any man who would have thrust an exploring hand and arm in there would have been too feeble of wit to care for what he caught.

We were directed, then, to another farm nearby, where there were said also to be kittens. Tamer ones — but only relatively speaking. Of which two were reported to be more or less gray. Gray enough, at least, to satisfy a child's eye, in uncertain light. One of those never showed himself at all. The other we briefly had a hand on. Then he, too, was gone through the weeds to some secret place we could not find. The situation was getting desperate.

To shorten the tale, we did not come home failures. We brought a kitten. An orange-and-white striped one, not to be mistaken for gray in any light. Unlike the others, he submitted peaceably to being picked up. When he was stroked, the small motor inside him made noises of satisfaction. In that hour of deciding which one of all those kittens would become a city cat, while all the others remained country cats, the course of his future life was set by purest chance.

I cannot say whether being a city cat is at all finer. He will live indoors. And is apt to be petted more. And may sleep on someone's pillow. On the other side of the balance sheet, there are city dogs, less tolerant beasts than farm dogs. And there are the wheels of cars on city streets.

But never mind that. It's done. He has become a citizen of my friend's household. Gray cats are forgotten entirely. This orange cat is finer than any imaginable. He has a name: Marmalade. He travels mostly by being carried. His throat must be sore from purring. His was the accidental gift of an amiable nature.

He trusted. And that made all the difference.

Goodbye to Something

Enough time has passed that I no longer remember in any detail the childhood experience of changing schools.

I vaguely recall — or think I do — a bleak interval of nausea on morning waking. But was it measurable in months or weeks, or only days? I expect I could recognize even now, even through the mask of years, the face of the teacher who struck my knuckles repeatedly and savagely with a ruler for writing with the left hand. Except for those fragments, though, that whole year has been represented by an utter blankness where memory ought to be.

Now a daughter of mine has been overtaken by just such a crisis of change. And through her I have been put in touch again with certain of those old feelings I had managed to block from mind.

Summer has been worst. Pain imagined is always more terrifying than pain itself. Her world of friendships, of frail alliances, of places and objects known, was doomed to be disassembled and rearranged. Her dearest classmate also was changing schools — but to a different one. During the daytime these awful facts could be forgotten in the giddy whirl of summer's play and busyness. But at evening, and especially at bedtime, they came crowding back again. She speculated on the future the way a condemned prisoner speculates about what might lie past the edge of the executioner's blade.

There has hung over her, more than anything, the expectation of loneliness — a dread of such force as to make smiles abruptly vanish and cries of momentary pleasure trail away into moans of remembered grief. Not once in all the summer, when she and her friend have managed to be together, have I heard her on parting speak the word *Goodbye*. Its meaning has changed. It has become freighted with too much finality.

Now summer has nearly passed and the date with the future soon must be met. Wearing new sneakers, she will be sent forth into the alien world, not daring even to hope she might find her way. The geography of the new school will be strange, its rules unfamiliar. Her classmates will be, for a long time, only acquaintances. And the novelty of all this will coincide with — will worsen — the alarming differences she has begun to sense and see in herself at a changeling age of girlhood.

Eventually, one supposes, new friends will come forward out of those ranks of unknown faces. Rare is the time, and mean the place, where that does not sooner or later happen. Her own virtues will be discovered, as well as her demerits. She will be known for what she is and what she is not, which is essential to the comfort of belonging.

Best of all, perhaps, she will come to understand that entry into that new world did not require her to leave the old one entirely behind; that change is not necessarily loss; that where she has come from is no less real a place than where she is or happens to be bound for. Such a realization is important to a traveler of any age, whether the passage is to a distant land or only into some uncharted region of experience. Without it, there can be no safety, no coherence to a life.

I think she may already be sensing that. For just the other evening, when she and her friend, that old and abiding friend, had spent some hours together, they were able for the first time in many weeks to speak aloud the hateful word.

"*Goodbye,*" they said to one another, quietly and cautiously at first. And found, to their mutual surprise, that it had begun to be emptied of danger. In the course of a friendship, goodbyes are only commas after all, not closings of the book. In the blue dusk, then, they could be heard to cry the word again and again, from yard to receding car. Joyfully — as if it were an affirmation. As if, by speaking it fearlessly, they denied its power to intervene between them.

Change is still threatening. Her world still is in disorder, her smiles less frequent than they used to be and will be again. But on that evening she made a start.

On the Road

I am left unsatisfied by any day of travel that does not end with the parched throat and bone-weariness of a forced march. Only by the severity of the ordeal can I know for certain that I have gone somewhere .

Some people — I know them — plan their journeys in scrupulous detail. They limit the number of miles they will drive each day to a sensible, a leisurely number. Each night's lodging along the way is chosen on account of some documented virtue. The hotel dining room is telephoned weeks in advance to learn what dessert *flambé* will be on the menu on the night in question. Inquiry is made as to the dimensions of the swimming pool and the availability of sauna baths.

These travelers pass cross-country in a civilized way, arriving well rested and assured of amenities.

Intermediate points do not interest me. My eye is fixed on destinations. I settle in the driver's seat. My hands lock in a death grip on the wheel and we strike forth cheerlessly upon the highway, embarked on a single-minded careen toward wherever it is we are finally bound.

Daybreak, if I have anything to say about it, finds us already briskly in motion. Except for stops for gasoline and carry-out boxes of greasy victuals, I do not mean for any of my passengers to set foot on earth again until the moon has ascended far up in the east, cries of lamentation have risen loudly in the rear seat and my own eyes have glassed over.

Where we may call the night's halt is anybody's guess. Finding a room at nearly midnight along a major tourist route in peak season requires patience and resourcefulness. Our luck this trip has run to smallish motor courts operated by families of immigrant East Indians, located next to 24-hour restaurants with names like *EAT* and *TRUCKERS WELCOME.*

There, under the naked bulb, while wife and children sink moaning into the sleep of drugged exhaustion, I consult the maps and lay plans for the next day's rampage across several states.

Scenery means almost nothing. Mountain ranges are traversed unseen in darkness, their majesty detectable only as a slight stuffiness in the ears. Our memories of the various sectors of the continent are not of foliage or topography but of the comparative fastidiousness of public rest areas along the interstate highways. Tonight, for example, one of the children remarked we must be going north because of the lesser number and smaller size of the bugs striking the windshield.

As I've said, not all people travel this way. But we do, and obviously we are not alone.

Not many hours ago we pulled into a service station to fuel the car and ask advice on how to bypass the next city, avoiding the hazard of being distracted and delayed by some interesting sight to see. A small boy was sitting on a chair in the station's office — a boy of 12 years, looking long-faced and bewildered.

The lad was from somewhere in Illinois, the attendant said. His parents had stopped for gas. He had gone to use the rest room. His parents had finished gassing the car and had driven on north without him. That had been 30 minutes or more ago. When the parents noticed he was missing, presumably they would come back. Would, that is, if they could remember where it was they'd gotten fuel. Now there is a family whose whole attention is concentrated, as mine has always been, on the real purpose of any journey, which is to click off the miles and get to the end of it.

The episode of the forgotten boy seems to have made a large impression on my own children. They know my nature behind the wheel. Very close together, very wide awake they sit in the rear seat. They do not ask the possibilities for dinner. They do not inquire to know when we will stop for the night — how soon, or in what town.

And they do not speak of any need for comfort stops. Above all, not of those. However long until bed, they do not mean to leave the car again.

Brevities

Two days' hard drive has delivered us out of the suffocation of the plains and into a country of deep sky and pine-edged waters and three-blanket nights. That is the wonder of residing not in some postage-stamp principality but in a continental nation.

Oceans bound us. In brackish waters of the south, alligators sulk and dream their reptilian hunger among the drowned mazes of the mangrove roots. Mountains heave up their rocky spines and then, on their western flanks, sink away to sun-scalded desert. The prairie reaches northward to the start of these deepening woods. And so vast is the whole that no one of these — swamp, prairie, peak or forest — begins to describe it. They are only its incidental features.

Our family is together now, after half a summer spent largely apart. I was traveling on business. Our daughters were at camp. Their mother, in our absences, tended the weedy garden of all our affairs and kept life in its remembered shape. Here, again, we are all under one roof.

We might have made a fire last night in the wood stove, but didn't. The hour of coming in from fishing was late. The blankets on the shelf against the log wall were many. And, anyway, it is fine, in the deep of August, to go cold to bed and feel the warmth arriving. Before sleeping, I went out barefoot on the grass at the lake's edge to watch the stars.

Here, where no other light intrudes, they are past numbering. The far edge of our galaxy, seen outward through its longest axis of a hundred billion exploding suns, made a band of perfect clarity across the night. Much nearer — though still infinitely distant — the aurora borealis, the northern lights, were making a display, sending long bars of energy up from the horizon, faint in one moment, pulsing brighter the next. In more than 40 years of coming to this north country I've seen them so well only once before. And that was in my own childhood, standing at the edge of this same water.

The northern sky, and the changeless country of these northern summers, express somehow the larger, longer calculations.

Enormous the land — vast its power and its possibilities. But the galaxy spins on across eternity. Terrible cool discharges of magnetic energy agitate the nights of a certain sector of an inconsequential planet. And does it matter a bit who is watching, if anyone is? Or in what year? Or from what political jurisdiction?

Only to us, perhaps. And yet, in great ways and small, the pageant proceeds.

Yesterday, a pair of wild mallard ducks, traveling by foot from the pothole where they'd nested, stood their ground and stopped the car to get their clutch of fuzzy hatchlings across. Last night, among the reeds just past the boat dock — where starshine on the water made a broken second sky — a loon was swimming where her own young, a single one or two at most, must have been hidden.

The display of light in the north ended. And I went back inside the cabin, bare feet wet, chilled through in late August, and looked at my daughters asleep — the citizens of a vast country and of a vaster cosmos.

But citizens only of a moment's time.

Childhood, like the northern summer, is of such a sweetness that surely it was made to last. You would think that — would wish it, and sometimes almost believe it. Then, in the fierce demonstration of brevities, the young are fledged, ice beards the reeds and, sudden as regret itself, the season turns.

Equinox

Crisp leaf scuttles across the clipped fur of summer's lawn. Daisies wither and marigolds claim the field. In full sunlight, one season holds; in pooled shade, already it is the next. The milk-pale reach of sky is full of cicadas' rasping. Cat lies squinty on the window ledge, waiting, smelling change.

As close as that, we are, to a kind of embarkation — the passage across another of those lines that divide our years. In youth, we transited with aching slowness. But with the practice of more than half a life, the lines flash by with dizzying speed. One moment there are kites aloft and birdfoot violets in the grass; the next, frayed monarch butterflies southbound and mourning doves in a line on the wire; and after that a creak of shoes in snow. All in a blur, impossible to slow, much less prevent.

So fleet is the autumn that the savoring of it must be mainly in anticipation. In stadiums where games are fought, the young will send up frosty cheers an afternoon or two — then melt away to vanish in the stream. In an hour of wind or pelting rain, all the leaf glory of October woodland will be beaten down to mulch the sleeping spring. Like a stone in flight, the season leaves no lasting track.

The single way to stay the rush might be to aim a telescope into the deep of night, through ages of forgotten time at suns whose fire has failed, then measure the reality of your moment against that immensity of theory and illusion. The leaf, the cat, the marigolds, the children and you are all, however transient, of surer substance than that eternity of frozen worlds. And to know it might let one resume the swift journey with neither sadness nor alarm.

Paterfamilias

S ay what you will about the bleak simplicity of very small places and the lives passed there. They have a continuity. Nothing, and no one, is entirely forgotten. Ever.

A hundred miles away and racing homeward on the interstate, I saw the sign with its familiar name. Had noticed it before in late years — but this time turned and followed the two-lane blacktop across the folded hills until it delivered car and me onto the single business street of the place the sign had promised.

From all appearances, a town moribund. Old houses in whose dooryards nothing stirred. A block of squat brick buildings, windows boarded. Wind whispering dryly through riotous weeds. At a distance ahead, the figures of two men standing — those two the only proof of life — watching the event of my car's approach.

That was my father's town. More exactly, it was the town to which he came as a boy from the farm nearby. Some of the storefronts were boarded even then, I think he said. As quickly as nature allowed, at age 19, he fled the farm and that place and came to the city where he spent the rest of his years. His older brother and his mother, my grandmother, stayed. Then the mother grew aged and took a small house just down from the boarded stores and the brother soon sold the farm and also left.

My father rarely spoke at all of his boyhood years. He remembered the snows. And his kneecap getting broken by a baseball. Little besides that.

A son's duty, and also surely a son's devotion, drew him back on visits. But not often. The mud road was difficult, frequently impassable. The car was old. It took the better part of a day going. Sometimes gas was hard to find. These trips, which might have been twice yearly, seemed not to give him any pleasure. He was saddened by his mother's frailty. Saddened, too, I think, by the rusted and pinched look of the place — the blind buildings, the broken men, the three-legged dogs and all the other creatures and things that seem to collect where roads end.

My suspicion is that not a city day arrived, hard as some of those days must have been, when he did not give silent thanks for escaping the other life he might have had.

We went with him on those visits, of course, and were displayed. Attended country churches and were introduced to gaunt people worn out in the service of the land. Sat before enough plates of fried chicken to start a franchise. Wandered the single street. Listened to the wind blow. Watched time pass.

My own memories are as lean as his were. Catching bullfrogs in the reservoir and eating their legs. Seeing some men stirring sorghum in a vat over a fire in a vacant lot. Getting an electrical shock from the battery an older boy had used to power a wooden car that actually moved.

From the day my father's mother died, when I was 10 or so, we never went there again. The few memories receded — and were not missed.

The house where we visited is gone now. My father is gone, and his brother, too. The reservoir has become a dry, sunken place in someone's pasture. The street in front of the derelict buildings has, however, been paved. And directly in its center the two men stood watching as my car approached. They didn't move, so I stopped before I hit them. And then got out.

"The town hasn't changed much," I said — or some similar inanity. Something they perfectly well knew. Then added, by way of explanation, *"My father came from here."*

"Name?" one of them asked.

He was a man of nearly a hundred years, but obviously still keen enough, inspecting me with a lively curiosity. That he would remember was unimaginable. Not across such a reach of time as that. Theoretically, though, it could be possible. So I spoke my father's name.

They turned the sound of it in their heads. Their faces brightened. And they began to recite the history of that side of my family: the other names, the location of the farm, the fact of its having been sold and the name of the man who bought it. The identities and fates of relatives previously not even heard of. No longer was I just a stranger who had stopped in a car. Their store of information about me — or at least about all who preceded me — was, though dated, very complete. This in spite of lifetimes having passed.

"There's a fellow down the street, last house on the south side," the old man said. "He'll tell you just about anything you'd want to know."

The truth is there wasn't anything I wanted to know. So I thanked them and turned the car around. And, without stopping at that house, drove past the boarded buildings again and away from there for what I expect will be the last time ever.

The Stone

The years overtake one another now in a dizzying race. And while I would neither hold them back nor turn them back, their velocity has begun to be unsettling. One evening not long ago I watched my younger daughter go off to her first job. She had been employed to sit several hours with the smaller children of friends.

The last time I noticed, other men's daughters were coming to our house for that same purpose. I remember all of them —

all still appearing in my mind's eye at about my daughter's age, 11 or 12. Although of course they have grown up and gone away, to school or in several cases to marriage and the start of families of their own. My recollection of childhood is of a languorous eternity. But that is the perspective clung to from an age when dogs and friends and all the people in our lives were known to last forever.

In reality, childhood is shorter than any dream.

The small boy across the street, whose basketball used to thump against the backboard in the long evenings of summer, has grown into a man. Several houses up the block, as I write this, a different boy plays now at throwing a football in his yard.

He is barely of school age. The football helmet engulfs his head like a tub. Inside it resonates the sound of an imagined crowd. Tomorrow he will play that game on a larger field. And then, too quickly, will have to leave all games aside for different and more serious contests. All of this will occupy the slightest moment, no longer than it takes to look away and then look back again.

And while it is happening — while that boy and my daughters and all of them are rushing on, without knowing it, toward the wonder and pain of their own whole lives — I will somehow remain fixed in place, like a stone in a moving stream, arrested forever at age 28 or whenever it was exactly that I stopped feeling my own years advance.

I recall, from my own boyhood, hearing older people discuss this phenomenon. I thought it was self-pity speaking, the regret of chances missed or of lives not fully lived. Now I know that what I heard in their voices was not self-pity but only the same amazement I have come to feel. For it is a fact, this acceleration of time — as sure as the seasons or the revolution of the planets or any other truth in nature. I do not intend to speak of this to my daughters, though. They will learn it soon enough.

To them, time still is something measured by a clock. A clock whose hands, in the last hour of school or when awaiting some scheduled pleasure, often refuse to move at all. Next month can, with effort, be imagined. The interval of a year is a cosmic abstraction.

That first paid engagement at the neighbors' house has been followed by others. My daughter has begun a bank account for her earnings. Very straight and prompt she strides away to her responsibilities. Carried along by the stream, and also a part of it, she is propelling time forward in eagerness and faith. I watch from a window as she goes off through the evening, and I am the stone, powerless to slow the stream's flow. Able only to sense the current passing around, then on. Quickly on.

Shadows

The dog grows old and fat and has developed a taste for roast duck in sherry sauce. Our pets are mirrors of ourselves. The house begins to show the wear of time. Cold drafts whine at the door corners. The basement is a jungle of things saved and things forgotten. Our dwellings personify our natures and the patterns of our lives.

The children's talents have begun to be manifest. One imagines the future at their command, but it is only partly so. All the past is in them, too. Our children replicate most of our mistakes.

We cast long shadows.

My father's unhandiness with tools, his defeat in the face of the smallest task of domestic repair, have become mine in turn. But so, I think, has something of his credulous faith in the goodness of the people he met. From my mother has come a fondness for the out-of-doors and silent places, a certain romanticism and an ear for melancholy.

My wife's father had a gift for gardening and for working with wood. Thus, when I see her with trowel in hand among her flowers, or rubbing stain into an old piece of furniture to restore its luster, I see him very much alive in her.

Her mother was a wonderfully humorous and idiosyncratic lady. She loved words and, in her speech, combined them in phrases and usages peculiarly her own — at once so utterly odd and so perfect that they lodged forever in the mind. My wife speaks those phrases still. And, just the other day, I heard one of them spring unbidden to the lips of one of the girls. For all time, for as many generations as our line endures, they will continue to be spoken and heard.

Examine carefully enough any of the components of one's attitudes and behavior — the values one holds, the habits one obeys — and the origin nearly always can be discovered.

The belief in the transcendent power of ideas I can trace back to a particular professor to whom I had the luck to be exposed in the 18th through the 21st years of my life. My sense of the worth of the journalist's craft has come mainly from the newspaper folk with whom I have been privileged to work. From a friend I stood beside in frozen duck marshes at an impressionable age there came an intemperate passion for winter dawns and sunsets and the whisper of quick wings in the darkness. From my wife, an addiction to the majesty of mountains.

And so it goes. We are born understanding nothing, caring about nothing. Everything, or nearly everything, is borrowed. Tennyson spoke of that, although more eloquently, as you'd expect. In the poem, "Ulysses," the aged wanderer looks back across a life of far adventure and says: "I am a part of all that I have met."

As we all are — all of us borrowers. The sum of our borrowings becomes the creature called ourselves, and presently we are borrowed from in turn. Nameless and unattributed, these oddities and small glories pass then into the collective experience of our kind.

That is the longest shadow we cast. There is no particular fame in it, and it is far from what some people have in mind who speak of immortality. But, for most of us, it may have to do.

An Autumn Walk: On Hunter Creek

October, tiring of being a spectacle, has ripened into mere perfection.

So steep and narrow is this valley that the sun can cross it in six hours only. Before 10 o'clock, the morning is still beginning. And after 3, the evening already is coming on. Pale and deep the sky is — that fraction of it which can be seen ahead, winding like a placid river between the furred hills. I have been following a smaller stream than that one, although, being also bounded by the valley, its course is the same.

Two dogs travel with me. One, my own, on purpose. The other by accident. She is a yellow Labrador, sleepy-eyed and full of years. Her owner reckoned she'd follow a while and then turn back. But she hasn't, and I believe she won't.

To a dog's mind, as to a man's, there is no finer use for such a golden day than walking. But men carry maps. They know where the walk ends; they have destinations. Dogs travel in trust. They bed at night where the man does. Beyond a certain point — after many crossings of the water and the traversing of stony ledges — there no longer is any way back for them. Only ahead, where the man goes, following the sky river where it leads.

The stillness is vast at midday. Somewhere an insect is clicking in the grass. Migrant tanagers are passing through, chittering over the thickets together like scraps of scarlet paper on a breeze to southward. Faintly, as the valley bends farther away from the road, yard dogs can be heard to challenge endlessly across the reach of hills.

Nearer, some small fish breaks the surface of his pool. The sun striking down through water as clear as air shows every pebble. Shows two crayfish advancing to war with claws upraised. But does not reveal the fish himself. The fish is magic.

The woodland opens on one side into a meadow where cattle are pasturing. What is a man doing there, come from a direction they have not known men to use? What do the dogs intend? Jaws arrested in chewing, the cow faces turn together.

Those are the events that fill a day.

We came once upon something quite amazing. A field of eggs — goose eggs, by the look of them, half again larger than a hen's. This in a little sandy glade between the trees. No vegetation was to be seen. That patch of ground was barren except for all the eggs, dozens of them, maybe hundreds, lying inexplicably on the sand in every direction.

I took one up. It had the feel and weight of an egg, and the shape exactly. It clicked like an egg when you tapped it with a fingernail. But then I noticed at the lesser end a tiny darkened dimple. The others had them, too. The dimple was the place where a stem had attached — and examining the ground more closely I could see the remnant of the vines, blasted by frost and desiccated to threads, leaving only their fruit detached and lying there in curious display.

So they were only gourds, after all. Of some wild sort I had never seen before. But wonderful to come across and be, for a moment, so childishly deceived by.

Now the sun has passed behind the west wall of Hunter's valley. And I have stopped to camp the night. Above is still a daytime sky. But evening has pooled already on the water and in the thickets bordering it, and a blue line of shadow advances quickly up the hills.

A small fire is welcome against the chill. Coffee boils at the edge of the flame.

The old Labrador inspects each item taken from the pack. There is nothing her nose describes as food. She shoulders close. It is the hour for eating. She has come farther than she intended to, and now, at the end of the march, there is only disappointment. So she withdraws several paces and lies down, a martyr, frowning at the fire.

A golden day or not, its conclusion is not as she'd imagined it would be. But that is what comes of too much trusting. No one ever warned her against taking up with a bad provider.

An Autumn Walk:
In Sweden Hollow

A great blue heron rises from some upstream shallow and comes, a croaking shadow, stately and huge, planing around the river's bend and thence on out of view. A kingfisher, too, goes off to roost, rasping a curse at his luck.

The sky behind the ridge pales to lemon. In that last light, minnows of the stream make little flashes as they strop their sides against the stones. Somewhere nearby must be a cave, for now bats come streaming overhead in convoy, trailing the night behind them. The light goes out, except for light of fire. Then finally that.

The dogs have bedded in the leaves. Their heads are facing away into the largeness of the woods. They are shivering with cold. They are thinking of home, and wondering why they are not there. They wonder what any of it means.

The man has a bedroll and is inside it, on his back. Looking up — leaving any danger to the dogs. He is looking at the stars, flung out with a brilliance and nearness he cannot remember ever having seen. Meteors burn their sudden messages down the night.

In the distance, owls converse.

The man, too, though his coming here was deliberate, is thinking of home and bed. The ground is hard. The darkness long. The woods, as always, much stranger in the night. He sleeps, then. But in a small hour something wakes him. He strikes a match to see the time. It is just past two o'clock in the morning.

A heavy dew has fallen, and then has frozen. There is a veneer of ice on every leaf and blade of grass, and even on the sleeping bag, which makes a crackling sound and sheds the ice in fine sheets as he settles himself again. It is a lonely hour, he thinks. In a lonely place, in lonely cold.

A plane goes over, its lights winking, so high the sound of its engine cannot be heard. Who travels the sky at such a strange hour? What urgent errand calls them? Surely they are more desperately alone up there even than a man in the frozen woods.

And then, finally, he hears again the noise that woke him.

It is the cry of geese. Not a great migration. Only a family of them, from the sound of it, or possibly several families. Unseen and unseeable. Disembodied voices, their progress markable very precisely from star to star. No map to lead them, and no rest at all this night. Their home a whole long continent. Their company only other disembodied criers in the dark.

What use to speak of loneliness after that? the man thinks, feeling at once very settled and safe in his ice-encrusted bedroll on the frosty earth. He remembers the maps in his pack. He knows his way.

Secure in that, he quickly sleeps.

An Autumn Walk: On Bryant Creek

The river makes a turn, the outer current rushing close against a sheer wall of stone that over millennia its flow has cut. There is no more place for walking. The bank on that side pinches down until there is only cliff and water. The traveler crosses there if he means to continue. There is no other way.

It is a small thing in the telling. But the doing of it is the work of half an hour.

First one must decide for certain that there is no choice. Then sit to remove boots and socks and roll the trousers up. And, while doing so, let the mind grow reconciled to how achingly cold the water will be on a late October morning after a night of frost. And how sharp the stones underfoot — made sharper by the bearing down of a heavy pack. These crossings are a requirement of following a highlands stream afoot — several such crossings in a day. One remembers each of them as an individual experience. They do not grow old.

Unshod and sitting on the bank, one finds endless things to consider. The purpose of the journey. Other discomforts against which the impending one may be qualitatively compared. And things nearby in nature.

In this season, you tread the forest in a silent rain of falling leaves. Some drift down directly onto the stream, where, crisp and curling at the edges, they ride the current as easily as boats. They ride longest and best in the great slow pools. That is the place the leaf boats were made for, where they float lightly and secure. But arriving presently at a rapid, suddenly they spin and tumble and are carried under — becoming not boats any longer but only drowned leaf-litter in the race, and one day, finally, somewhere, sodden wrack on the bottom.

Maybe the leaf boats contain the lesson of haste.

One likes to think that, anyway, as one sits in comfort in those minutes until, with a wrench of pain and courage, one must thrust one's feet into the icy water onto the sharpness of the stones and make one's way — whimpering and begging mercy — to the other side.

And then, having accomplished it, one has to sit and let the air and sun do their drying work. And brush off the grit and sand. And draw on socks and shoes again, luxuriating in the satisfaction of having the ordeal behind. And by the time you have done all this, a half-hour has passed, without progress except laterally across the water and, occasionally, some lazy excursion of the mind.

As I make these notes, I have just completed such a crossing — the fourth today. And sitting here, feet bare and drying, I have seen a joyous thing. Just down the stream, here in the deepest woods, several hundred blackbirds have come to water. One does not ordinarily think of blackbirds as pretty creatures. Their cry is unpleasing. Sometimes in their flocking they shift and flow together like smoke across a field, and that is curious to watch. But scarcely more.

From somewhere, though, and on their way to somewhere, these birds have arrived at this particular point on the stream. And they have come with purpose, ignoring me entirely, though they are just on the next gravel bar and really very close. A dapple of sunlight through the trees falls on the bar at whose edge the main body of the flock is splashing and drinking among the reeds.

Out a little from that is a shoal where the river rushes shallow over stones. Some of the bolder members, several dozen of them, have ventured out onto the rocks, bathing there, slipping down into the water and then clambering out again, fluffing themselves to dry, wings shining in the sun-sparkle off the river.

And over all this scene there has arisen a huge chirruping and chattering that is impossible to mistake for anything but joy.

They are only blackbirds still — common and ungainly things. But in this moment there is music in them. It fills the air and fills the woods around. And I cannot help thinking, as I watch them now, how rare and wonderful it is to be privy to the exceeding happiness of so great a number of individual lives.

Where they will go from here I can't guess. Their days, I suppose, are short. But long after the exact sound of them has faded, and even after I have perhaps forgotten what sort of birds they were, I will remember the immensity of their joy. In speaking their hearts' music, it has not mattered that they were common. What counts is not the singer. It's the song.

Notes in Bottles

I doubt that there are many writing people alive who have not been overtaken, on certain gray days of the spirit, by a sense of the futility of words.

It is a dubious sort of occupation, putting one word after the other. When writing goes well, it is the next best thing to being unemployed. And when it goes poorly, real unemployment is apt soon to be achieved. The possible combinations of letters on the page are endless, the chance of finding exactly the right one remote. Even if found, to whom will it speak — or will it speak to anyone? The effect hardly ever can be measured.

Thoughts like these send writing folk into fits of intermittent despair, making them wish, too late, that they had taken up stonemasonry or basket weaving or some other craft whose product was of provable use. Then, from an unexpected quarter, reassurance comes. And it seems both possible and sensible to write again.

Not many nights ago, an audience sat in a theater to see performed a stage play whose author had been a friend of many of those present.

I remember when he first mentioned his plan for that piece of writing. And also his relish for the challenge that lay ahead. There were problems to be solved along the way — questions of fact and theatricality to be dealt with and reconciled. And after that, the words had to be found. It was fascinating to hear him discuss these matters. His enthusiasm was boundless. He was, I think, that rarest kind of writer: modest to excess about his own gift, yet convinced absolutely of the grandeur of the purposes to which language can be put.

By the time we sat in that theater the other night, our friend had passed from life. And yet the occasion was anything but sad. For the humor, the fine sensitivity, the tenderness and discernment of the man were there, imperishable, in the lines he had written and the play he had made.

A day or so after that, looking for something in a drawer, I came across a bundle of letters held with a rubber band. They were letters that had found their way to me in Europe many years ago, written by my parents when they were not a great deal older than I am now.

I opened and reread those. And, again, the emotion of the moment was not sadness but keen pleasure — much like the pleasure of reading them the first time at cafe tables in strange cities so long ago. The news still seemed fresh. I could see my mother's face and my father's clearly; could see their hands moving across the paper as they sat writing at the table in a room I still know so well. No time at all seemed to have passed.

It was not uncommon, in those days, for a fortnight to intervene between their posting of an envelope and its delivery in Strasbourg or Cattolica or Alicante or some other stop along the way. But the distance and the delay were meaningless. That is the power of language — specifically of the written word. The elapse of time may be more than a fortnight; may be generations, even. And the separation — as with my parents, now, and with the writer of the play — may be vastly greater than any ocean. But the power is undiminished.

Writing people, being so sketchily employed, tend also to be insecure and the prey of hopelessness. The empty page looms before them in a confusion of possibilities. They doubt that they will ever get the words exactly right, and mostly they are correct. Only after much practice do they grow at ease with their deficiencies, content to leave a record of having tried.

Her Birthday

Chronology begins to blur. Certain of the details of our life together recede. What remains is a more general sense of texture and of themes.

November has contained the best of times and the worst — great sadness, much happiness, the excitement of large rearrangements. Twice in this season we have changed houses. Twice we have lost a parent. There has been, with all, the predictable run of celebrations and of hurts.

November happens also to be the month in which, skeptically and with diminishing comment, she permits her birthday to be observed. I know her feeling exactly. Were it not for the fine enthusiasm of the children, one might as soon let the date go by unnoticed.

We do not yet particularly feel our age, so we are not much given to self-pity. We still can climb a mountain trail with anyone I know. Our discouragements heal as quickly as they ever did. We have discovered downhill skiing in our middle years. All the same, the subject of time — time's certain consequence, the deadline it imposes — has come to occupy a corner of our thoughts, though not yet morbidly.

With what I've said here, with the odd mixture of joys and punishments that our years, like anyone's, have brought, is it any wonder that birthdays, the mile markers on a journey of finite length, sometimes produce uncertain weather of the heart?

The other evening the television was playing unnoticed some children's special left on after our daughters had gone to their beds. I turned from whatever I was doing to ask a question, and found that, just for an instant, she was unable to reply. She had happened to glance up from her book and an image on the screen had unaccountably touched her — touched some memory, or some regret in her, perhaps.

She could not quite speak. Just shook her head, astonished, and made a little shrug. It was absurd, and afterward we laughed about it. Although it set me thinking.

How many regrets, or even how many fragile, wistful notions, do the people nearest us carry? Do we ever know? With her I can't really say since, unlike me, she is private about such things. I notify the world of all my complaints, promptly and noisily. She buries hers away. But surely there must be some. One does not pass from girlhood through working bachelorhood, through marriage and the early years of children and finally to a second, later career without collecting some wounds and disappointments along the way. Some of them may even have to do with me, though, naturally, I have not the slightest notion what they'd be.

No life is easy. Least of all a woman's life, hedged round eternally, it must seem, by other people's needs, their claims of time. It would be amazing if she did not wonder, sometimes — just speculatively — about other and more self-directed shapes a life can take.

Thoughts like these occurred to me a day or so afterward while I was circulating through stores, looking for some remembrance to mark the day. Perfume had been mentioned, a routine sort of gift, but at least a findable one. The woman at the counter was very elegant, very helpful. She anointed bits of cotton, then daubed her pale wrist with several of the currently famous musks.

Surely I would want perfume, she said. *Cologne was only the brass section playing, perfume the full orchestra.*

Why, yes. Perfume, of course!

This one is $48 the quarter-ounce.

Large is my devotion, and great my guilts. But I fled out of there without a purchase. And when later she opened her few packages they contained humbler, more durable articles than can be manufactured from the civet's oil.

Two small sea shells to speak of tides lapping and things abiding. And a calendar to give the promise of another year.

The Great Uncle

There is no way of defending a child against terrible losses. But how do you even explain them?

Someone has been gone these several months, now — a great uncle, great in years, in gentleness, in understanding. A child's world needs to be inhabited by people of many ages. Without it ever having been explicitly discussed, this uncle had come to fill the place of two grandfathers also gone to death, one of them never known.

His home, as the little girl knew it, was a summer cottage on the shore of a Minnesota lake. There was another, different sort of home for winters, in some place called Omaha. But that was an abstraction.

The lake was where he really lived. He would sit in his chair in front of the cabin, the lake wind stirring his silver hair, his pipe gone cold in his teeth and a stack of newspapers beside him on the grass. His face was always brown from the fishermen's sun. He would be looking out across the water in a far-eyed way, but not actually looking — remembering more than he was seeing, but never with regret. And never so lost in thinking of what had been that, if the little girl happened to find him sitting there, he would not return from that to warmly share with her the pleasure of all that still was and might yet be.

And presently, when the afternoon wind had laid and the light was right on the water, he would collect his gear and, with anyone else who cared to, go down to the boat and out to some favorite reed bed or rocky point to ring another evening down. If there was a place for her, the little girl would go along to watch and to be near. She thinks of each of those times now like a gift.

Some small part of every summer that she can remember was spent there. And she imagined, with that faith that only children have, that nothing so important would ever really change. But in this year, in the place called Omaha, the great uncle died. In spite of tears and prayers, in spite of frantic bargains proposed to the Universe in the loneliness of a child's bed at night, he died and was gone. The grief hardly could be supported, but she tried.

Just the other day a letter came, and with it the word that — painful as it was to consider — the cabin might have to be sold. It was, after all, such a long way from Omaha and the family remaining there. The place would be used so little now. How could it be kept up as it should? Anyway, selling it was a possibility. There had been feelers.

With that, all the sense of loss came flooding back.

"Then we'll have to buy it," she said immediately.

No, it's farther from here than from Omaha. So the problems would be the same — worse.

"But if strange people live there," (tears coming freely now) "it might mean we couldn't ever go there again. Or even see it again."

And that, of course, was true.

Her mind was racing. "Maybe it won't happen right away.

Maybe I'll have time to grow up. And then I'll buy it."

What use is there in saying, at such a moment, that it is no more possible for an adult than for a child to own and keep safe everything that he or she has loved? Anyway, the place was just the touchstone. That wasn't what she mourned. Not really that at all.

"He knew the tree where the lady bugs stayed."

Her small shoulders shook.

"He could always think of something to do . . . catch frogs or something."

It was a fact; there were no empty days around him.

"Who else will tell us all the secrets of the fish?"

Who, indeed?

And finally, her face and her heart a ruin: "What are we going to do?"

What has there ever been for anyone to do, except to confess the pain and try, in spite of it, to keep alive a willingness to take the splendid risks of caring?

The Circle Route

Memory is an unruly servant, like the butler in one of those dated English comedies. For years you imagine that he is in your employ, then one day you discover he has really become master of the house. You issue commands, but they are ignored. The butler has a capricious will of his own.

In a strange city a fortnight ago I observed a young couple out wheeling their bundled infant in a carriage one evening. They stopped at a bench in a little street-side park and took the baby from its buggy and sat holding and playing with their newborn while, in the sharp air, the life of the sidewalk flowed by.

Hours later, back in my hotel room, there came over me a sudden realization that I could no longer remember the physical sensation of holding my own children as infants in my arms. This discovery produced so keen a pang of regret that I actually gave a little cry aloud.

That I did hold them — many times — I knew perfectly well. I even could call up a mental picture of the act, and some indistinct recollection of the pleasure it gave. But that was all an exercise of intellect. The true feeling of it, the exact *tactile sensation,* had been altogether lost. Had those quiet moments been swept under and away by too much busyness? Was I simply inattentive? Or does it happen the same way to everyone? That I can't say.

But as I look at my daughters now, plunging on toward young womanhood, more than half their time in our care already elapsed, it is distressing to know that so rich an interval of one's life has fled beyond any power of deliberate recall.

And yet, treacherous as memory is apt to be, it also is capable of wonders of quite the opposite sort.

Toward the end of this summer past, we were together, those daughters and I, in a boat on a lake in the far north. As night came on, we determined to pursue a particular kind of fish. But where on all that water was it to be found, and how were we to know? Darkness was deepening and far across the lake, from a bay behind a dark wooded point, the loons were sending up their cry of desolation.

Something more than 40 years ago, in the starry cold of just such a northern night, I had crouched in the bottom of the boat on that very lake while my parents puzzled out and answered that same question about the fish. I had not thought about that in all the years since. But now, with memory as the navigator, I steered the boat to a place on the water that seemed as if it might be the right one.

With each oar stroke the picture in my mind came clearer. The risen moon was in the proper place. The curve of the reed bed was unquestionably the same. Suddenly, then, I was certain. The years rolled away with a rush, and my parents were there in the boat with us, as alive as they had ever been, their sharp cries of surprise ringing out over the water as they swung the many fish aboard.

In absolute faith we cast out our lines. And, of course, the fish we sought — those and no others — were there.

Old as that memory was, it was as powerful and vivid as life itself. Which must mean that nothing really is ever lost, only oddly catalogued. Surely you have heard people of great age discuss this curiosity. The most distant events, they say, come readily to mind in exact detail. It is the recent ones that are clouded or mislaid entirely.

They declare this a terrible vexation. But I count it to be a fine promise, at least where the matter of my daughters' early childhood is concerned. The memory of them in my arms years ago is irretrievable now. But with any luck I will survive long enough for that to become a matter of fairly ancient history.

The girls will go out of our house. Their lives will take independent shape. They will have children in their time, if they choose to. And, if they do, the probability — the certainty, you might almost say — is that those children will sometime be presented to me to hold.

And just as happened on the lake that summer night under a certain slant of moon, all the clutter of years will pass from mind. In that instant, an old man will be very young once more. The life in his arms will be his own daughters as they were. And all he imagined to be forgotten will be securely his again.

On Leaving

Just after breakfast they came through a cold slant of autumn rain and carried the home away. Not the house itself — though they'd have managed that, too, if it had been in the bargain — but everything between its walls. Casually one of them would circle a bureau, its drawers still full, measuring it with his eye. Then lay on hands and walk away with it. Two hours it took them, no more. Then, somewhat numbed, the transient family made its final tour, shoes clattering on bare oak floors, too-loud voices echoing as in a cave.

Gone — all of it! Well, not quite all. The cold hearth, ash-dusted, still held its memories of February fires. Here, the nursery the children had come home to. Here, scratches made by crib legs — here vagrant crayon marks low against the door frame. Here, the dining room where good talk had run too late into the night. On the wall, a paler rectangle where hung — still does, for the image is perfectly clear in their eyes — a picture that pleased them all.

For a moment, although chill from doors standing open, the place is not empty at all. The fire burns up, the laughter can be heard and the soft, sure breathing of babies in the night. Then the leavers go out, taking all that with them, and let fall a latch whose key they no longer own.

Pristine it stands behind them. All the echoes gone. Waiting, impassively, for new people to come and write the wholly different, no less tender markings of their lives on its same walls. A house is only stone and boards after all. Remembered, it forgets the rememberers.

From a high branch of the leafless mulberry a slaty jay looks down, watching them go — the van, the car, the people. It is all the same to him. He has more important matters to consider. Winter is coming on and the bird feeder stands empty. And he is hoping for a change of luck. Those last ones kept a cat.